Bryophyte Floristics and Ecology in Grand Canyon National Park

Natural Resource Technical Report NPS/SCPN/NRTR—2012/602

Theresa Ann Clark

Northern Arizona University
Department of Biological Sciences
P.O Box 5640
Flagstaff, AZ 86001-5640

July 2012

U.S. Department of the Interior
National Park Service
Natural Resource Stewardship and Science
Fort Collins, Colorado

The National Park Service, Natural Resource Stewardship and Science office in Fort Collins, Colorado publishes a range of reports that address natural resource topics of interest and applicability to a broad audience in the National Park Service and others in natural resource management, including scientists, conservation and environmental constituencies, and the public.

The Natural Resource Technical Report Series is used to disseminate results of scientific studies in the physical, biological, and social sciences for both the advancement of science and the achievement of the National Park Service mission. The series provides contributors with a forum for displaying comprehensive data that are often deleted from journals because of page limitations.

All manuscripts in the series receive the appropriate level of peer review to ensure that the information is scientifically credible, technically accurate, appropriately written for the intended audience, and designed and published in a professional manner.

This report received formal peer review by subject-matter experts who were not directly involved in the collection, analysis, or reporting of the data, and whose background and expertise put them on par technically and scientifically with the authors of the information.

Views, statements, findings, conclusions, recommendations, and data in this report do not necessarily reflect views and policies of the National Park Service, U.S. Department of the Interior. Mention of trade names or commercial products does not constitute endorsement or recommendation for use by the U.S. Government.

This project was funded by the National Park Service through the Colorado Plateau CESU Cooperative Agreement #H1200-004-0002 (Task NAU-227).

This report is available from Southern Colorado Plateau Network (http://www.nature.nps.gov/scpn/products.cfm), and the Natural Resource Publications Management Web site (http://www.nature.nps.gov/publications/nrpm/) on the Internet.

Please cite this publication as:

Clark, T. A. 2012. Bryophyte floristics and ecology in Grand Canyon National Park. Natural Resource Technical Report NPS/SCPN/NRTR—2012/602. National Park Service, Fort Collins, Colorado.

Contents

Figures

Figures *continued*

Tables

Tables *continued*

Errata

Pages	Error	Correction
26 (Table 4), 46, 59, 62 (Figure 22), B8, C10, D2, E7	*Trichostomum tenuirostre*	*Pottiopsis sweetii*
25 (Table 4), 31, 60, 62 (Figure 22), B7, C2, D2, E2	*Sciuro-hypnum plumosum*	*Sciuro-hypnum oedipodium*
26 (Table 4), 44, 58, B7, C9, D3, E6	*Syntrichia laevipila*	*Syntrichia pagorum*
44, B7, C9, D4, E6	*Syntrichia montana*	*Syntrichia virescens*
26 (Table 4), 45, 62 (Figure 22), B7, C9, D2, E6	*Tortella alpicola*	*Tortella tortuosa*
45	Collection #192a (catalog number 1C6767) was changed from *Tortula inermis* to *Tortula hoppeana*	

Abstract

Our understanding of bryophyte floristics and ecology in the aridlands of North America is dwarfed by that of temperate and tropical systems across the continent. Bryophyte diversity remains underestimated and community patterns remain largely unexplored. A notable deficiency exists regarding rock habitat, despite the ubiquity and variability of this substrate in these arid environments. Along a mile-high elevation gradient, Grand Canyon National Park (GRCA) harbors broad ecological continua, including a spectrum of rock types and climatic variation encompassing much of that found within the American Southwest. Indeed, GRCA provides the ideal location in which to study aridland bryophytes. As a result of such an effort, this report presents an expanded bryophyte flora (bryoflora) and ecological investigation of rock bryophyte communities in GRCA.

This bryoflora of GRCA was compiled from over 1,500 field specimens and summarizes the local distribution and habitat-specificity of 155 confirmed bryophyte taxa (153 species, 2 varieties). Records include 28 taxa newly reported for Arizona and 113 new to GRCA, some of which mark significant range extensions (e.g. *Gyroweisia tenuis* and *Gymnostomum calcareum*). Three taxa remain undescribed or new to science. In summary, the bryoflora of GRCA 1) is collectively distributed across the entire elevation gradient in low abundance but high frequency, 2) is dominated by desiccation-tolerant members of the families Pottiaceae, Grimmiaceae, and Bryaceae, 3) includes three species of conservation concern, and 4) is most diverse in the high-elevation mixed conifer forests of the North Rim.

The ecological investigation quantified patterns in rock bryophyte communities throughout the pinyon-juniper, ponderosa pine, and mixed conifer forests of GRCA, and related them to the surrounding environment. The study sought to determine if bryophyte communities differed significantly within the three forest types, which track changes in temperature and precipitation across a 1,000 m elevation gradient; furthermore, it was desirable to determine if forest type could provide a simple framework for monitoring patterns in this bryophyte community. Bryophytes were sampled using a 100 x 1 cm transect placed randomly on three rocks at each of 104 sites along trail corridors stratified by forest type. Three main findings emerged. 1) Bryophyte richness, cover, diversity, and evenness differed significantly ($R^2 = 0.10 - 0.19$), although inconsistently, between two of the forest types. 2) Community composition on rocks differed significantly ($R^2 = 0.19$) among all forests. 3) Elevation and rock type were most strongly related to community composition. Results suggest that a combination of large and fine-scale environmental variables is needed to understand and monitor rocks bryophyte communities in GRCA.

Overall, this two-part investigation provides a foundation for future research in the community dynamics of aridland bryophytes in the American Southwest, including phytogeographical comparisons, climate-change research, and ecological modeling. Lastly, this report will inform national park service and public land management agencies about important considerations in the conservation of bryophyte diversity in the aridlands of North America.

Acknowledgments

Funding to support many aspects of this project was provided by the Southern Colorado Plateau Inventory and Monitoring Network, National Park Service. Glenn Rink, John R. Spence, and Larry E. Stevens contributed additional bryophyte collections that enhanced the floristic data set and contributed several state and park records. John R. Spence, Ph.D., Tina Ayers, Ph.D., Lisa Thomas, MS, and Phillip Turk, Ph.D., provided valuable assistance with research design and manuscript review. GIS sampling design and map creation were generously completed by Jodi Norris and Kristin Straka. Matthew Lau offered assistance with R and insight regarding multivariate analyses. Field volunteers helped record data and contributed towards a timely and safe experience in the far reaches of Grand Canyon: Larry Brown, Glenn Rink, Jessica Collins, Jessica Clark, Jess Waterhouse, Christina Bentrup, Ann Connolly, Emily Warren, Emily Palmquist, and Luke Evans. Many bryologists helped with species identification of challenging families: Roxanne Hastings, John Spence, Terry McIntosh, Norton Miller, Dale Vitt, Brent Mishler, Nancy Slack, and David Wagner. I would especially like to thank Roxanne Hastings and Terry McIntosh for their contributed hours helping me learn the complex taxonomical variation of the Grimmiaceae. I am grateful for the assistance and support of these aforementioned people, in addition to the encouragement of friends and family throughout this endeavor.

1 Introduction

Bryophytes are the smallest land plants. Nowhere is this more pronounced than in the American Southwest, where the typical moss stands no taller than a few millimeters, occupies an area the size of a quarter, and is camouflaged by a microhabitat as cryptic as the plant itself. Despite their low profile, bryophytes warrant considerable attention as important contributors to biological diversity and many ecosystem functions. Research continues to reveal the critical role that bryophytes play in many ecosystems, even in the American Southwest where bryophyte productivity is limited (Nash et al. 1977). Despite these tangible values, bryophytes are often overlooked by botanists, ecologists, and land managers alike.

Grand Canyon National Park (GRCA) provides an opportunity to improve our understanding of bryophyte diversity and ecology in this region, thanks to its rich geology and mile-high elevation gradient, which encompasses a large proportion of the environmental variation present in the Southwest. Consequently, the park will likely support a proportionally rich bryophyte flora (bryoflora). Furthermore, GRCA is located on the Colorado Plateau, a large, topographically diverse region for which bryophyte floristics and ecology have been poorly studied over the past 50 years. Contrary to popular belief, a large number of bryophyte species inhabit dry environments away from waterfalls and springs. These species are able to thrive in hot, dry habitats like those found throughout GRCA. Most accomplish this by tolerating periods of complete desiccation, entering a resilient stage of dormancy similar to that exhibited by a virus (fig. 1). The taxonomic diversity of aridland bryophytes may not approach that of hydrophilic taxa, but new species are discovered yearly and the known distributions of many continue to expand as collecting in arid regions of the world continues.

This report presents the results from three summers of bryological field work in GRCA. The results are divided into two parts. Chapter 3 presents a comprehensive floristic inventory of bryophytes in the park, which summarizes the data associated with historic and modern bryophyte collections. The floristic analysis describes the distribution patterns of species throughout GRCA and the microhabitats suitable for each. Chapter 4 is an investigation of bryophyte community ecology on rock habitat throughout the pinyon-juniper, ponderosa pine, and mixed conifer forests of GRCA. This research explored ecological relationships between large-scale environmental variation and patterns in epilithic bryophyte richness, abundance, diversity, evenness, and community composition.

1.1 Background: Ecological role of bryophytes in the arid Southwest

In the American Southwest, bryophytes are small in stature and so low in biomass that they are easily overlooked. Paradoxically, bryophytes play as critical a role in arid ecosystems as they do in temperate and tropical ones, where they

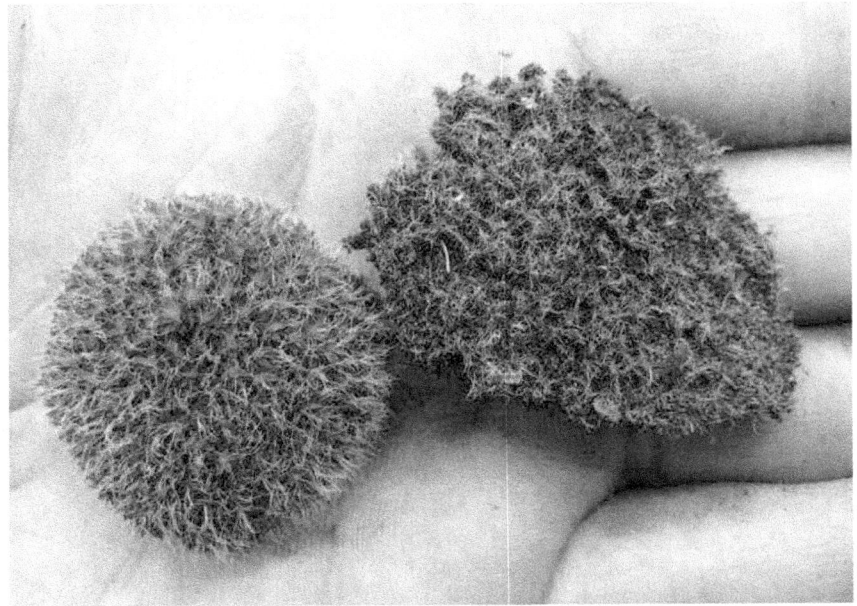

Figure 1. Many bryophytes tolerate the arid climate of Grand Canyon NP. by going dormant. **Right**: *Syntrichia ruralis* in its dry, dormant condition with leaves infolded. **Right**: *Syntrichia ruralis*, seconds after being sprayed with water. Like many desert adapted bryophytes, this species absorbs moisture rapidly like a sponge. The unfolding of its radially arranged leaves resemble a bouquet of flowers opening in fast motion.

cover entire surfaces of trees, logs, and rocks. Collectively, bryophytes are a pervasive group of plants, found throughout the world on every continent, where they substantially enrich biodiversity in most ecosystems (Crosby et al. 1999, Rydin 2009). Their diversity is greatest in moist temperate and tropical rainforests, while their biomass is greatest in boreal bogs (Rydin 2009). Even arid regions, like the American Southwest, support large numbers of these cryptogamic plants which form a notable proportion of local plant diversity (Hedenas 2007, Stark 2004, Stark & Brinda 2011).

Perhaps leading to this ubiquity was their emergence as one of the first organismal groups to colonize land some 400 million years ago. Since the beginning of terrestrial life, bryophytes have contributed to succession, soil stabilization, seedling establishment, biogeochemical cycling (water, carbon, and nutrients), symbiotic relationships, and habitat creation for macro and micro-invertebrates (Belnap & Lange 2003, Longton 1992, Wieder and Vitt 2006). Today, bryophytes continue to perform

these functions and others. Furthermore, their simple biology makes them sensitive biological indicators that will continue to provide important feedback relevant to pollution and global climate change (Slack 2011).

In arid ecosystems, the functionality of bryophytes is often augmented by other small and cryptic organisms, namely algae, bacteria, liverworts, lichens, and cyanobacteria, which co-establish with bryophytes to form biotic soil crust. Collectively the interwoven crust community has a significant impact on several main processes in aridland ecosystems and can be found colonizing exposed soil in much of the Southwest (Belnap and Lange 2003; fig. 2).

- The high water-holding capacity of bryophytes and neighboring algal-fungal networks aids in water uptake and retention by soil following rain events, in otherwise sandy soils (Belnap & Lang 2003). The crust allows neighboring vascular plants to access water that would otherwise readily evaporate, a vital role when water is the limiting factor to plant growth (Proctor 2009).

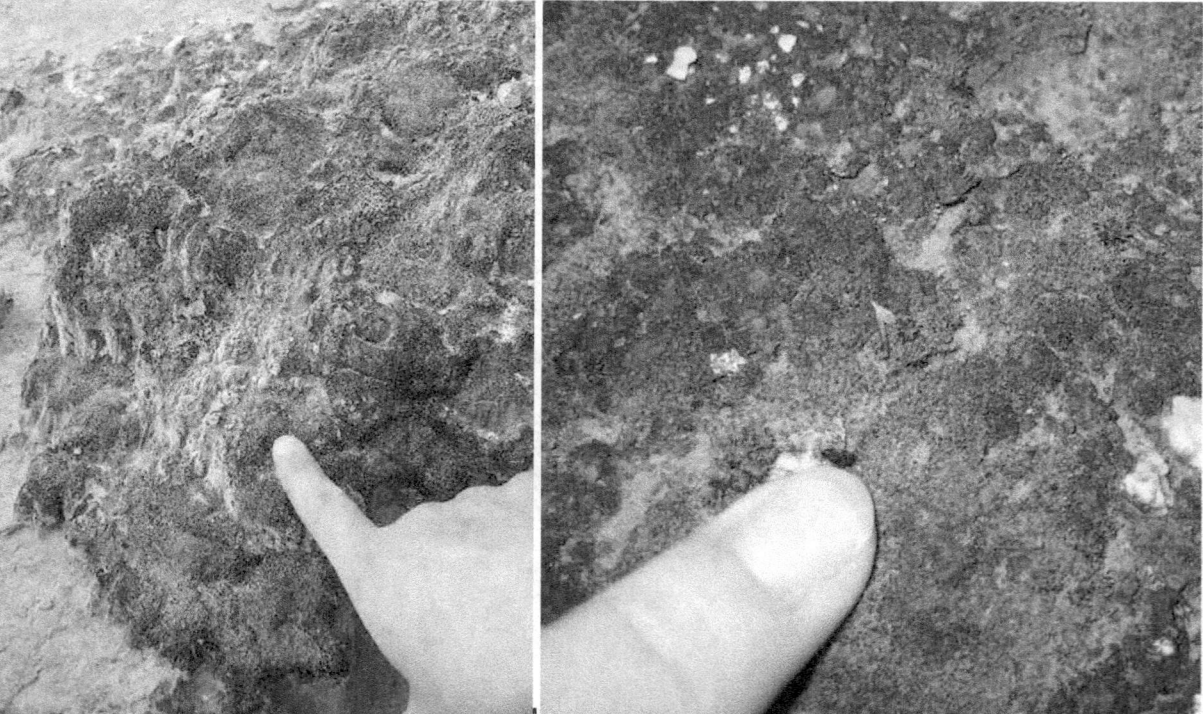

Figure 2. Well established soil crust communities on the South Rim (**left**) and North Rim (**right**) of Grand Canyon NP. Mosses usually compose a higher proportion of soil crust assemblages on the North Rim, giving these crusts a much greener appearance when moistened by morning dew or a rain event.

- This water-holding capacity, combined with the binding properties of soil crust increases the integrity of soil surfaces and prevents erosion from wind and water. (Eldridge 1998).

- The moist, stable surfaces provided by soil crust facilitate seedling germination and have been shown to impede establishment of invasive species in some studies (Morgan 2006).

- Bryophyte communities across all arid substrata (e.g. soil, logs, trees, rocks, waterfalls) offer vital habitat to micro- and macro-invertebrates such as nematodes, tardigrades, rotifers, mites, and insects. These organisms, which are the foundation of many food webs, seek out homes and nurseries in the buffered microclimates and protective architecture provided by bryophyte mats and cushions (Belnap 2003, Vanderpoorten & Goffinet 2009).

These are only a few of the known processes facilitated by bryophytes globally, but they clearly illustrate their importance to the health of aridland ecosystems like those found throughout much of GRCA.

1.2 Gaps in understanding bryophyte floristics of Grand Canyon National Park

Our current understanding of bryophyte floristics in Arizona remains inadequate, and is limited largely to the historic work of John Bartram (1924, 1927), James McCleary (1953, 1954, 1959, 1962), and Inez Haring (1947, 1961). The most recent additions to the state flora were two checklists contributed by Haring (1961) and Johnson (1978) more than 30 years ago. Modern floristic research will undoubtedly uncover species new to the state, and GRCA continues to provide a pristine and ecologically-rich region in which to focus such efforts. Over the past 50 years, though, this resource has barely been tapped for bryophyte research.

Inez Haring (1941, 1946) reported 69

species for GRCA, which, today, represent only about 17% of the approximately 450 bryophyte species known to occur in Arizona (Brian 2000, J. R. Spence unpublished data). Turning to other organismal groups for comparison suggested that many bryophyte species may await discovery in GRCA. Specifically, the contemporary vascular plant and lichen floras of GRCA represent ~31% (1201/3900) and ~21% (203/969) respectively of their state floras (Bates et al. 2010, Boykin and Nash 1995, SEINET 2011, Spence et al. in preparation). It seemed reasonable to surmise that a comparable proportion of bryophyte species could inhabit the park because broad environmental continua are known to increase the diversity of bryophytes as they do vascular plants, and most organisms for that matter. The geology, topography, climate, and biotic communities across the canyon's approximately 2,300 m elevation gradient vary on a scale unmatched by any other state or national park in the American West. The myriad of resulting microhabitats available to bryophytes along these continua should support a proportionately rich community, one that may represent a large component of the state's bryophyte diversity.

1.3 Gaps in understanding rock bryophyte ecology in the forests of Grand Canyon National Park

Understanding bryophyte community ecology in arid regions is critical to conserving the diversity and functionality of these plants. The bryophyte work of Inez Haring in GRCA (1941 & 1946) was mostly limited to floristics; her 1946 park checklist noted the distribution of resident species across five life zones, but did not include a quantitative investigation of these relationships at any scale— the community ecology of bryophytes in GRCA, therefore, remained unexplored from a quantitative standpoint and reflected a broader deficit in our understanding of rock bryophyte community ecology in Arizona and other semiarid regions of North America. Relevant research had addressed bryophyte ecology only incidentally in the pursuit of understanding soil crust functionality (e.g. Belnap 2002, Beymer and Klopatek 1991, Warren 2003), vulnerability (e.g. Anderson et al. 1982, Beymer and Klopatek 1992, Brotherson et al. 1983, Cole 1991), and, to a lesser extent, community patterns and processes (Bowker et al. 2000, Bowker et al. 2006, Kleiner and Harper 1977, Ponzetti et al. 2007, Rivera-Aguilar et al. 2006, Thompson et al. 2005).

Aside from soil crust research, I could find only three studies that deliberately investigated bryophyte community ecology on dry substrata in arid or semiarid regions of North America. These included an examination of forest epiphytes in a semi-arid valley of Montana (McCune and Antos 1982), a descriptive comparison of the microhabitat niches of aridland bryophytes on various substrata in California (Sagar and Wilson 2009), and a distribution analysis relating epilithic (rock-dwelling) species frequency to microhabitat features and photon flux within a chaparral-oak woodland in San Diego County, California (Alpert 1985). As mentioned above, the diverse range of habitats, vegetation communities, topography, and climatic conditions in GRCA provided a prime opportunity to study bryophyte community ecology in an arid ecosystem.

I chose to investigate the ecology of bryophyte communities on dry rock throughout the pinyon-juniper, ponderosa pine, and mixed conifer forests of GRCA for four reasons. First, my pilot study indicated that bryophytes occur more frequently on dry rocks throughout GRCA than on any other dry substratum (soil, trees, or logs). Additionally, I determined that bryophytes are most common at higher elevations where the pinyon-juniper, ponderosa pine, and mixed conifer forests prevail. And finally, pilot data and floristic work, including my own, suggested that rocks are the most species-rich dry substratum in the canyon.

Secondly, there is an explicit deficiency

in our understanding of how epilithic bryophyte communities respond to environmental gradients in arid systems. The challenges posed by sampling and identifying these scarce and taxonomically complex species may be cause for this deficiency.

Thirdly, changes in climate, forest architecture, and tree species are broadly known to affect patterns in bryophyte species richness, composition, and productivity (e.g. Asada et al. 2003, Corrales et al. 2010, Frahm and Gradstein 1991, Frahm and Ohlemüller 2001, Nash et al. 1977, Rambo and Muir 1998, Weibull 2001, Weibull and Rydin 2005, Vanderpoorten & Engels 2003); the forests of GRCA track a significant climatic continuum, crossing over 1,000 m of elevation and exhibiting structural and compositional differences that may further alter the microclimatic conditions experienced by bryophytes in the understory. Specifically, precipitation and temperature generally increase from the low-elevation pinyon-juniper forest to the ponderosa pine, and finally, to the mixed conifer forest, located at the highest elevations in GRCA (Pearson 1920, Daubenmire 1943, Moir and Ludwig 1979, White and Vankat 1993, Whittaker 1967, Woodbury 1947). Additionally, canopy closure and herbaceous ground cover increase from the open pinyon-juniper woodland to the dense mixed conifer forest, dominant tree species change, and the frequency of hardwoods increases. Collectively, these large and finer-scaled environmental gradients create unique habitats that I predicted would influence the bryophyte communities therein.

Lastly, I considered the challenges faced by bryologists and non-bryologists to manage and monitor these cryptic rock bryophyte communities in the aridlands of the American Southwest. Although bryophytes are known to respond acutely to environmental variation at fine scales, including physical properties of their substrata (e.g. Wiklund and Rydin 2004, Pharo and Beattie 2002, Sagar and Wilson 2009, Turner and Pharo 2005), as well as microclimatic conditions offered by topography and surrounding vegetation (e.g. Bowker et al.

2006, Eldridge and Tozer 1997, Weibull and Rydin 2005), it seemed appropriate to begin with a large-scale investigation. If forest type could significantly predict a large proportion of variation in rock bryophyte communities, then this macro-scaled three-level factor would provide a practical framework for understanding and monitoring rock bryophyte communities in GRCA.

I predicted that bryophyte richness, abundance, diversity, evenness, and community composition would differ significantly among the pinyon-juniper, ponderosa pine, and mixed conifer forests of GRCA. Additionally, I hypothesized that site-level variation in slope, aspect, potential direct incident radiation, rock type, and shade cover would predict additional variation independent of forest type and elevation. To my knowledge, no comparable investigations have been undertaken for epilithic bryophytes in arid regions of North America.

2 Study area: Grand Canyon National Park

2.1 Location

Grand Canyon National Park (GRCA) is located in northern Arizona and contains 446 km (277mi) of the Colorado River, which stretches 2,253 km (1,400 mi) from its headwaters in the Rocky Mountains of Colorado to its mouth, at the Gulf of California (Hirsch et al. 1990). The Colorado River is the largest river in the American Southwest with a 640,00 ha (518,000 acres) watershed, which drains portions of Colorado, Arizona, New Mexico, Utah, California, Nevada, Wyoming, and northwestern Mexico (Kammerer 1992). The canyon corridor averages 29 km (18 mi) wide and flows southwest down a 580 m (1,900 ft.) elevation gradient from Lake Powell to Lake Mead. GRCA encompasses 4,927 km² (1,902 mi²) of land in Coconino and Mohave Counties, and marks the convergence of four North American biomes: the Great Basin, Mohave, and Sonoran Deserts and the Colorado Plateau.

The park is situated in the southwest corner of the Colorado Plateau Province, a physiographic region that was uplifted without deformation. Centered approximately on the Four Corners region, the Colorado Plateau encompasses 33,700,000 ha (83,300,000 acres) spanning parts of Arizona, New Mexico, Colorado, and Utah. Within GRCA, the Kaibab and Kanab Plateaus border the Colorado River to the north and constitute the North Rim. The Coconino Plateau forms the canyon's South Rim and is approximately 300 m (1,000 ft.) lower than its northern counterpart. The Colorado River at the boundary of Lake Mead National Recreation Area is the lowest point in the park at 366 m (1,200 ft.) while Point Imperial is the highest at 2,683 m (8,803 ft.) on the Kaibab Plateau. This topographical relief of about 2,300 m (7,500 ft.) creates an extensive ecological-climatic gradient across GRCA.

2.2 Climate

Grand Canyon National Park has a continental and arid climate that ranges from relatively cool and moist on the North Rim to hot and dry in the lower reaches of the Inner Canyon (Sellers & Hill 1974; fig. 3). Climate data from the following three weather stations represent climatic variation found within the park: Phantom Ranch Station (771 m) at the Colorado River, Grand Canyon NP 2 Station on the South Rim (2,068 m), and Bright Angel Ranger Station on the North Rim (2,560 m). GRCA experiences a bimodal precipitation pattern that occurs predominantly as summer monsoons and winter snowfall, but varies greatly depending on elevation (Sellers & Hill 1974).

On the North Rim, annual precipitation ranges from 353 mm–1,143 mm (13.9 in–45.0 in.), with a mean annual precipitation of 515 mm (25 in.; WRCC 2011). The South Rim has a semi-arid climate with drier summers and milder winters than the North Rim, and receives approximately one third less precipitation, with a mean of 406 mm (16 in.). The Inner Canyon is the driest region of GRCA and lower reaches experience a desert climate that receives half the precipitation of the South Rim, mostly in the form of summer monsoon storms (WRCC 2011, Sellers & Hill 1974). Annual precipitation in the Inner Canyon, ranges from 119 mm to 417 mm (4.7 in–16.4 in), with a mean of 229 mm (10 in; WRCC 2011).

Mean winter lows are most extreme in January on the North Rim (-9°C, 16°F) and most mild at the base of the Inner Canyon (3°C, 38°F) (WRCC 2011). Highs in the summer average 39°C (103°F) in the Inner Canyon, while both the South and North Rims are much cooler, averaging about 28° C (83°F) (WRCC 2011).

Plant growth in GRCA is limited by frost and extreme aridity (Huisinga et al. 2006). The Inner Canyon rarely receives

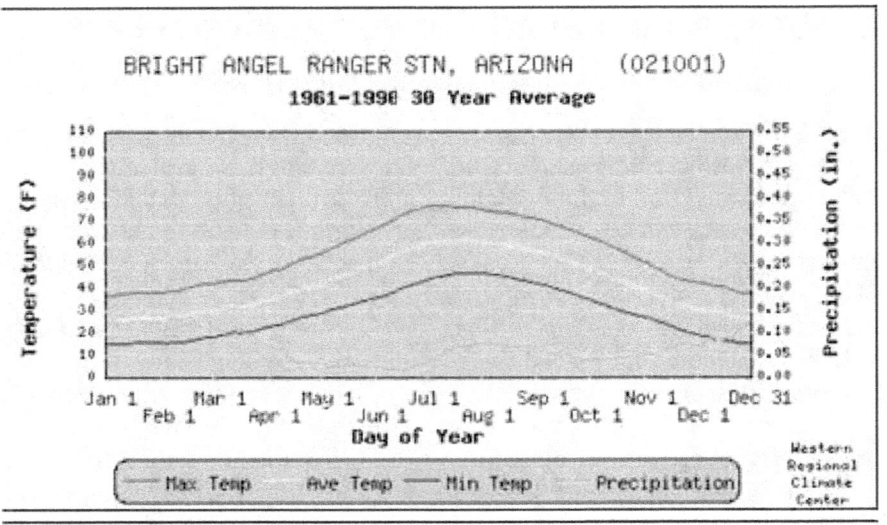

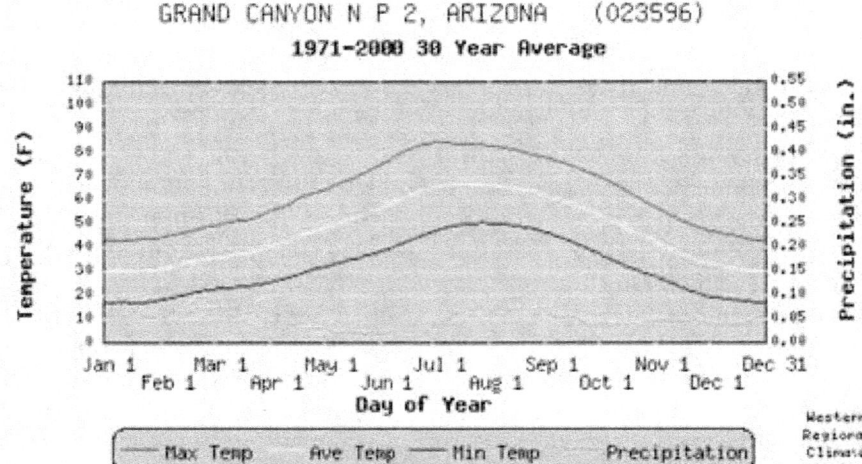

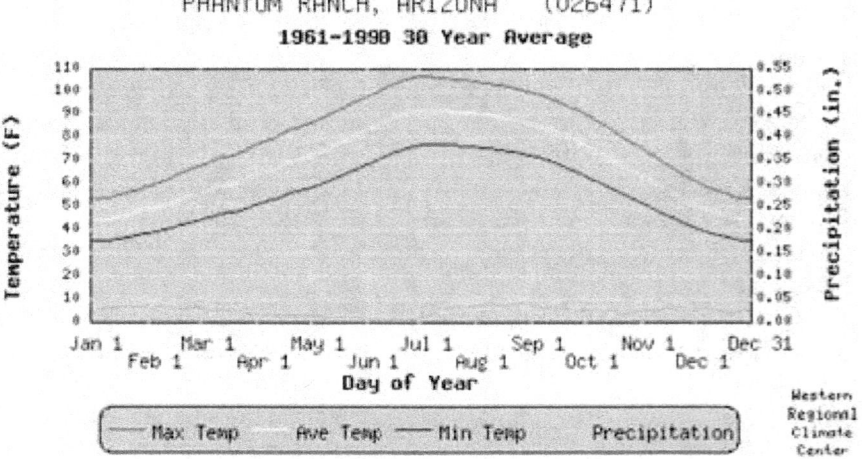

Figure 3. Climate of Grand Canyon NP (GRCA) at three elevations. Top: High elevation climate regime at Bright Angel Station (Grand Canyon NP 2 Station) on North Rim at 2,068 m. Middle: Intermediate elevation climate regime at Grand Canyon NP 2 Station on the South Rim at 2,107 m (1971–2000). Bottom: Low elevation climate regime at Phantom Ranch Station at the base of the Inner Canyon along the Colorado River at 771 m. (Graphs courtesy of WRCC.)

frost, experiencing between 234 and 365 frost-free days annually, but lack of moisture limits the growing season for most plants to just after the summer monsoons and winter rainfall (Huisinga et al. 2006, WRCC 2011). On the North Rim, there are fewer frost-free days (21 to 155), but increased moisture availability enables a longer growing season (WRCC 2011, Huisinga et al. 2006). Although the number of frost-free days on the South Rim is greater (97 to 167), the growing season is not effectively longer due to the opposing effect of heat stress (WRCC 2011, Huisinga et al. 2006).

2.3 Geology

The layered rock walls of Grand Canyon reveal much of the geologic history of North America, and the fossil record therein traces the evolution of life from the Precambrian through the Permian (McKee 1982). During the early Pliocene Epoch, between 7 and 9 mya, the Colorado Plateau uplifted and provided the mile-high land mass which would be carved by the Colorado River over the next 3 to 5 million years (McKee & McKee 1972). This fine example of aridland erosion has revealed 11 major formations that were primarily deposited by ancient swamps, seas, oceans, and coastal dunes (Breed and Roat 1976).

The oldest rocks (c.a. 1.7 bya) of Grand Canyon occur at the base of the inner gorge and are primarily crystalline granite that forms slopes and sheer cliffs. These rocks are divided into two formations— the Vishnu Group and Zoroaster Gneiss—which are composed predominantly of mica schist and felsic gneisses (Damon and Giletti 1961, Noble & Hunter 1916). A group of younger Precambrian rocks was deposited next during the Proterozoic Era, and today forms a discontinuous layer at the top of the gorge, known collectively as the Grand Canyon Supergroup (Breed and Roat 1976, Ford et al. 1972). These younger Precambrian strata are the oldest sedimentary rocks in the canyon and include basaltic lavas, dolomites, shales and hard sandstones (Breed & Roat 1976). The

many formations of this group rest at a 10°–12° angle to the nearly horizontal Cambrian strata that lie above (Breed & Roat 1976). This angular relationship between the Grand Canyon Supergroup and these Cambrian strata is called the Great Unconformity (McKee 1982).

The remaining sedimentary rocks in Grand Canyon rise approximately 1,500 m (5,000 ft.) above the Precambrian gorge. These Paleozoic rocks were deposited during the early Cambrian between 550 and 250 mya and are rich with plant and animals fossils (Breed and Roat 1976). The oldest three formations, a sandstone-mudstone-limestone sequence, create a broad terrace known as the Tonto Platform. This group forms a shelf up to 5 km (3 mi) wide in the lower reaches of the Inner Canyon. The soft Bright Angel Shale formation forms gentle mudstone slopes 60 to 140 m (200–450 ft.) tall that grade into the shelf of the Tonto Platform, which is comprised of the Tapeats Sandstone formation. Where the Bright Angel Shale formation has completely eroded away, the hard Tapeats Sandstone formation is exposed (McKee 1936). Composed of coarse sand grains, Tapeats Sandstone is the oldest of the Paleozoic rocks and ranges from 30 to 90 m (100–300 ft.) thick. The upper cliffs of the Tonto are formed by the Muav Limestone formation, which rises above the terrace 150 to 800 feet (Breed and Roat 1976).

Directly above the Muav Limestone, the Temple Butte and Redwall Limestone formations collectively create a tall, continuous cliff that occurs throughout the canyon (Breed and Roat 1976). Composed of dolomite, the Temple Butte Limestone was deposited during the Devonian Period (370 mya) and forms a narrow band in the eastern canyon, which progressively widens to over 300 m (1,000 ft.) in the western section of the canyon (McKee 1937). The Redwall Limestone was deposited above during the Mississippian Period (330 mya) and forms a relatively uniform red cliff approximately 500 feet tall (McKee and Gutschick 1969). Composed of a grey limestone, this formation is superficially stained red by the overlying Supai Group. Springs and caves commonly occur in this stratum because of its high porosity.

During the Pennsylvanian and Permian Periods (310 mya), red beds of the Supai Group were deposited (White 1929). Today, this group forms a broad sequence of ledges and cliffs that span about 200 m (650 ft) and whose strata are composed of fine-grained, step-forming sandstones and slope-forming shales (Breed and Roat 1976). The Hermit Shale formation above forms slopes of red siltstone that average 300 feet in thickness. Atop this slope is a tall, white cliff formation called the Coconino Sandstone, which ranges from 15 to 90 m (50–300 ft) thick (McKee 1933). This white formation of quartz sand grains was deposited by desert dunes in the early Permian (270 mya). The remaining 180 m (600 ft) that lead to the canyon's rim crosses cliffs of the Toroweap and Kaibab Formations. These sandstone and limestone rocks were deposited during the mid-Permian (273 mya) by an advancing and retreating sea. The lithological composition of these two formations is highly variable throughout the canyon, and includes limestones, sandy limestones, sandstones, and beds of chert (McKee 1938). The Kaibab Formation tops both canyon rims and produces a gray-brown podzolic soil (USDA 1938).

2.4 Vascular plant communities

Many plant communities exist along the altitudinal relief from the Inner Canyon to the North Rim (Daubenmire 1943; Warren et al. 1982). These biotic communities have been described under several classification systems, but broadly include plant associations of river and stream riparian zones, desert scrubland, pinyon-juniper woodland, ponderosa pine forest, mixed conifer forest, and sub-alpine forest (fig. 4; Merkle 1954, 1962, Moir and Ludwig 1979, Rasmussen 1941, Warren et al. 1982, White and Vankat 1993).

2.4.1 Riparian and wetland habitats

These aquatic, semi-aquatic, and moist habitats comprise springs, seeps, marshes, and riverside margins. Springs and seeps create micro-climates that maintain higher levels of moisture, shade, and humidity than the surrounding canyon (Spence 2008). The magnitude of their buffering effect varies, but overall these oases greatly increase the diversity of vascular plants, often offering refuge to endemic and rare species. The marshes and riverside riparian communities along the Colorado River corridor are predominantly deciduous woodland vegetation consisting of non-native tamarisk (*Tamarix ramosissima*) and arrow weed (*Pluchea sericea*), which grow along sandy banks (Stevens et al. 1995).

A less abundant, but stable marsh community is maintained by flood control from Glen Canyon Dam. After dam construction in 1963, the abundance and size of marshes dramatically increased in response to a reduced flooding regime (Stevens et al. 1995). This allowed the establishment of fluvial wet and dry marshes, which expanded along the river and along return-channels and backwaters where fine sediment collects (Stevens et al. 1995; Turner and Karpiscak 1980). These marshes include various emergent and seasonally flooded communities (NatureServe 2010).

A common assemblage on silty loam soil is the cattail-reed community (e.g. *Typha domingensis, Phragmites australis, Juncus* spp.), while loamy sand supports a horseweed-Bermuda grass association (e.g. *Conyza canadensis, Polygonum aviculare, Cynodon dactylon*) (Stevens et al. 1995, Warren et al. 1982). Additionally, sections of the river rarely inundated support horsetail-willow dry marshes on sandy soils (e.g. *Equisetum* × *ferrissii, Salix exigua, Andropogon glomeratus*) (NatureServe 2010, Stevens et al. 1995, Warren et al. 1982). The post-dam environment along the Colorado River has enabled the establish-

Figure 4. Major biotic communities in Grand Canyon National Park. **A.** Mixed conifer forest community, restricted to the North Rim (Widforss Trail). **B.** Ponderosa pine forest community, common on the North and South Rims (Cape Final Trail). **C.** Pinyon-juniper woodland community, common along the South Rim and the upper reaches of the Inner Canyon down to ~1500 m (Rim Trail). **D.** Desert scrub community, present below ~1500 m in the Inner Canyon (North Kaibab Trail). **E.** Spring riparian community, scattered at various elevations, but prevalent in the Redwall Limestone formation (Roaring Springs). **F.** River riparan community, present along the Colorado River and its tributaries.

ment of a new riparian community that colonizes river banks previously scoured every year by spring floods (e.g. *Tamarix ramosissima, Salix* spp., *Baccharis emoryi, B. salicifolia, Prosopis glandulosa* var. *torreyana,* and *Pluchea sericea* (NatureServe 2010, Stevens et al. 1995).

2.4.2 Desert scrub and grassland

Outside the riparian river corridor, desert scrub and desert grassland communities inhabit terraces and slopes along the Inner Canyon. Although these xerophytic plants are adapted to extreme heat and prolonged drought, their distribution throughout this landscape is restricted by the lower reaches of frost, which typically extend to the Supai Formation (1,500 m, 5,000 ft.). The low-elevation desert flora of Grand Canyon is diverse in part because it contains species otherwise exclusive to one of the four North American deserts,

the Great Basin, Mohave, Sonoran, and Chihuahuan. Many species in the cool desert community of GRCA are found throughout Marble Canyon where species characteristic of the high-elevation Great Basin Desert occur (e.g. *Coleogyne ramosissima, Ephedra torreyana, Atriplex canescens, Opuntia basilaris, Bouteloua eriopoda, Bromus tectorum, Artemisia tridentata, Lycium pallidum*) (NatureServe 2010, Warren et al. 1982).

Warm desert communities occur in GRCA from the convergence of the Little Colorado River to the Grand Wash Cliffs in the west, and reflect species characteristic of the Mohave and Sonoran deserts which reach their western and northern limits, respectively, in Grand Canyon. Common species in this mixed community include *Acacia greggii, Canotia holacantha, Ephedra fasciculata, Gutierrezia sarothrae, Ambrosia dumosa, Encelia farinosa,* and *Larrea*

2.4.3 Pinyon-juniper woodland

The pinyon-juniper woodland is one of two dominant forest communities on the South Rim. This open, dry ecotype also extends below the South Rim along slopes of the Bright Angel Shale formation, down to about 1,900 m (6,234 ft) (Woodbury 1947). On the North Rim, this community occurs in a narrow strip along the rim of the canyon at an elevation outside its niche. The community is sustained by a topographical-climatic phenomenon known as the "rim effect", in which hot, dry updrafts from the Inner Canyon create climatic and soil conditions similar to those present at lower elevations (Halvorson 1979). The fully developed pinyon-juniper woodland of the South Rim is dominated by widely-spaced, small coniferous trees, namely Colorado pinyon (*Pinus edulis*), one-seed juniper (*Juniperus monosperma*), Utah juniper (*Juniperus osteosperma*), and Rocky Mountain juniper (*Juniperus scopulorum*) (Howell 1941). However, in steeply sloped drainages and within small ravines, ponderosa pine (*Pinus ponderosa*) and Gambel oak (*Quercus gambelii*) often replace the ubiquitous pinyon and juniper species (Merkle 1952). Several deciduous trees and shrubs including Gambel oak, cliff-rose (*Purshia stansburiana*), serviceberry (*Amelanchier utahensis*), and sagebrush (*Artemisia* spp.) occur scattered between the broadly spaced dominant trees (Merkle 1952).

The sparse understory of the pinyon-juniper woodland is predominantly Arizona fescue (*Festuca arizonica*), blue grama grass (*Bouteloua gracilis*), and prairie June grass (*Koeleria cristata*), which grow in clumps beneath the conifers (Merkle 1952). Banana yucca (*Yucca baccata*), hedgehog cacti (*Echinocereus* spp.), and beehive cacti (*Mammillaria* spp.) occur infrequently, reflecting the hot, dry climate of this ecotype (Howell 1941).

In the warm temperate climate below the North and South Rims, deciduous shrubs become more abundant and diverse, but are restricted to non-vertical slopes in the Toroweap, Hermit Shale, and Supai Formations. Common species include hop hornbeam (*Ostrya knowltonii*), pale hop tree (*Ptelea trifoliata*), flowering ash (*Fraxinus cuspidata*), and grease bush (*Glossopetalon nevadense*) (Warren et al. 1982). Silk tassel (*Garrya* sp.) is an unusual local phenomenon on these slopes.

2.4.4 Ponderosa pine forest

Ponderosa pine replaces Colorado pinyon and one-seed juniper at approximately 2,200 m (7,300 ft.), marking the ecotone into the ponderosa pine forest on the South and North Rims (Merkle 1952, 1962). Pure stands of ponderosa pine forest are common on the South Rim, however pinyon-pine and one-seed juniper frequently dominate ridges and slopes (Merkle 1962). On the North Rim, white fir (*Abies concolor*) is sporadically associated with ponderosa pine at low elevations (White and Vankat 1993). Grasses (*F. arizonica, Elymus elymoides, K. cristata*) are the pervasive understory plants of the open ponderosa pine forest, however sagebrush (*A. tridentata*) occurs in several stands on both rims (Merkle 1962). Infrequent secondary shrubs include rabbitbrush (*C. depressus*), cliff rose (*P. stansburiana*), and Gambel oak (*Q. gambelii*), while common herbs are Hill lupine (*Lupinus hillii*) and redroot buckwheat (*Eriogonum racemosum*) (Merkle 1962, Warren et al. 1982).

2.4.5 Mixed conifer forest

Extensive mixed conifer stands occur above 2,500 m (8,250 ft.) and are thus restricted to the North Rim's Kaibab Plateau (Merkle 1962). However, the South Rim supports small pockets of this high-elevation community in north-facing cool-air drainages along the sloping Toroweap Formation (Merkle 1954). The mixed conifer forest has the highest diversity of tree species in GRCA. Various associations of ponderosa pine, white fir, blue spruce (*Picea pungens*), Douglas fir (*Pseudotsuga menziesii*), and aspen (*Pop-*

ulus tremuloides) comprise this cold and relatively moist temperate forest (Merkle 1962, White and Vankat 1993). White fir and ponderosa pine are the most frequent and uniformly distributed species, although white fir density greatly exceeds that of ponderosa pine (Merkle 1962). Its relatively closed understory is also the most diverse and dense of all forest types in the canyon (Merkle 1962, White and Vankat 1982). Common shrubs include juniper (*J. communis*), creeping barberry (*Mahonia repens*), manzanita (*Arctostaphylos patula*), New Mexican locust (*Robinia neomexicana*), and rose (*Rosa arizonicum*). Prevalent herbs and grasses are frequent in open woods and meadows, and include bird's food trefoil (*Lotus utahensis*), Virginia strawberry (*Fragaria ovalis*), yarrow (*Achillea millefolium*), mutton grass (*Poa fendleriana*), pine dropseed (*Blepharoneuron tricholepis*), and mountain muhly (*Muhlenbergia montana*) (Merkle 1962, White and Vankat 1993).

2.4.6 Subalpine forest
A cold, mesic subalpine forest occurs at the highest elevations (2,800 m, 8,700 ft.) on the North Rim (Merkle 1954). Here, the canopy becomes more homogenous and closed, dominated by Engelmann spruce (*Picea engelmannii*) and subalpine fir (*Abies lasiocarpa*), two drought-intolerant species (Merkle 1962, White and Vankat 1993). Fire-tolerant quaking aspen co-occurs most frequently in areas that have burned. The dark understory supports the lowest diversity and cover of shrubs and herbs in the canyon. Common species include creeping barberry, common juniper, Porter's licorice root (*Ligusticum porteri*), mutton grass, and squirreltail (*Elymus elymoides*) (Merkle 1962, White and Vankat 1954). However, high-elevation open meadows on the Kaibab Plateau are rich in wildflowers, grasses, and herbs (Merkle 1962), and are locally represented in a region called the Basin.

2.5 Previous bryological work in Grand Canyon National Park
Historically, bryophyte collecting in Grand Canyon National Park has been incidental or of short duration. In the 1930's and 1940's, the first vascular plant collectors to visit GRCA documented 25 bryophyte species, which occurred mainly at seeps, springs, and waterfalls (Clover and Jotter 1944, Hawbecker 1936, Patraw 1932). Seven bryophyte species from the North Rim's Kaibab Plateau were included in Hawbecker's 1936 revised check-list of plants of Grand Canyon National Park. During the summers of 1938 and 1939, Clover and Jotter (1944) explored 1,060 km (660 mi) of the Colorado and Green Rivers from Greenriver, Utah to Boulder Dam, Nevada. Their expedition navigated through Grand Canyon for 42 days and, while collecting concentrated on vascular plants, 18 bryophyte species were recovered from various springs, waterfalls, and side-canyons along the Colorado River.

The only comprehensive floristic investigation of bryophytes in Grand Canyon was that of Inez Haring, who spent three months in the canyon during the fall of 1941 and 1946. Haring's final 1946 checklist documented 64 species, 31 genera, and 12 families of bryophytes. She collected along trails on the North and South Rims, and visited Dripping Springs, Indian Gardens, Rowe's Well, and several other Inner Canyon localities. Concentrated collecting time was spent at moist, forested sites in the eastern portion of the canyon, east of Point Sublime. Her most westward and eastward collections were made at Kanab Creek in Slide Canyon and at Waterloo Hill, west of Desert View, respectively (Haring 1946). *Grimmia* was the most common genus collected, although the 6 reported species surely underrepresented the actual richness of this genus within the canyon (Haring 1946). Three common species, *Syntrichia ruralis*, *Gemmabryum caespiticium*, and *Bryum lanatum*, were ubiquitous across the elevation range sampled (Haring 1941). Although her survey traversed much of the park's altitudinal relief, Haring's collections inadequately represented below-rim and dry habitat throughout the park. Her work qualitatively described the habitats and distributional patterns of bryophytes, but lacked the quantitative data necessary to elucidate ecological community patterns within GRCA.

In the 50 years since the work of Haring, bryophytes have not been the focus of subsequent plant collecting in GRCA (Brian 2000). However, five bryophyte species have been reported new to the park as components of vascular plant and bryophyte checklists for Arizona (McCleary 1953, 1954, McDougal 1947ab, 1948). Of these records, two were erroneous; one was a synonym, and one a duplicate record (McCleary 1953, 1954).

3. Bryophyte floristics in Grand Canyon National Park

3.1 Objectives

There were ten objectives for this floristic endeavor:

1. Expand the known bryoflora of GRCA by collecting bryophytes from a variety of biotic communities within six defined geographic regions (collection regions) in the park and by incorporating modern collections made since the 1940s.

2. Voucher collections of each taxon with curated specimens to be housed in appropriate herbaria.

3. Produce a contemporary checklist based on modern and verified historic collections.

4. Report the local distribution and microhabitat specificity of each bryophyte species.

5. Determine common species associated with major substrata in the six collection regions.

6. Report collection regions and substratum types supporting high regional diversity.

7. Determine significant range extensions for species new to Arizona and GRCA.

8. Note species of conservation concern and their respective habitats in the park.

9. Qualitatively assess if the low-elevation bryoflora in GRCA appears to hold characteristic species from the four North American deserts, which surround the park.

10. Offer management implications for protecting vulnerable bryophyte habitats and species of conservation concern in GRCA.

3.2 Methods

In order to produce a comprehensive bryoflora for GRCA, I compiled and reviewed historic and modern collections made prior to and after 1960, respectively, and contributed my own set of specimens, which were collected between 2007 and 2010. The details of processing specimens and summarizing their associated data follow.

3.2.1 Historic collection review

The Grand Canyon Herbarium houses 324 historic bryophyte specimens, most of which were collected and deposited by Inez Haring prior to 1946, and are hereafter referred to as the historic collections. I reviewed the majority of these on loan at the Deaver Herbarium (ASC) of Northern Arizona University, Flagstaff. I did not examine a partial set of duplicates made by Inez Haring that are housed at the Museum of Northern Arizona, Flagstaff; nor did I examine the collections of Clover and Jotter (1944), which reside at the University of Arizona Herbarium (ARIZ), Tucson. Twenty-five of the collections referenced in Clover and Jotter (1944) are on loan at the Deaver Herbarium (ASC). I will review these collections, and, if necessary, create an addendum to this report. Finally, I updated the nomenclature of all historic specimens to correspond with the current Bryophyte Flora of North America, Volumes 27, 28, and 29 (FNA eds. 2007+). However, I also referenced recent work (Huttenen and Ignatov 2004, Ignatov and Huttenen 2002) in the family Brachytheciaceae, for which several genus treatments remained incomplete as of January 2012.

3.2.2 Modern floristic collecting

The modern floristic collection constitutes a compilation of my own collections from field sampling and a set of mostly unidentified collections contributed by Glenn Rink, John Spence, and Larry Stevens.

3.2.2.1 Contributed modern collections. The botanists mentioned above donated 150 bryophyte specimens, which they had collected in GRCA over the course of 53 field days between 1998 and 2005. I identified the majority of these collections at the Deaver Herbarium, and incorporated the named specimens into the floristic analysis and the GRCA voucher collection. Details on curation are outlined in section 3.2.3.

3.2.2.2 Modern field sampling.

Modern collecting was authorized by the National Park Service. I collected over 1,310 specimens over the course of 56 field days during the spring and summer months from March 2007 to April 2010 (fig. 5). The goal of field sampling was to balance species capture with an estimation of species frequency in different habitats across the park's varied landscape.

I divided GRCA into six collection regions: (1) the North Rim, (2) the South Rim,(3) the Inner Canyon (below the South and North Rims to 0.5 km from the Colorado River), (4) the Colorado River (1 km corridor), (5) Lake Mead vicinity (most eastern tail of GRCA, west of the lake), and (6) Marble Canyon. Trail corridors within all but the latter two regions were visited in order to efficiently and safely explore most of the topographic, geologic, and climatic variation present therein (fig. 5). I attempted to make collections from all unique microhabitats encountered along trails in order to maximize species capture. Little field time was allotted to Marble Canyon and the Lake Mead vicinity due to accessibility challenges. These areas should be further explored by bryolo-

gists in the near future. A field summary for GRCA follows, listing the trails, elevations, and vegetation types traversed by modern and historic (before 1950) collectors as well as the minimum number of field days based on collection records. The Catalog of Accepted Taxa summarizes the distribution and frequency of each species across GRCA.

3.2.2.3 Field summary for historic and modern collections.

North Rim collections (NRim). Historic and modern collectors have spent approximately 64 days collecting bryophytes on the North Rim's Kaibab Plateau, of which 38 days comprise modern collecting time (table 1). The majority of collections were made between Powell Plateau and Walhalla Plateau, two regions dominated by mixed conifer and spruce-fir forest and interspersed with patches of open meadow and ponderosa pine forest. The following trails were sampled intensively by the author: Cliff Springs, Widforss, Cape Final, Point Imperial, and Ken Patrick. I made collections at many forested sites, springs, ponds, and open meadows including Little Park Lake vicinity, Robber's Roost, Cape Royal, Bright Angel Point, Upper Thompson Spring, and Greenland Lake. Other modern and historic collections have been

Figure 5. Modern bryophyte collection sites visited in Grand Canyon NP, Arizona, over the course of 56 field days during the spring and summer months from March 2007 to April 2010. Inset illustrates park location within the Colorado Plateau of the American Southwest.

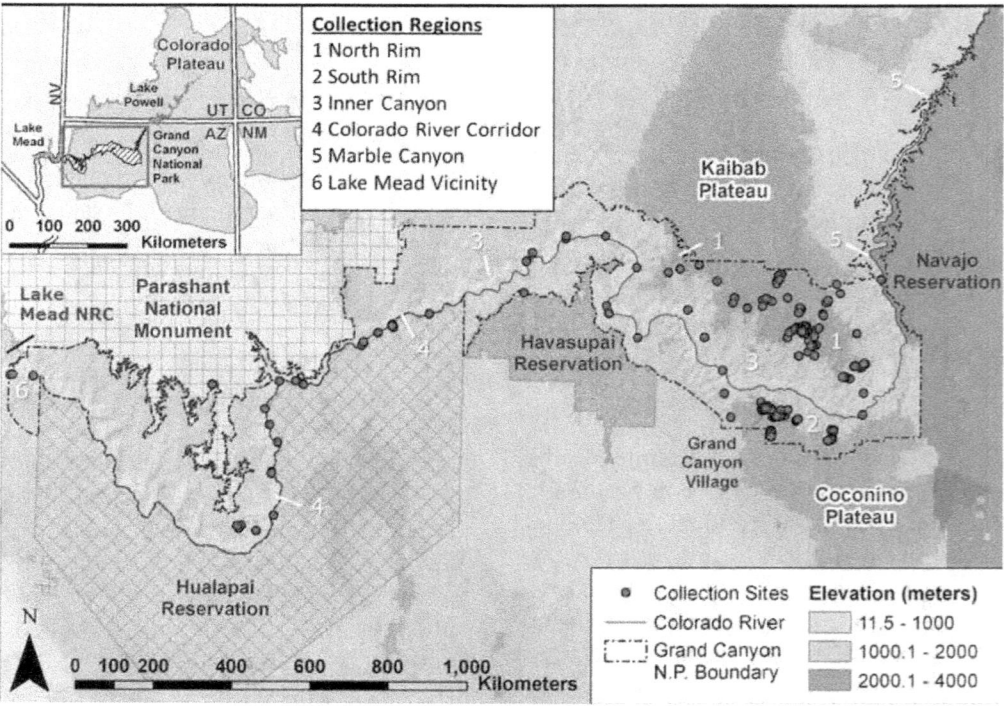

Table 1. Tally of bryophyte taxa and field collection days by collection region. For each collection region, the estimated number of field collecting days, state records, park records, species richness, and family richness is listed. The number of taxa found restricted to one region (Species unique to region) is also listed. The tally of acrocarpous (Acrocarp) and pleurocarpous (Pleurocarp) moss taxa and liverwort species is given by region.

Collection region	Field days (historic; modern)	AZ records	Park records	Species and varieties	Families	Species unique to region	Acrocarp moss taxa	Pleurocarp moss taxa	Liverwort species
GRCA	156 (47; 109)	28	107	155	33	–	115	29	11
North Rim	64 (26; 38)	20	58	93	27	36	64	20	7
South Rim	30 (16; 14)	1	23	43	12	5	38	5	0
Inner Canyon	78 (12; 66)	18	69	105	23	16	85	16	4
Colorado River	18 (0; 18)	8	35	49	12	6	43	4	2
Lake Mead	1 (0; 1)	2	13	20	7	1	19	1	0
Marble Canyon	2 (0; 2)	0	1	4	4	1	1	2	1

made at Neil Spring, Milk Creek, Castle Lake, Slide Canyon, Big Springs, North Canyon Spring, Aspen Canyon, De-Motte Park, Powell Saddle, Nankoweap Basin, Marble Flats, and The Basin.

South Rim collections (SRim). Botanists have spent a total of 30 days collecting bryophytes in the South Rim region, a relatively flat section of the Coconino Plateau from the westerly Pasture Wash to the easterly locations of Desert View and Waterloo Hill. Pinyon-juniper woodland lines the rim, while ponderosa pine forest covers the remainder of this region. I collected heavily over 14 days along the Arizona Trail near Grand Canyon Village and the entire lengths of Rim Trail and Shoshone Point Trail. In the past, Inez Haring covered additional ground at Pasture Wash, Rowe's Well, Lipan Point, Desert View, and Waterloo Hill, as well as scattered locations in Grand Canyon Village.

Inner Canyon collections (Inner). A total of 78 days have been spent surveying bryophytes below the North and South Rims. Vegetation communities in the Inner Canyon begin as mixed conifer forest below much of the North Rim, and as pinyon-juniper woodland below much of the South Rim. The desert scrub communities begin around 1,500 m and continue to the Colorado River. Modern collectors sampled intensely in this region for approximately 66 days

(table 1). Specifically, I sampled the following trails intensively: Bright Angel, North and South Kaibab, Waldron, Boucher, and Grandview (to Miner Spring). I also sampled at Havasupai Canyon (<1/4 mi past GRCA border), Elves' Chasm, and Hermit Trail. Other collectors have sampled minimally in many canyons (Lava, Kwagnut, Nankoweap, Kanabownits, Green Springs), along creeks (Basalt, Clear, Unkar, Manzanita, Cave, Kanab, Shinumo), at waterfalls (Muav, Vasey's Paradise) and at springs (Kanabownits, Angel, Monument Creek, Indian Gardens).

Marble Canyon collections (Marble). Much terrain remains unexplored in the upper portion of GRCA and no historic collecting occurred here. The park boundary begins below the rims and there are few trails, thus access is largely restricted to the Colorado River. Modern collectors John Spence and Larry Stevens briefly visited springs on two separate days: Saddle Canyon, Buckfarm Canyon, and Keystone Spring.

Lake Mead vicinity collections (Mead). This region also remains largely unexplored. Accessing this area is dangerous and difficult as the terrain consists of intricately branching drainages surrounding Lake Mead, which is at a historic low (< 330 m). The vegetation is desert scrubland. No historic bryophyte collecting has been done in this region. I spent one day in January of 2009 collecting in the vicinity of Lake Mead just east of the GRCA boundary and west of the Grand Wash Cliffs (table 1).

Colorado River Corridor collections (River). Modern collectors have spent a total of 18 days sampling bryophytes within a 1 km corridor of the Colorado River (table 1). At least several days were spent along the Colorado River by Clover and Jotter, but their specimen data was not available for review. Riparian vegetation occurs on sloping and flat banks where beaches have formed. Otherwise, steep cliffs that line the river are largely inaccessible. Springs and travertine seeps occur here. Above this narrow margin, the sparse desert scrub vegetation of the Inner Canyon begins. I spent 10 days in the fall of 2007 collecting along the river from Bright Angel Creek to Diamond Creek. Efforts were focused along the riparian zone and at springs (Pumpkin, Warm, Artesian, 194-Mile, the Parashant, 220-Mile, 205-Mile), seeps (few are named except Ledges), mouths of side canyons (Nankoweap, Clear Creek, Forester, Havasu, Deubendorff, Mohawk, Saddle) and silty banks of the riparian zone (few are named except Fat City Beach and Hell's Hollow). In the *Catalog of Accepted Taxa* (3.3.4), the abbreviation CRM will be used for the respective Colorado River Mile of a particular locality.

3.2.3 Floristic analysis
I compiled all available locality data associated with each historic and modern collection into one database, which enabled me to conduct a comprehensive floristic analysis. Specifically, I summarized patterns of species distributions throughout the six collection regions in GRCA. In addition to locality information, I included for each collection the specimen's genus, family, habitat type, collection date, bryophyte group (moss/liverwort), growth form (acrocarpous or pleurocarpous moss; leafy or thalloid liverwort), elevation, and record status (park/state). I summarized ecology and trait patterns for taxa and collection regions with the aid of R (R

Development Core Team 2011). The raw collections data will also be made accessible on SEINet (Southwest Environmental Information Network) for reference and specimen loans in concordance with the GRCA Herbarium and Deaver Herbarium (ASC). Collection dates of each specimen were used to estimate field collecting effort by each collector. The local elevation range of each taxon was estimated from the reported maximum and minimum elevations from which a taxon was collected in the park. Detailed microhabitat descriptions were used to summarize habitat variation of each taxon, but were less commonly available for historic collections.

3.3 Results

3.3.1 Historic collection review
I examined 285 of the 324 historic collections housed in the GRCA Herbarium, as the taxa corresponding to these collections had poorly resolved family treatments during the time they were determined in the 1940's (e.g. Bryaceae, Grimmiaceae, and Pottiaceae). Correct determinations were assumed for the remaining 118 collections. After reviewing these 285 questionable specimens, I updated the nomenclature of 87 and assigned new determinations to 67, which left 38 specimens unresolved (Appendix A). Most of these collections represented duplicate taxa and so the number of incorrectly identified taxa was much fewer. The 38 unresolved collections will be reviewed by a specialist and if an addendum is necessary, it will become available online at http://science.nature. nps.gov/im/units/scpn/products.cfm. As a result of the historic collection review, I moved 26 previously reported taxa (Brian 2000, Haring 1944, 1946) to the *Catalog of Excluded Taxa* (3.3.5); this abridgement reduces the historic bryoflora of GRCA from 69 to 42 taxa. Several species in this list are tentatively excluded, awaiting review, including 6 species that were documented in the historic checklists of Clover and Jotter (1944) and Hawbecker (1936). Notably, of the 42 confirmed historic bryophyte taxa, all but 8 species (*Philonotis fontana, Funaria muhlenbergii, Leptobryum pyriforme, Pohlia cruda, Orthotrichum pellucidum, Orthotrichum pumilum, Pterygoneurum*

Table 2. Species new to the state of Arizona. For each species, the frequency of collection from unique localities is listed as either Freq (10–20), Infreq (5–10), or Rare (<5), followed by the specific number of localities where the species was found, all collection regions in which a taxon was found, elevation, global distribution, description of range extension, and the observed habitat (cwd=coarse woody debris) are listed for each new bryophyte record. Cardinal directions are abbreviated.

Species	Frequency (# localities)	Collection region(s)	Elevation (m)	Global distribution	Range extension	Growth form & sex	Habitat
Barbula convoluta	infreq (5)	N.Rim, Inner	2400–2600	British Colombia, scattered U.S. (CA, ID, IL, MT, OR, TX, UT, WA)	Southern extension	dioicous acrocarp	shaded soil, rock
Didymodon fallax	rare (4)	Inner, River	500–1400	Global including bordering states	Not significant	dioicous acrocarp	riverside, seep, waterfall
Didymodon nevadensis	infreq (9)	N.Rim, Inner, River, Mead	500–2400	British Columbia, W. U.S. (CO, NV, NM, NB, TX)	Not significant	dioicous acrocarp	soil, limestone/travertine, riverside
Didymodon nicholsonii	rare (2)	Inner, River	700–2400	W. North America	Southern extension	dioicous acrocarp	riverside, shaded soil
Didymodon rigidulus var. icmadophilus	infreq (6)	N.Rim, Inner, River	700–2700	Global, border states	Not significant	dioicous acrocarp	crust, shaded soil, rock, riverside
Didymodon tectorum	rare (1)	N.Rim	2000	W. U.S. endemic (CO, KS, MD, NM)	Western extension	dioicous acrocarp	rock
Fissidens obtusifolius	rare (2)	River, Inner	500–700	Ontario, Alaska, E. & central U.S.	American Southwest	acrocarp	travertine, streamside
Gemmabryum badium	rare (3)	N.Rim, Inner	1700–2500	W. Eurasia, CA, NV	Southern extension	dioicous acrocarp	dry soil, sandstone
Grimmia caespiticia	rare (1)	N.Rim	2400	W. North America, NY, Greenland	American Southwest; southern extension	dioicous acrocarp	sandstone
Grimmia sp. nov.	rare (1)	Inner	1700	TBA	TBA	monoicous acrocarp	sandstone
Gymnostomum calcareum	rare (4)	N.Rim, Inner, River	700–2400	Global, rare in U.S. (CA, MO, & NC)	American Southwest	dioicous acrocarp	moist soil, streamside, spring
Gyroweisia tenuis	rare (1)	River	700	Global, patchy & rare in N. North America	American Southwest; southern extension	dioicous acrocarp	seep
Hypnum cupressiforme	rare (2)	N.Rim, Inner	1000–2500	global, restricted to CO, NM, & ND in contiguous U.S.	Not significant	dioicous pleurocarp	soil, cwd
Imbribryum sp. nov.	rare (1)	N.Rim	2500	SW U.S.	Not significant	dioicous acrocarp	spring

Table 2 continued

Species	Frequency	Collection region(s)	Elevation (m)	Global distribution	Range extension	Growth form & sex	Habitat
Leskeella nervosa	rare (2)	N.Rim, Inner	2400–2700	Greenland, Iceland, Asia, Europe & scattered in Canada & U.S.	Not significant	pleurocarp dioicous	spring
Asterella graciis	rare (1)	N.Rim	2400	W. U.S. & Canada	Southern extension	thalloid	limestone, spring
Pohlia camptotrachela	rare (1)	N.Rim	2700	W. U.S. & British Columbia	American Southwest; southern extension	dioicous acrocarp	pond margin moist soil
Pseudoleskea patens	rare (1)	N.Rim	2500	W. U.S. and N. North America,	Southern extension	dioicous acrocarp	soil, rock
Rosulabryum flaccidum	infreq (7)	N.Rim, Inner	1700–2600	Ontario, West Indies, & scattered U.S. (CA, CO, MD, MO, NV)	Not significant	acrocarp	limestone tree soil
Rosulabryum laevifilium	rare (3)	N.Rim	2400–2600	Europe, Canada & most of U.S.	Southern extension	dioicous acrocarp	limestone, cwd
Schistidium agassizii	rare (2)	N.Rim	2500	N. North America	Southern extension	monoicous acrocarp	wet rock, moist soil
Schistidium atrichum	infreq (7)	N.Rim, Inner	1500–2500	W. U.S. north to Alaska	American Southwest; southern extension	monoicous acrocarp	limestone, sandstone
Schistidium confertum	infreq (8)	N.Rim, S.Rim, Inner	1500–2700	W. U.S. north to Alaska	American Southwest; southern extension	monoicous acrocarp	limestone, sandstone, soil over rock
Schistidium dupretii	rare (2)	N.Rim, Inner	2000–2500	N. North America	Southern extension	acrocarp	limestone
Schistidium frigidum	rare (1)	N.Rim	2400	North America excluding E. & midwestern U.S.	Southern extension	monoicous acrocarp	rock
Schistidium papillosum	rare (2)	N.Rim	2500	Scattered throughout North America	Southwestern extension	monoicous acrocarp	sandstone
Trichostomum planifolium	rare (1)	Inner	700	Mexico, Asia, & W. North America (CA, NV, NM, CO, UT).	Not significant	monoicous acrocarp	soil over rock
Targionia sp. nov.	infreq (5)	Inner, River	700–2100	SW U.S.	Not significant	thalloid	soil, streamside

ovatum, Abietinella abietina) have been found at least once more by modern collectors associated with this project.

3.3.2 Modern collections

Modern collections have contributed 113 new taxon records to the park, yielding a total of 155 taxa (species and varieties) and increasing the known bryoflora of GRCA over threefold. Of these new taxa, 28 are newly reported for the state of Arizona (FNA eds. 2007+; table 2) and three remain undescribed or new to science (*Grimmia, Imbribryum,* and *Targionia* spp.nov) (see section 3.3.4. ***Catalog of Accepted Taxa***). To this end, I have contributed over 1,310 collections, including 90 records for GRCA and 26 records for Arizona. Other modern collectors have contributed 19 GRCA records and 3 state records, although some of these overlap my own. Specifically, Glenn Rink enumerated 18 GRCA and 2 state records, John R. Spence contributed 11 GRCA and 3 state records, and Larry E. Stevens contributed 7 GRCA records.

The three undescribed taxa are in the process of being taxonomically circumscribed. The North American *Grimmia* specialist, Roxanne Hastings, confirmed one *Grimmia* specimen that I had collected to be unlike any other described in the literature. This *Grimmia* specimen appears to resemble a subset of *Grimmia* species that occur in Europe and are members of the subgenus Gastrogrimmia. The undescribed thalloid liverwort, *Targionia* sp.nov., is likely a species which has been collected several times by other bryologists in the Southwest, but which remains formally undescribed at this time. Lastly, the new *Imbribryum* was collected by North American Bryaceae specialist John Spence; he is currently working on the description, which will be published in The Bryologist in the near future.

3.3.3 Floristic results

3.3.3.1 Taxonomic diversity.

The 155 confirmed taxa comprise 33 families, 75 genera, 153 species, and two

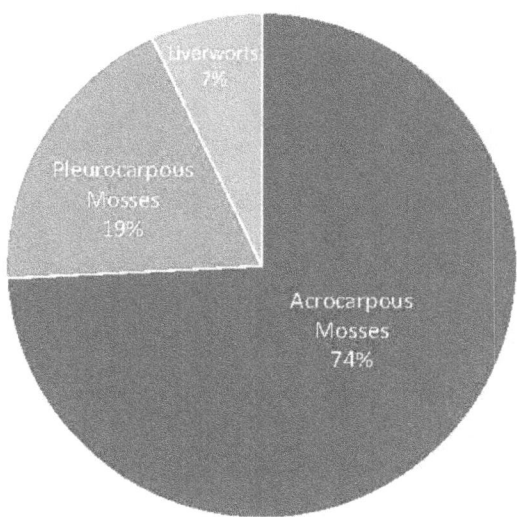

Figure 6a. Bryophyte demographics in Grand Canyon NP (GRCA). The bryoflora of GRCA constitutes 144 mosses and 11 liverwort species (including several varieties). Acrocarpous mosses possess many morphological adaptations to aridity and are known to comprise the largest proportion of aridland bryofloras.

Figure 6b. In contrast, liverworts are the least resilient to desiccation. Throughout the collecting history of Grand Canyon NP, *Frullania inflata,* has been reported once beneath a shaded mixed conifer forest near the edge of the North Rim. This species was found growing on a large limestone outcrop within a cool air drainage. (Photo courtesy of John Brinda.)

varieties. The bryoflora includes 144 mosses and 11 liverworts (fig. 6), listed below in the ***Catalog of Accepted Taxa*** (3.3.4).

The most frequently collected family in GRCA is Pottiaceae with 49 species and two varieties, followed by Grimmiaceae (18 species), Bryaceae (17 species), and Brachytheciaceae (10 species) (fig. 7). All other reported families are currently represented by fewer than 7 species, and most include one or two species. The most richly collected genera are *Grimmia* (11 species), *Didymodon* (8 species, 2 varieties), *Tortula* (7 species), *Syntrichia* (6 species), *Gemmabryum* (5 species), and *Ptychostomum* (5 species). The majority of remaining genera are represented by one species. The following eight species are classified as abundant

Figure 7. Family demographics of bryophytes in Grand Canyon NP (GRCA). Distribution of 155 bryophyte taxa (153 species and 2 varieties) among families in GRCA. The three most abundant families constitute acrocarpous mosses, while the fourth most abundant family, Brachytheciaceae, consists of is a pleurocarpous mosses with many resident species restricted to riparian areas in GRCA.

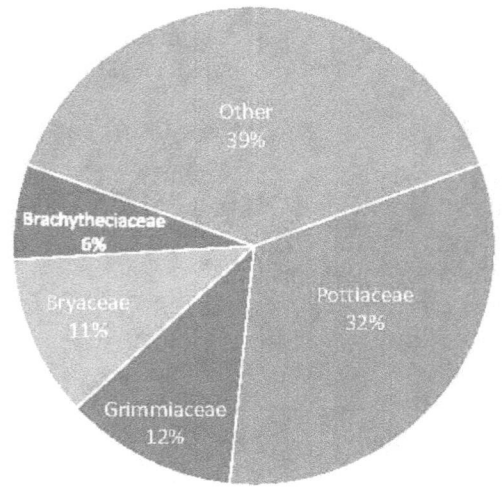

Figure 8. *Syntrichia ruralis* is one of the largest and most abundant xerophytic bryophytes in Grand Canyon NP (GRCA). It displays broad environmental tolerance and has been collected across the entire elevation gradient in GRCA. Furthermore, the species can grow on many substrata, including dry to moist soil, tree bases, downed wood, and rock. (Photo courtesy of J.C. Schou)

Figure 9. Observed bryophyte richness among substrata in Grand Canyon NP (GRCA). Total number of bryophyte species found in riparian/wetland habitats or growing on various dry substrata in GRCA. Most species, for which there are multiple collection records, were found on several substrata. Approximately half of the taxa found at riparian or wetland sites are mesic species restricted to this aquatic/semi-aquatic habitat throughout their known ranges.

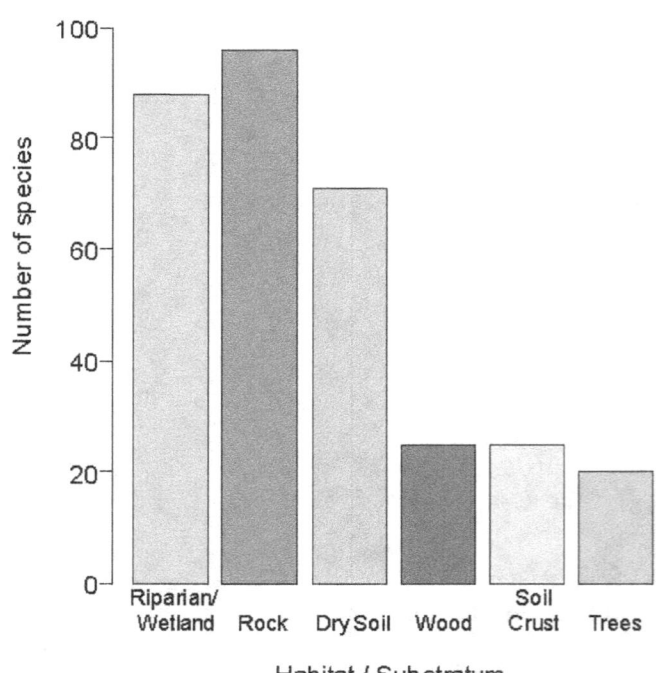

Table 3. Distribution of common species among collection regions. The most commonly collected bryophyte species in Grand Canyon NP, each collected at 10 or more distinct localities in the park. The documented distribution of each species throughout the park is indicated by marking (X) in all collection regions in which it was found. Species new to the park are indicated. Observed habitat from historic and modern park collections is noted (cwd=coarse woody debris).

Species	Total localities	N. Rim	S. Rim	Inner Canyon	Colorado River	Marble Canyon	Lake Mead	Growth form	New to park	Observed habitat
Gemmabryum kunzei	21	X	X	X	X		X	acrocarp	X	soil over rock; soil; riverside; streamside
Syntrichia ruralis	51	X	X	X	X		X	acrocarp		soil over rock; soil; tree; cwd
Bryum lanatum	17	X	X	X	X		X	acrocarp		soil over rock; soil; crust; roadsides
Grimmia anodon	17	X	X	X	X		X	acrocarp		limestone; sandstone; cwd
Syntrichia caninervis	20	X	X	X	X		X	acrocarp	X	soil over rock; crust; dry soil; limestone
Weissia ligulifolia	16	X	X	X	X		X	acrocarp		shaded soil; soil over rock; streamside
Grimmia pulvinata	14	X	X	X	X		X	acrocarp	X	limestone; sandstone; concrete; cwd
Tortula inermis	15	X	X	X	X		X	acrocarp		soil over rock; shaded soil; sandstone
Gemmabryum caespiticium	25	X	X	X	X		X	acrocarp		soil over rock; limestone; cwd; crust
Pseudoleskeella tectorum	21	X	X	X			X	pleurocarp		limestone; tree; cwd; sandstone
Dicranoweisia crispula	14	X	X	X			X	acrocarp	X	cwd; limestone; tree; sandstone
Grimmia plagiopodia	16	X	X	X			X	acrocarp		limestone; sandstone; crust
Didymodon vinealis	17	X	X	X	X		X	acrocarp	X	soil over rock; shaded rock; seep; waterfall
Brachythecium collinum	30	X	X	X				pleurocarp		limestone; cwd; soil
Ceratodon purpureus	21	X	X	X				acrocarp		cwd; soil; rock; crust
Grimmia alpestris	21	X	X	X				acrocarp	X	limestone; sandstone
Brachythecium fendleri	20	X	X					pleurocarp	X	rock; soil over rock; tree; cwd
Encalypta vulgaris	16	X	X	X				acrocarp		soil over rock; soil
Syntrichia norvegica	12	X	X	X				acrocarp	X	soil over rock; rock; tree
Timmia megapolitana subsp. *bavarica*	15	X	X	X				acrocarp		shaded soil; soil over rock; rock
Gemmabryum valparaisense	12	X	X	X	X			acrocarp	X	moist soil; riverside; spring; seep
Conardia compacta	11	X		X		X		pleurocarp		limestone; soil over rock

Table 3. *continued*

Species	Total localities	N. Rim	S. Rim	Inner Canyon	Colorado River	Marble Canyon	Lake Mead	Growth form	New to park	Observed habitat
					Collection regions					
Hypnum revolutum	15	X		X				pleurocarp		rock; tree; soil
Tortula obtusifolia	10	X		X				acrocarp		soil over rock; limestone; shaded soil; sandstone
Polytrichum juniperinum	11	X						acrocarp		soil; soil over rock; spring
Grimmia orbicularis	21		X	X	X			acrocarp	X	limestone; sandstone; soil over rock; travertine
Eucladium verticillatum	15			X	X			acrocarp		seep; spring; streamside
Rhynchostegium aquaticum	10			X	X	X		pleurocarp		spring; waterfalls; stream; rock

Table 4. Species unique to each collection region. Species found within (restricted to) only one collection region in Grand Canyon NP (GRCA). Growth form of mosses is either pleurocarpous (Pleurocarp) or acrocarpous (Acrocarp), while liverworts have either leafy or thalloid forms. The number of localities at which each species was found is indicated. Frequency categories are defined for the park based on the number of localities where a species was found: rare (<5), infrequent (5–10), common (>10), or abundant (>20). Species that have been documented to occur in Parashant NM, Arizona and Big Bend NP, Texas are indicated. Species that were restricted to mesic habitat (springs, seeps, riparian, ponds, waterfalls) in GRCA are also indicated.

Region	Species	Growth form	# of localities where species was found	Frequency	Elevation (m)	Parashant NM	Big Bend NP	Mesic only
North Rim	*Asterella gracilis*	thalloid	1	rare	2500			
	Atrichum selwynii	acrocarp	2	rare	2500			
	Brachythecium nelsonii	pleurocarp	1	rare	2300			X
	Bryoerythrophyllum recurvirostrum	acrocarp	3	rare	2500–2600	X	X	
	Campyliadelphus chrysophyllus	pleurocarp	1	rare	2500		X	
	Cephaloziella divaricata	leafy	4	rare	2500–2600			
	Chiloscyphus polyanthos var. rivularis	leafy	1	rare	2400			X
	Cratoneuron filicinum	pleurocarp	2	rare	2300–2400			X
	Distichium capillaceum	acrocarp	2	rare	2500–2600			
	Drepanocladus aduncus	pleurocarp	2	rare	2500–2700			
	Drepanocladus longifolius	pleurocarp	1	rare	2700			X
	Encalypta rhaptocarpa	acrocarp	4	infr	2200–2500			

Table 4 continued

Region	Species	Growth form	# of localities where species was found	Frequency	Elevation (m)	Parashant NM	Big Bend NP	Mesic only
	Eurhynchiastrum pulchellum var. pulchellum	pleurocarp	2	rare	2400–2500		X	
	Frullania inflata	leafy	1	rare	2500	X		
	Gemmabryum subapiculatum	acrocarp	1	rare	2700			X
	Grimmia caespiticia	acrocarp	1	rare	2400			
	Hypnum pallescens	pleurocarp	1	rare	2500			X
	Imbribryum sp. nov.	acrocarp	1	rare	2500			X
	Leptobryum pyriforme	acrocarp	4	rare	2400–2600		X	
	Orthotrichum obtusifolium	acrocarp	1	rare	2500			
	Philonotis fontana	pleurocarp	5	infr	2300–2500		X	X
	Pohlia camptotrachela	acrocarp	1	rare	2700			X
	Pohlia cruda	acrocarp	2	rare	2500–2600		X	X
	Polytrichum juniperinum	acrocarp	11	common	2400–2700			
	Pseudoleskea patens	pleurocarp	1	rare	2500			
	Pseudoleskea radicosa var. compacta	pleurocarp	2	rare	2600–2700			
	Pterigynandrum filiforme	pleurocarp	1	rare	2500			X
	Ptychostomum bimum	acrocarp	1	rare	2500			
	Riccia glauca	thalloid	1	rare	2700			
	Rosulabryum laevifilium	acrocarp	3	rare	2400–2600			X
	Schistidium agassizii	acrocarp	2	rare	2500		X	
	Schistidium frigidum	acrocarp	1	rare	2400			
	Schistidium papillosum	acrocarp	2	rare	2500			
	Sciuro-hypnum plumosum	pleurocarp	1	rare	2400			X
	Syntrichia papillosissima	acrocarp	1	rare	2600	X		
	Tortula hoppeana	acrocarp	1	rare	2500			
South Rim	Brachytheciastrum velutinum	pleurocarp	1	rare	2100			
	Grimmia sessitana	acrocarp	1	rare	2100			
	Orthotrichum pellucidum	acrocarp	1	rare	2100			
	Pterygoneurum subsessile var. subsessile	acrocarp	1	rare	2100	X	X	
	Zygodon viridissimus var. rupestris	acrocarp	1	rare	2100			

Table 4 continued

Region	Species	Growth form	# of localities where species was found	Frequency	Elevation (m)	Parashant NM	Big Bend NP	Mesic only
Inner Canyon	Abietinella abietina	pleurocarp	1	rare	1600			
	Amblystegium serpens	pleurocarp	4	infr	1500–2500		X	
	Didymodon tectorum	acrocarp	1	rare	2000			
	Fissidens grandifrons	acrocarp	5	infr	700–1700			X
	Funaria muhlenbergii	acrocarp	1	rare	1600	X		
	Grimmia sp.nov	acrocarp	1	rare	1700			
	Hygroamblystegium varium	pleurocarp	7	infr	900–2400			X
	Marchantia polymorpha	thalloid	2	rare	1600–1800			X
	Microbryum starckeanum	acrocarp	1	rare	700	X	X	X
	Mnium arizonicum	acrocarp	1	rare	1900			X
	Pterygoneurum ovatum	acrocarp	1	rare	1800	X		
	Rosulabryum torquescens	acrocarp	1	rare	1300	0	0	0
	Syntrichia laevipila	acrocarp	2	rare	1300	X	X	
	Tortella alpicola	acrocarp	1	rare	1800	X		
	Trichostomum planifolium	acrocarp	1	rare	700			
	Weissia controversa	acrocarp	2	rare	1700–2500		X	
Colorado River	Entosthodon sp.	acrocarp	3	rare	500 - 600			
	Fissidens fontanus	acrocarp	1	rare	500	X	X	X
	Fontinalis hypnoides	acrocarp	1	rare	600		X	X
	Funaria hygrometrica var. calvescens	acrocarp	1	rare	700			
	Gyroweisia tenuis	acrocarp	1	rare	700			X
	Trichostomum tenuirostre	acrocarp	1	rare	400			
Marble Canyon	Mannia fragrans	thalloid	1	rare	900			X
Lake Mead	Aloina bifrons	acrocarp	1	rare	500	X		

(>20 localities): *Syntrichia ruralis* (fig. 8), *Brachytheciastrum collinum, Gemmabryum caespiticium, Gemmabryum kunzei, Grimmia orbicularis, Grimmia alpestris, Pseudoleskeella tectorum,* and *Ceratodon purpureus*). An additional 20 species are classified as common and have been collected between 10 and 20 times at distinct localities across the canyon (table 3).

3.3.3.2 Distribution of bryophyte taxa by collection region. At this time, the greatest number of bryophyte species and varieties have been documented for the Inner Canyon (105 taxa) and the North Rim (93 taxa) collection regions (table 1); of these, 56 have been collected in both regions. The North Rim has the largest number of taxa found in no other collection region (36 species, table 4), and it shares 30 species in common with the South Rim, for which 43 taxa have been found. Five of these are singleton species collected from only one locality in the park (*Brachytheciastrum velutinum, Grimmia sessitana, Orthotrichum pellucidum, Zygodon viridissimus,* and *Pterygoneurum subsessile*). In the Colorado River collection region, 49 taxa have been reported, 6 of which are currently exclusive to this region. The last two collecting regions have had very limited collecting. Twenty species are confirmed for Lake Mead and four for Marble Canyon. Unique to the documented bryoflora bordering Lake Mead is *Aloina bifrons,* while *Mannia fragrans* is unique to Marble Canyon.

3.3.3.4 Species distribution and diversity among substrata. The substrata available to bryophytes in GRCA include rock, soil, trees, downed wood, soil crust, and riparian areas. Considering all known collection records, riparian/ wetland areas and dry rocks support the largest number of bryophyte species in GRCA (fig. 9). Specifically, 95 confirmed species have been found on dry rocks in GRCA, although this number includes species growing directly on rock and those growing on soil over rock. Many of the former are confined to this habitat, while many of the latter also occur

on soil independent of rock. In total, 88 species have been reported to occur associated with seeps, springs, waterfalls, ponds, streams and the Colorado River, although only 45 appear restricted to these aquatic and semi-aquatic habitats (figs. 9 &10). Common soil microhabitats for bryophytes include exposed mineral soil, soil beneath sagebrush (*Artemisia tridentata*), and soil bordering rock bases, grass clumps, and tree roots. Dry soil (excluding crusts) in GRCA supports at least 71 species. Downed wood, soil crust communities, and trees support much lower diversity (25, 25, and 20 taxa, respectively). The most common microhabitats associated with dead wood included the undersides and crevices of decaying logs partly to fully decorticate. Note that, with the exception of dry rock, mean site-level richness for any one of these habitats was not measured in this study, and is certainly much lower than these inventory numbers, which report cumulative species richness for each substratum (See section 4.0).

3.3.4 Catalog of Accepted Taxa

The data associated with each species record below reference all historic and modern collections for a given taxon. Species are listed in alphabetical order by family, genus, and species. Asterisks precede taxa that are new records to GRCA (*), Arizona (**), and science (***). Each species name and authority is followed by its collection frequency class, park distribution category, elevation range, and observed habitat. Localities are provided for locally rare taxa only.

The elevation associated with each modern collection was determined using a hand-held Global Positioning System (Garman GPS set to NAD 83), and estimated for historic collections.

Collection frequency classes are based on the number of distinct sites at which a species was collected and are rare (< 5 sites), infrequent (5-10 sites), common (10-20 sites), and abundant (>20 sites).

Park distribution categories are defined

as either widespread (+), local (-), or scattered (#) throughout the suitable habitat of a particular species.

Elevation range reports the lowest and highest collection sites in meters.

Collection regions are listed next in bold and are ordered to reflect decreasing elevation: NRim, SRim, Inner, Marble, Mead, River; the number of distinct localities at which the species was found is noted in parentheses after each region, and is followed by a list of unique habitats/substrata for which a species was collected.

Selected collectors and collection num-

bers are referenced in brackets for each unique habitat per taxon.

Collections are from the author unless otherwise noted: John Spence (JS), Glenn Rink (GR), and Larry E. Stevens (LES).

Cited historic collections were made by Inez Haring (IH), Rose Collom (RC), Louis Schellbach (LS), and H.C. Bryant (HB). If a species was collected by Haring (1941, 1946), its historic name is listed last in brackets.

Relevant taxonomic or biogeographical information and State/Park record details follow under Notes.

✶✶✶✶✶

Bryophyta (Mosses)

Amblystegiaceae

Amblystegium serpens (Hedwig) Bruch: Rare-, 1500–2500 m. NRim(3): Ken Patrick Trail below Neal Spring, on moist limestone rock in shaded drainage [113], Robber's Roost, on moist slope at built-up spring with water trough [459], Lower Neal Spring, on moist limestone rock at spring [IH: 3732]. Inner(1): Upper Unkar Creek, in vicinity of spring on moist soil [GR: 6809]. [*A. juratzkanum* Schimp.]

Campyliadelphus chrysophyllus (Bridel) Kanda: Rare-, 2500 m. NRim(1): Milk Spring, in mixed-conifer forest along Point Sublime Road, substratum unknown [GR: 7658]. Notes: This species was cited by Clover and Jotter (1944). [*Campylium chrysophyllum* (Bridel) J. Lange]

Conardia compacta (Müll. Hal.) H. Robinson: Infrequent+, 1000–2500 m. NRim(6): on moist limestone rock or cliff, partly to fully shaded, often near springs and seeps [456, GR: 7658, H: 3709, 3741]. Inner(4): at base of seep on sandstone and limestone rock [214], on moist rock along edge of stream [LS: 3714]. Marble(1): Saddle Canyon Spring, on moist rock [JS: 5306]. [*Amblystegium compactum* (Müller Hal.) Austin]

*Drepanocladus aduncus (Hedwig) Warnstorf: Rare-, 2500 –2700 m. NRim(2): 1 mi W of Crystal Creek near Point Sublime Rd., on a N-facing limestone outcrop [GR: 8948], Upper Little Park on soil bordering dried pond, partly-shaded [79].

*Hygroamblystegium varium (Hedwig) Mönkemeyer: Infrequent#, 900–2400 m. Inner(6): submerged and emergent in cascades and springs [1114], on seeping walls of hanging gardens [GR: 7265, 7270]. Notes: All species of this genus previously recognized in North America are now treated as synonyms of *H. varium.* (e.g. *H. noterophilum, H. tenax, H. fluviatile, H. orthocladon*). These former species have been lowered to the rank of subspecies or variety and encompass the wide range of morphological variation in *H. varium*, which is often correlated with habitat. The variety corresponding to *H. orthocladon* was reported by Clover and Jotter (1944), but has not been located. [*Amblystegium noterophilum* (Sull. & Lesq.) Holz.; *Amblystegium irriguum* (Hook. & Wilson) Schimp.]

Leptodictyum riparium (Hedwig) Warnstorf: Infrequent+, 600–2700 m. NRim(5): on base of *Populus tremuloides* in shaded forest [450], on moist soil and downed wood in open mixed conifer forest and bordering perennial ponds [128], on upturned soil exposed in tree fall [72]. River(1): on submerged and emergent rocks at spring in vicinity of the Colorado River [674]. [Nomenclature unrevised]

Bartramiaceae

Philonotis fontana (Hedwig) Bridel: Infrequent#, 2300 –2500 m. NRim(4): on moist soil in open meadow and bordering a small pond [IH: 3721]. Inner(1): at spring on unknown substratum [LES ns, 8/6/2000]. [Nomenclature unrevised]

*Philonotis marchia (Hedwig) Bridel: Rare#, 800–900 m. Inner(1): Kanab Creek, on damp soil at seep [JS: 5349]. River(2): Nankoweap Creek, on damp soil

streamside [JS: 5325], Cottonwood Creek Spring, on damp soil [LES ns, 10/23/2000].

Brachytheciaceae

Brachytheciastrum collinum (Schleicher ex. Müll. Hal.) Ignatov & Huttunen: Abundant+, 1600–2700 m. NRim(>20): common on downed wood in shaded forest [77], common on soil abutting rocks and logs [147], frequent on dry limestone and sandstone rock, usually shaded [96]. SRim(3): on shaded soil beneath rock overhangs and *Artemisia tridentata* [164], on limestone rock in shade [IH ns 10/3/1944]. Inner(9): frequent on shaded limestone rock with or without soil [200], on downed wood [125], at spring [RC: 1183]. [*Brachythecium collinum* (Schleich. ex Müll. Hal.) Schimp.]

*Brachytheciastrum fendleri (Sullivant) Ochyra & Zarnowiec: Common+, 1700–2600 m. NRim(5): on sandy soil beneath limestone overhang [387], on sandstone and limestone rock [319], on base of large *Populus tremuloides* [300], on fallen branch [299]. SRim(1): on soil in crevice of limestone rock, partly shaded [161]. Inner(6): on tree bases and roots, including *Pinus ponderosa* [343], on shaded soil usually abutting roots and beneath rock overhangs [831], on base of *Quercus gambelii*, fully shaded [367].

*Brachytheciastrum velutinum (Hedwig) Ignatov & Huttunen: Rare-, 2100 m. SRim(1): section of Arizona Trail near Grand Canyon Village, on limestone outcrop in *Pinus ponderosa* forest [1212].

*Brachythecium frigidum (Müll. Hal.) Bescherelle: Rare#, 800–2600 m. NRim(1): North Canyon Spring, emergent on rock in stream [JS: 5467]. Inner(3): Roaring Springs, submerged or emergent on rocks in cascades & streams [1109]. Angel Spring, submerged [GR: 8602], Hermit Spring [LES ns, 8/30/2000].

*Brachythecium nelsonii Grout: Rare-, 2300 m. NRim(1): Big Spring Canyon at Big Springs [LES ns, 6/22/2001].

*Brachythecium rivulare Schimper: Rare#, 700–2600 m. NRim(2): Robber's Roost Spring [LES ns, 8/4/2000], Cliff Spring, emergent on limestone rock in pool [JS: 5449]. Inner(1): Elves' Chasm, on damp limestone rock [JS: 5337].

Eurhynchiastrum pulchellum (Hedwig) Ignatov & Huttunen: Rare#, 2400–2500 m. NRim(2): on rock and soil at moist sites in mixed conifer forest and in vicinity of a spring [GR: 8837, IH: 22]. [*Eurhynchium strigosum* (F. Weber & D. Mohr) Schimp. and *Eurhynchium diversifolium* Schimp.]

Oxyrrhynchium hians (Hedwig) Loeske: Rare#, 1000–2600 m. NRim(1): North Canyon Spring, emergent on rocks in stream [JS: 5465]. Inner(1): Vicinity of Mystic Falls in Nankoweap Canyon, near waterfall and hanging garden [GR: 7271]. [*Eurhynchium hians* (Hedw.) Jaeger & Sauerb.]

Rhynchostegium aquaticum A. Jaeger: Common+ 500–1600 m. Inner(7): submerged and emergent on rock, often limestone, at springs in flowing streams and cascades [537], at hanging garden [GR: 7301]. Marble(1): on limestone rock at spring [JS: 5311]. River(1): on travertine spring adjacent to the river and lacking shade [664]. Notes: This species was reported by Clover and Jotter (1944). Recent molecular phylogenetic analysis of the morphotype previously called *R. riparioides* in North America suggests that two distinct lineages exist globally (S. Huttunen et al. 2007); until further resolution is available, a broad circumscription of *R. aquaticum* is prescribed in FNA. [*Rhynchostegium riparioides* (Hedw.) Card.]*Sciuro-hypnum plumosum* (Hedwig) Ignatov & Huttunen: Rare-, 2400 m. NRim(1): Castle Lake, along edge of pond on moist soil and rock [GR: 8795]. Notes: This genus was recently segregated from Brachythecium primarily on the basis of smaller size, autoicous sexual condition, and rough setae (Ignatov and Huttunen 2002).

Bryaceae

Bryum argenteum Hedwig: Infrequent+, 700–2400 m. NRim(1): component of soil crust associated with grasses in open *Pinus ponderosa* forest [871]. SRim(2): on bare soil between coniferous litter or within soil crust beneath open *Pinus ponderosa* or pinyon-juniper forest [917]. Inner(6): on calcareous rock in crevices or over a thin layer of soil, exposed or partly shaded [1031], on shaded soil beneath rock overhangs [902].

Bryum lanatum (P. Beauvois) Bridel: Common+, 500–2600 m. NRim(5): frequent along roads or trails on moist soil [104]. SRim(4): frequent on soil or as component of soil crust amongst pine litter on flat ground in Pinus ponderosa forest [920]. Inner(5): frequent on soil over limestone or sandstone rock in open or shaded situations [188], component of soil crust on a N-facing slope without shade [593]. Mead(1): on moist, sandy soil below grasses over a N-facing slope [1014]. River(2): above beach on exposed soil or in shade of cliff [700]. [*Bryum argenteum* var. *lanatum* (P. Beauv.) Hampe]

****Gemmabryum badium* (Bruch ex Bridel) J. R. Spence: Rare#, 1700–2500 m. NRim(1): Widforss Trail, on soil at base of rock over a SW-facing slope [973]. Inner(2): Grandview Trail, on sandstone rock [1213], North Kaibab Trail, on steep bank composed of gravely soil, E-facing with filtered light [358c]. Notes: Previously reported in North America from only Nevada and California, this marks the first occurrence of this rare species in the American Southwest.

Gemmabryum caespiticium (Hedwig) J. R. Spence: Abundant+, 500–2600 m. NRim(>10): common on moist and dry soil in closed or open canopy forests [265, 470, 884], infrequent on rock and soil over rock [94, 269], rare component of soil crust in open woods with grasses [870] rare on logs [140]. SRim(6): infrequent component of soil crust in open woodlands on dry, gravely soil [794, 920], on soil over log [RC: 1250]. Inner(10): common on soil over limestone and sandstone rock in exposed situations [183, 412], infrequent directly on shaded limestone rock [347], infrequent on moist soil bordering tree roots and rocks [383], infrequent on sandy or gravely soil in exposed situations [1078], on seeping rock [1095], on S-facing shale rock [GR: 7308], on soil over log in shaded mixed conifer forest [1043]. River(2): rare at edge of the river on sandy soil and travertine [644, 654]. [*Bryum caespiticium* Hedw.]

*Gemmabryum kunzei (Hornschuch) J. R. Spence: Abundant+, 400–2700 m. NRim(6): infrequent on soil over calcareous rock [69, 1053], infrequent on dry or shaded soil along rocks and tree roots [322]. SRim(1): on soil in rock crevice, S-facing and exposed in *Pinus ponderosa* forest [842]. Inner(4): on soil over limestone and sandstone ledges without shade [183], on sandy, moist soil along streamlet [498]. Mead(1): component of moist soil crust near seep at base of N-facing cliff with calcareous deposits [1006]. River(9): frequent component of soil crust on sand above the high-water mark, without shade [638], frequent on dry, calcareous rock or with a thin layer of soil, shaded or open [732], frequent on dry soil abutting rocks [582], on dry river bank in shade of

Baccharis sp. [644].

Gemmabryum subapiculatum (Hampe) J. R. Spence & H.P. Ramsay: Rare-, 2700 m. NRim(1): Little Park Lake vicinity, NE of N. Rim entrance station, on moist soil with sedges and litter bordering a pond [143b].

Gemmabryum valparaisense (Thériot) J. R. Spence, in ed.: Common+, 500–2400 m. NRim(2): on wet soil at base of seeping wall, covered in calcium deposits and fully shaded [123]. Inner(6): frequent on moist soil at springs [87, GR: 6810], infrequent on rock in seepage areas [213], along moist bank of perennial streamlet [GR: 7054]. River(4): frequent above and below the high-water mark on muddy, silty soil [666].

***Imbribryum* sp. nov. J. R. Spence: Rare-, 2500 m. NRim(1): Basin Spring, in damp soil-filled crevices on sandstone outcrop [JS: 5906].

Plagiobryoides vinosula (Cardot) J. R. Spence: Infrequent#, 500–1900 m. Inner(3): on seeping limestone or sandstone walls [211, 493], on moist soil bordering pool at spring [809]. River(4): riverside on travertine and moist soil below high-water mark [685], riverside on seeping ledge and in cave behind a cascade [624], on exposed river floodplain on moist, silty soil [493].

Ptychostomum bimum (Schreber) J. R. Spence: Rare-, 2500 m. NRim(1): Upper Milk Creek upstream of Milk Spring, on soil in small meadow [GR: 7662].

Ptychostomum creberrimum (Taylor) J. R. Spence & H.P. Ramsay: Rare-, 2400–2500 m. NRim(1): North Kaibab Trail in a dry forested drainage, on moist, gravely soil bordering a tiny rock, partly shaded and NE-facing [283]. Inner(1): North Kaibab Trail, on tiny limestone rock over a moderate slope, NE-facing and with filtered light [353].

Ptychostomum pallescens (Schleicher ex Schwägrichen) J. R. Spence: Infrequent-, 2400 –2700 m. NRim(4): on moist soil abutting rocks and beneath overhangs in cool drainages, often partly shaded [248, 283], submerged in pool at spring [IH: 1365], on decaying branch bordering a dried pond, partly-shaded and <1 cm above ground [78b]. Inner(2): on soil over log in shaded mixed conifer forest [1043], on moist gravely soil abutting rocks and tree roots in mixed conifer forest [321]. [*Bryum pallescens* Schleich. ex Schwägr.]

Ptychostomum pseudotriquetrum (Hedwig) J. R. Spence ex D.T. Holyoak & N. Pederson: Rare-, 1700–2600 m. NRim(2): North Canyon Spring, on moist soil [JS: 5468], Upper Thompson Spring [LES ns, 8/3/2000]. Inner(1): Muav Falls Canyon in Upper Bright Angel Creek, at seep [GR: 7272].

Ptychostomum turbinatum (Hedwig) J. R. Spence: Rare#, 1100–2500 m. NRim(1): North Kaibab Trail, on moist soil of a vertical collapsing bank beneath *Acer grandidentatum*, partly shaded and E-facing [321]. Inner(2): Indian Gardens, on seeping wall at spring, partly shaded [IH ns 9/9/1940], Kwagunt Canyon at a perennial stream W of Banta Point, streamside on moist soil [GR: 7048]. [*Bryum turbinatum* (Hedw.) Turner]

**Rosulabryum flaccidum* (Bridel) J. R. Spence: Infrequent#, 1700–2600 m. NRim(6): on limestone rock in shaded drainages often on moist soil over rock [111, 951], on base of *Populous tremuloides*, partly shaded [1081], on moist soil of N-facing slope [1024]. Inner(1): on soil beneath rock overhang, fully shaded and NW-facing in pinyon-juniper community [826]. Notes: Known from bordering states, this record fills a distributional gap for this species in the western United States.

**Rosulabryum laevifilium* (Syed) Ochyra: Rare-, 2400–2600 m. NRim(3): Widforss Trail, on soil below sandstone rock [970], Robber's Roost, on moist base of coniferous stump, fully shaded and N-facing, surrounded by dense vegetation [429], North Kaibab Trail, on gravely soil and limestone boulder [356]. Notes: Known previously from Canada and the majority of the US, this record extends the southernmost limit of the species' range in North America.

Rosulabryum torquescens (Bruch ex De Not.) J. R. Spence: Rare-, 1300 m. Inner(1): North Kaibab Trail, <1/2 mi from Cottonwood Campground, on loose soil between small rocks and partly shaded by Gutierrezia [GR: 1133].

Cratoneuraceae

Cratoneuron filicinum (Hedwig) Spruce: Rare-, 2300–2400 m. NRim(2): Lower Neal Spring, on rock along stream in open coniferous forest [IH: 3726], Big Spring Canyon at Big Springs [LES, 6/22/2001]. [Nomenclature unrevised]

Dicranaceae

Dicranoweisia crispula (Hedwig) Milde: Common+, 500–2700 m. NRim(14): frequent on downed wood in mid to advanced stages of decay, <0.2 m above the ground [75, 998], on base of *Populus tremuloides* and *Pseudotsuga menziesii*, <0.1 m above the ground [312, 1089], infrequent on limestone and sandstone rock [435, 463], rare on downed burnt logs [288]. Inner(1): on sandstone rock [1213], on log [1041]. Mead(1): on log over steep slope in desert, lacking shade [1021].

Ditricaceae

Ceratodon purpureus (Hedwig) Bridel: Abundant+, 1800–2700 m. NRim(33): common on dry and moist soil in shaded or open woods, along roadsides, along tree bases, logs, and rocks, or amongst coniferous litter [109, 463, GR: 7113, 7658], common on soil over downed wood and occasionally burnt wood in mid to advanced decay, <0.2 m above the ground, often partly shaded [870, 958, GR: 7664], infrequent on limestone and sandstone rock [424, 981], on upturned soil from fallen tree [471]. SRim(5): on open or shaded soil as a component of crust in *Pinus ponderosa* forest [794, 916], abutting roots of *Pinus ponderosa* [840]. Inner(3): on soil over sandstone and limestone rock outcrops [204, 402], on N-side of log in advanced decay [997].

Distichium capillaceum (Hedwig) Bruch & Schimper: Rare-, 2500–2600 m. NRim(2): Fred Harvey Mule Pond, along crevice of limestone rock in vicinity of pond and near edge of mixed conifer forest [IH: 3730], North Canyon Spring, on moist soil and downed wood [JS: 5470a].

Encalyptaceae

Encalypta rhaptocarpa Schwägrichen: Infrequent#, 2200–2500 m. NRim(5): on dry gravely soil on a steep bank and over limestone outcrop in shaded drainage [358, 301], in mixed conifer forest on dry soil below boulder on a steep slope [89], on sandstone boulder, fully shaded [87].

Encalypta vulgaris Hedwig: Common+, 2000–2700 m. Frequent on dry soil over rock crevices or beneath overhangs, partly shaded. NRim(4): on soil over limestone rock and beneath rock overhang [1068, IH: 24-E], on seeping rock

[1071], on soil at base of Juniperus sp. [IH ns 9/1/1940]. SRim(3): on soil in crevices and holes of limestone rock [932, IH ns 8/18/1940], shaded beneath a rock overhang [IH ns 8/17/1940]. Inner(9): on soil in crevices of sandstone and limestone rock, usually partly shaded [205, GR: 6804], on soil over seeping rock [1096].

Fissidentaceae

Fissidens fontanus (Bachelot de la Pylaie) Steudel: Rare-, 500 m. River(1): Warm Springs, submerged on travertine at edge of river [652].

Fissidens grandifrons Bridel: Infrequent#, 700–1700 m. Inner(5): submerged in flowing channel and cascades, on wet rock bordering channel in small cave, on vertical walls bordering large waterfall [518], at hanging garden [GR:7265], at spring [GR: 7223].

**Fissidens obtusifolius* Wilson: Rare#, 500–700 m. River(1): Warm Springs, riverside on travertine wall below the high-water mark [663]. Inner(1): Elves' Chasm, on moist stream bank and in hole on limestone rock, fully shaded [500, 503].

Fissidens sublimbatus Grout: Infrequent+, 500–2600 m. NRim(3): on loose soil bordering log in mixed-conifer forest [858], on crevices of limestone rock, partly shaded [259]. Inner(3): on fully shaded soil below sandstone overhang [1099], on exposed soil in crevice of pegmatite cliff [738], in vicinity of spring along base of large boulders on moist, red clay soil [817]. Notes: One specimen was collected by Haring in 1944 [IH ns 9/29/1944], but was not included in her 1946 publication; the specimen was much later reported for GRCA by Brian (2000).

Fontinalaceae

Fontinalis hypnoides Hartman: Rare-, 600 m. River(1): About 3 miles from Lees Ferry at the Artesian spring bordering the Colorado River below Lava Falls CRM 180.1, submerged in the river [676].

Funariaceae

Entosthodon spp. Schwägrichen: Rare#, 500–600 m. River(3): Mouth of Parashant Canyon in dry tributary, component of soil crust beneath *Acacia* sp. and *Larrea tridentata* [715], Ledges in vicinity of CRM 151, on moist clay soil behind small water fall, NE-facing [618], mouth of 194-Mile Canyon, river left on dry soil abutting rock on rocky slope, partly shaded [702]. Notes: The taxa collected at these three localities may represent different species.

Funaria hygrometrica var. *calvescens* (Schwägrichen) Montagne: Rare-, 700 m. River(1): Trinity Camp CRM 91, on moist soil near river [JS: 5328].

Funaria hygrometrica var. *hygrometrica* Hedwig: Infrequent+, 1300–2500 m. NRim(5): in mixed conifer forest on disturbed soil of roadside and campground lot [1126b], over steep slope and abutting base of limestone boulder, SW-facing [973], on limestone rock by pond [IH: 3604]. Inner(3): on dry and moist exposed soil along trails [IH: 3685, IH ns 9/9/1940].

Funaria muhlenbergii Turner: Rare-, 1600 m. Inner(1): head of Hermit Creek Canyon, trailside on soil above rock [IH ns 9/7/1940]. Notes: This species has been collected once by Haring, but was not reported in her publications (1941, 1946). Brian (2000) includes this species in her checklist and cites the locality of a specimen collected by Clover & Jotter (1944) from Conquistador

Isle, CRM 122; however, this specimen has not been located for verification.

Grimmiaceae

Grimmia alpestris (Weber & Mohr) Schleicher: Abundant+, 1500–2700 m. NRim(>15): common on acidic limestone rock, exposed or partly shaded [273], frequent on sandstone rock, exposed or partly shaded [85]. SRim(6): common on acidic limestone in *Pinus ponderosa* forest, usually without shade [919, IH: 3789]. Inner(5): frequent on sandstone rock, sunny and dry [409], rare on limestone rock, partly shaded beneath conifers [369]. Notes: This species was collected by Haring (1946), but was misidentified in all collections as either *Coscinodon calyptratus* (Drumm.) C. Jens. [*G. calyptrata* (Hook.) C.E.O. Jensen ex Kindb.] or *Grimmia ovalis* (Hedw.) Lindb. [*G. commutata* Hüb.]. This species is known to occur on acidic sandstones, but many of the limestones in GRCA are very acidic, and so this species was collected frequently on both sandstone and limestone rock throughout the park.

Grimmia anodon Bruch & Schimper: Common+, 500–2700 m. NRim(8): common on dry limestone rock, exposed or partly shaded [247, 949], rare on decaying logs, partly shaded [75]. SRim(8): common on limestone rock in *Pinus ponderosa* or pinyon-juniper forest, often along exposed cliffs of the canyon rim with or without shade [184, 926], frequent on sandstone rock [160]. Inner(1): in a riverside cove above the high-water mark on soil between dolomite rocks and *Tamarisk* sp., partly shaded and N-facing [707]. Mead: on exposed calcareous rock in desert scrub, N-facing [1012].

**Grimmia caespiticia* (Bridel) Juratzka: Rare-, 2400 m. NRim(1): along Cape Final Trail in *Pinus ponderosa* forest on sandstone rock [880]. Notes: Restricted predominantly to western North America (excluding NY and Greenland), this record marks the first occurrence of the species in the American Southwest and thereby extends its southern limit.

Grimmia longirostris Hooker: Rare-, 2200–2700 m. NRim(2): Lower Neal Spring, on limestone rock in open woods [IH: 3784], Ken Patrick Trail, on cherty rock over a steep slope near edge of rim with high exposure [976]. SRim(1): Arizona Trail near Grand Canyon Village, on dry limestone rock in *Pinus ponderosa* forest [1209]. Inner(1): North Kaibab Trail, on small limestone rock over moderate slope, NW-facing with filtered light [368].

Grimmia moxleyi R.S. Williams in J.M. Holzinger: Rare-, 500–2100 m. SRim(1): Rim Trail, on dry soil over a tiny rock, E-facing with filtered light in pinyon-juniper woodland at edge of rim [176]. Inner(1): in the vicinity of Honga Rapids, [642]. River(1): in the vicinity of Fat City Beach [672]. Mead(1): Pearce Ferry vicinity near Grand Wash Cliffs, component of soil crust surrounded by calcareous rocks and grasses over a N-facing slope [1011]. Notes: This species is of conservation concern, rare within its limited distribution throughout Arizona, California, Nevada, and Mexico.

Grimmia orbicularis Bruch: Abundant+, 500–2100 m. SRim(3): on dry sandy soil over limestone rock in *Pinus ponderosa* forest [173], on limestone rock in open woods [IH: 3797]. River (>15): rare on diabasic rock and on soil at base of this rock, partly shaded or exposed [569a], frequent on limestone rock over exposed or shaded slopes [607], frequent on dry soil over and amongst rocks on exposed or partly shaded slopes above the beach [557, 630, 697], on a dry travertine rock ledge above a spring, partly shaded and N-facing [723]. Inner(>15): frequent on exposed sandstone rock [234], frequent on limestone rock, shaded or exposed [822], infrequent on exposed soil amongst rocks in dry channels [634], on dry travertine rock in vicinity of spring [507]. Mead(1): on N-facing limestone rock, component of soil crust, and on calcareous soil over rock in open desert scrub vegetation [1002]. Notes: This species was collected frequently by Haring (1946), but all collections were misidentified as either *G. decipiens* Renauld & Cardot, *G. pulvinata* (Hedw.) Smith, *G. plagiopodia* Hedw., *Coscinodon calyptratus* (Drumm.) C. E. O. Jensen [*G. calyptrata* (Hook.) C.E.O. Jensen ex Kindb.], *Grimmia ovalis* (Hedw.) Lindb. [*G. commutata* Hüb.], Schistidium apocarpum Hedw. Bruch & Schimp. [*G. apocarpa* Hedw. var. *gracilis* Röhl.], or *Bucklandiella sudetica* (Funck) Bednarek-Ochyra & Ochyra. [*Racomitrium heterostichum* (Hedw.) Brid.]

Grimmia ovalis (Hedwig) Lindberg: Infrequent+, 1300–2100 m. SRim(2): on limestone rock, exposed in open woodland [171]. Inner(4): on exposed limestone rocks [187, 1125], on sandstone rock along trail [1235].

Grimmia plagiopodia Hedwig: Common+, 500–2600 m. NRim(6): common on limestone rock, exposed to fully shaded in mixed conifer forest [268]. SRim(3): on limestone rock, exposed to fully shaded in open woodland [179]. Inner(6): frequent on dry, exposed sandstone rocks [415], rare on limestone rock, partly shaded [378]. Mead(1): component of soil crust within a runoff channel over a NE-facing slope in open desert scrub [1016].

Grimmia pulvinata (Hedwig) Smith: Common+, 500–2600 m. NRim(2): on dry sandstone rock, exposed to partly shaded in mixed-conifer forest [116]. SRim(3): on dry limestone, sandstone, or concrete, in open woodland lacking shade [181]. Inner(7): frequent on exposed sandstone and limestone rocks [221, 1131], on dry soil over log in advanced decay [1076]. River(2): rare on soil among rocks and on pegmatite rock in dry, open slopes above beach [690, 701]. Notes: This species was collected by Haring, but misidentified as *Coscinodon calyptratus* (Drumm.) C. Jens. [*G. calyptrata* (Hook.) C.E.O. Jensen ex Kindb.] [IH: 3773, 3775].

Grimmia sessitana De Notaris: Rare-, 2100 m. SRim(1): Rim Trail near edge of rim, on dry soil over low-lying rock embedded in an E-facing, gentle slope within open pinyon-juniper woodland [174].

***Grimmia* sp. nov.: Rare-, 1700 m. Inner(1): Grandview Trail, on a dry, reddish sandstone outcrop, trailside and N-facing in sparse pinyon-juniper and desert scrub vegetation [1205]. Notes: This specimen most closely resembles the European *Grimmia crinita* Brid. and will be described in a future publication.

Jaffueliobryum wrightii (Sullivant) Thériot: Rare-, 500–700 m. Inner(3): Havasu Canyon at the intersection of Beaver and Havasu Creeks, on a sloping NW-facing rock in an active tributary [237], CRM 220.0, on sloping pegmatite cliff 400 m from the beach, partly shaded and N-facing [737], Kanab Canyon, on soil over a Muav Limestone wall, partly shaded and N-facing [598]. River(1): mouth of Two-hundred and Five Mile Creek, river left, on dry soil in between limestone rocks over a steep, rocky SW-facing slope [719].

(*)Schistidium agassizii Sullivant & Lesquereux: Rare#, 2500 m. NRim(2): Ken Patrick Trail, in an ephemeral pool of water on a limestone rock [862], at the junction of Point Imperial Road and Cape Royal Road, along edge of rock over a hillside [IH: 19]. Notes: Known throughout northern North America, this record extends the southern limit of the species. I report this species as a

new state record, but not as a new GRCA record because this species was previously reported for the park by Haring (1946), but was overlooked and not cited for Arizona in the FNA treatment (FNA eds. 2007+). [*Grimmia alpicola* Hedw.]

**Schistidium atrichum (Müll. Hal. & Kindb.) W.A. Weber: Infrequent+, 1500–2500 m. NRim(5): on limestone boulder [1233], on moist limestone wall outcrop, E-facing [315], on a small sandstone rock over an E-facing slope, fully shaded and moist [98]. Inner(2): on moist limestone and sandstone rock, partly or fully shaded in mixed-conifer forest [385, 386]. Notes: This species is known from the western US north to Alaska. This is the first report for the southwestern US and serves to extend the southern limit of the species range in North America. This species was collected by Haring (1946) [IH: 3751, 3756], but incorrectly identified as *Schistidium confertum* (Funck) Bruch & Schimp. and *Grimmia apocarpa* var. *pulvinata* (Hedw.) G. Jones, an obsolete variety.

**Schistidium confertum (Funck) Bruch & Schimper: Infrequent+, 1500–2700 m. NRim(6): on limestone rocks in shaded or open situations [439, 1234], on a sandstone boulder over a moderate slope, fully-shaded and E-facing [87b], on soil over rock in meadow [69]. SRim(1): on rock in open woods [IH: 3773]. Inner(1): on sandstone rock [LS ns 12/13/1994]. Notes: Previously known from northerly western North America, this marks the first report of this species in the American Southwest. Haring (1946) and Louis Schellbach collected this species several times, but all specimens were incorrectly identified as either Schistidium dupretii (Thér.) Web. [*Grimmia dupretii* Thér.], *Grimmia atrofuscum* (Schimp.) Limp. [*Grimmia apocarpa* Hedw. var. *atrofusca* (Schimp.) Husn.], or *Coscinodon calyptratus* (Drumm.) C. Jens. [*Grimmia calyptrata* (Hook.) C.E.O. Jensen ex Kindb.]

**Schistidium dupretii (Thériot) W. A. Weber: Rare#, 2000–2500 m. NRim(1): Basin Spring, on limestone rock [IH: 3756]. Inner(1): Bright Angel Trail, on flat bench of exposed limestone cliff, NW-facing [206]. Notes: This record serves to extend the southern limit of the species' western range, which had been a belt stretching from CA to MT. This species was collected by Haring (1946), but was incorrectly identified as S. confertum (Funck) Bruch & Schimp. [*Grimmia apocarpa* Hedw. var. *conferta* (Funck) Spreng.] [IH: 3756]. However, I report the species new to Arizona because it was not recognized for the state in FNA (FNA eds. 2007+). Notes: Known previously throughout northern North America, this record extends the species' southern limit in the American west.

**Schistidium frigidum H. H. Blom: Rare#, 2400 m. NRim(1): Cliff Springs Trail, trailside on a small rock at toe of a NW-facing slope, 0.1 m above ground [120b]. Notes: Known throughout North America except for eastern and Midwestern US. This record extends the southwestern limit of this species in North America.

**Schistidium papillosum Culmann: Rare-, 2500 m. NRim(2): Widforss Trail near the rim, on sandstone slab with high exposure, N-facing and partly shaded [1064], in mixed conifer forest bordering Harvey Meadow, on a small sandstone rock over an E-facing slope, fully shaded and moist [96a]. Notes: Scattered throughout North America, this record extends the southwestern limit of this predominantly boreal species, which previously had only been reported for Colorado in the western US.

Hypnaceae

**Hypnum cupressiforme* var. *subjulaceum* Molendo: Rare-, 1000–2500 m. NRim(1): North Kaibab Trail near trailhead, on log in advanced decay, N-facing [1023c]. Inner(1): Lava Canyon, on soil [GR: 7011]. Notes: This species is largely restricted to higher latitudes, and otherwise reported in only three western states (CO, NM, ND), but additionally John Spence has material from Utah. Nonetheless, this record marks a southwestern extension to the species' distribution in North America.

Hypnum pallescens (Hedwig) P. Beauvois: Rare-, 2500 m. NRim(1): Ken Patrick Trail below Neal Spring, on bank of a dry streamlet, fully shaded [114].

Hypnum revolutum (Mitten) Lindberg: Common+, 1700–2700 m. NRim(9): frequent on limestone and sandstone rock, often N-facing and shaded [433, 1083a], rare on bases of Populus tremuloides, partly shaded [449], on log in shaded forest [1040]. Inner(5): frequent on limestone and sandstone rock, usually N-facing [994c], trail-side on dry slope [834], on subterranean roots of a shrub exposed from erosion, partly shaded [819a].

Hypnum vaucheri Lesquereux: Rare-, 1800–2100 m. SRim(1): Rim Trail, on dry soil over roots of *Pinus edulis* over a sloping cliff at edge of rim, exposed and N-facing [165]. Inner(1): Bright Angel Trail, on man-made calcareous rock wall, N-facing at toe of slope [31].

Leskeaceae

**Leskeella nervosa* (Bridel) Loeske: Rare#, 2400–2700 m. NRim(1): in vicinity of the N. Rim lookout tower near N. Rim entrance station, on downed log in advanced decay, fully shaded and 0.01 m above the ground in mixed-conifer forest [126b]. Inner(1): North Kaibab Trail at Coconino Sandstone rest area, in crevice of sandstone cliff top, dry and exposed at edge of cliff [398]. Notes: The Flora of North America cites the occurrence of this species in Arizona based on this GRCA record. Known broadly from Canada and the US, including the neighboring states of CO, UT and NM, this record marks a southwestern extension to the species' range.

**Pseudoleskea patens* (Lindberg) Kindberg: Rare-, 2500 m. NRim(1): Ken Patrick Trail along dry stream channel below Neal Spring, on dry to moist soil and rock in mixed-conifer forest [115]. Notes: Known previously from the western US and northern North America, this record serves to extend the southern limit of the species' range.

Pseudoleskea radicosa var. *compacta* (Best) E. Lawton: Rare-, 2600–2700 m. NRim(2): Robber's Roost, on boulders in mixed-conifer forest, N and E-facing [88, 480].

Pseudoleskeella tectorum (Funck ex Bridel) Kindberg ex Brotherus: Abundant+, 500–2700 m. Common on shaded rock, tree bases, and downed wood, usually N-facing. NRim(>15): common on limestone cliffs and outcrops, shaded [354], infrequent on bases of trees including *Populus tremuloides, Acer grandidentatum, Pseudotsuga menziesii* [1039], rare on logs in advanced decay, fully shaded and N-facing [941], rare on soil over sandstone outcrops [1046], on cherty rock, fully shaded in a hole [975]. SRim(7): frequent on N-facing limestone rock along the rim [903], rare on shaded tree bases of *Pinus edulis* and *Juniperus* sp.[750, 936], rare on shaded logs in advanced decay [757]. Inner(11): frequent on limestone rock, shaded and often N-facing [372], frequent at the base of boulders and cliffs on soil over rock, fully shaded [888], rare on bases of **Quercus gambelii** and *Juniperus* sp. [995, 1073], on subterranean roots of a shrub exposed from erosion, partly shaded [819]. Mead(1): on log over steep slope in desert scrub [1021]. [*Leskea williamsi* Best var. *filamentosa* Best; *Leskea tectorum* (Braun) Lindb. var. *flagellifera* Best]

Meesiaceae

Leptobryum pyriforme (Hedwig) Wilson: Rare-, 2400–2600 m. NRim(4): Robber's Roost, on moist soil [RC ns 8/31/1944], on moist limestone rock at open roadside spring [HB ns 9/28/1944], Kanabownits Spring, on moist soil [HB ns 9/29/1944], Tipover Spring, on moist soil around spring pipe [MB ns 9/29/1944].

Mielichhoferiaceae

**Pohlia camptotrachela* (Renauld & Cardot) Brotherus: Rare-, 2700 m. NRim(1): Little Park Lake vicinity, on moist soil and along edge of log with sedges bordering dried pond in open woods [129a]. Notes: Known previously in North America from the western US and British Columbia, this record extends the species' distribution to the American southwest.

Pohlia cruda (Hedwig) H. Lindberg: Rare-, 2500–2600 m. NRim(2): Basin Springs, in crevices below limestone rock, partly shaded [IH: 3724], North Canyon Spring, on moist soil [JS: 5470b].

**Pohlia wahlenbergii* (F. Weber & D. Mohr) Andrews: Rare#, 1800–2500 m. NRim(1): Robber's Roost, at spring within dry drainage at top of 20° slope, on moist soil along base of log, fully shaded and S-facing [457]. Inner(1): Kwagunt Canyon, on moist bank of perennial stream [GR: 7049].

Mniaceae

**Mnium arizonicum* Amann: Rare-, 1900 m. NRim(1): Bright Angel Trail, on moist soil at trailside seep, W-facing and partly shaded on steep slope [215].

Orthotricaceae

Orthotrichum alpestre Hornschuch ex Bruch: Infrequent+, 500–2600 m. NRim(4): on limestone boulder [478], on log [1044], on base of *Pseudotsuga menziesii*, <0.5 m above the ground [943c]. SRim(1): on underside of burnt log and on rocky ledge in open woods [IH ns 8/18/1940]. Inner(1): on log in advanced decay, N-facing, on steep slope [998a]. Mead(1): on exposed log on steep slope in desert [1020].

**Orthotrichum cupulatum* Bridel: Rare+, 2000–2600 m. NRim(1): on limestone rock in mixed-conifer forest [1214]. SRim(1): on limestone rock in *Pinus ponderosa* forest [1208]. Inner(2): on top of dry, vertical limestone cliff outcrop, partly-shaded, NE-facing [202], trailside at toe of 20° slope on roots of large *Pinus ponderosa*, fully shaded, E-facing [334b].

**Orthotrichum hallii* Sullivant & Lesquereux: Infrequent+, 2400–2500 m. NRim(4): frequent on fully shaded limestone cliffs and outcrops [945]. SRim(3): on partly shaded sandstone boulder [166], on long root of *Juniperus* sp. partly shaded [936]. Inner(2): on shaded bases of *Populus tremuloides* and *Pseudotsuga menziesii* [992a].

**Orthotrichum obtusifolium* Bridel: Rare-, 2500 m. NRim(1): Widforss Point Trail, on soil over partly shaded limestone rock in cool-air drainage [947].

Orthotrichum pellucidum Lindberg: Rare-, 2100 m. SRim(1): Coronado Point, on limestone boulder in woods [IH: 3616].

**Orthotrichum pumilum* Swartz: Rare#, 500–2400 m. Inner(1): North Kaibab Trail, on soil over base of *Pseudotsuga menziesii*, N-facing [992a]. Mead(1): Pearce Ferry, <1 mi E of the park border near the Grand Wash Cliffs, on base of *Quercus gambelii* on steep slope, N-facing [1018a].

Zygodon viridissimus var. *rupestris* Hartman: Rare-, 2100 m. SRim(1): section of Arizona Trail near Grand Canyon Village, on base of *Juniperus* sp., N and NW-facing [921b].

Polytrichaceae

Atrichum selwynii Austin: Rare-, 2500 m. NRim(2): at Milk Spring in mixed-conifer forest [GR: 7658b], near road by North Rim Lodge on soil in open woods [IH ns 9/2/1940], deep limestone sink along the Point Sublime Road on soil over log in advanced decay [GR: 7666b]. Notes: This species was collected by Haring (1946), but was misidentified.

Polytrichum juniperinum Hedwig: Common+, 2400–2700 m. NRim(11): common on dry to moist soil of meadows [70], and mixed conifer forest [469], rare on roadsides [IH: 27], on damp soil at vicinity of spring [GR: 7658]. [Nomenclature unrevised]

Pottiaceae

Aloina aloides var. *ambigua* (Bruch & Schimper) E. J. Craig: Infrequent#, 500–700 m. Inner(4): on soil over rock [505], in tributary on open bank of dry wash [714], on open soil with soil crust [596]. Mead(1): in soil crust at base of grass tufts on a N-facing, 20° slope, surrounded by calcareous rocks [1011c].

Aloina bifrons (De Notaris) Delgadillo: Rare-, 500 m. Inner(1): vicinity of Pearce Ferry, < 1 mi E of the GRCA border near the Grand Wash Cliffs, in moist soil crust at base of N-facing cliff near calcareous deposits from seep [1007a].

Barbula bolleana (Müll. Hal.) Brotherus: Infrequent+, 500–700 m. Inner(3): at spring along streamlets and on rock in vicinity of waterfalls [513], on seeping soil over vertical wall, partly shaded [604b]. River(5): riverside on open, muddy bank at the high-water mark, adjacent to spring [705], riverside on travertine wall below high-water mark, filtered light [660]. Notes: This species was cited in Clover and Jotter (1944), however this specimen was not included in Haring's 1946 checklist.

**Barbula convoluta* var. *eustegia* (Cardot & Thériot) R. H. Zander: Infrequent+, 2400–2600 m. NRim(4): on soil over rock lacking shade [967a], on moist, sandy soil over slope, partly shaded in forested drainage [473], atop dry, exposed boulder bordering stream, SW-facing [109c], in a dry, forested drainage, on gravely, silty soil beneath a rock overhang on 40° slope, partly shaded and E-facing [282]. Inner(1): trailside on steeply sloping bank composed of rocky, gravely soil, E-facing and with filtered light [358a]. Notes: This record begins to fill the distributional gap between the western US and scattered records (TX and IL).

Barbula indica var. *indica* (Hooker) Sprengel: Rare#, 400–1400 m. Inner(2): mouth of Kanab Canyon, on seeping soil over vertical wall, partly shaded [606], Miner's Spring on Grandview Trail, on moist, red clay soil below large boulders, NW-facing [816]. River(1): upriver from Granite Park, CRM 208.5, river right, on moist, muddy bank below the high-water mark with *Equisetum* and *Cynodon*, partly shaded and SW-facing [722].

Bryoerythrophyllum recurvirostrum (Hedwig) P.C. Chen: Rare#, 2500–2600 m. NRim(3): Ken Patrick Trail, in dry stream channel on dry soil at base of boulder covered by grape vines, NW-facing [111b], and on shaded soil along base of log [858], at Kanabownits Spring, substratum unknown [RC: 1191], Robber's Roost, in basin drainage on dry boulder, and on soil over small limestone rock [475]. Notes: This species was collected by Rose Collom in 1941, but was misidentified as *Didymodon tophaceus* (Brid.) Lisa. The species is reported in Brian's compilation (2000), but no voucher has been found to match the cited locality.

Crossidium aberrans Holzinger & E. B. Bartram: Common+, 400–2200 m. Inner(4): along a streamlet on moist, sandstone-derived soil [499], on sloping soil beneath Muave Limestone rock [602b], on sandstone wall [1238]. River(10): common soil crust component in open washes [709] or located at the bases of shrubs and rocks, partly shaded [670a], on limestone rock above beach [687].

Crossidium crassinervium var. *crassinervium* (De Notaris) Juratzka: Infrequent+, 500–700 m. Inner(3): at base of rock along streamlet, fully shaded [521a], on open soil and soil over rock lacking shade [241]. Mead(1): component of soil crust on N-facing slopes below grass tufts and in dry wash [1016c]. River(5): frequent soil crust component in open washes, partly shaded at bases of shrubs and rocks [1010], on rock above beach [565].

Crossidium seriatum H.A. Crum & Steere: Infrequent+, 400–700 m. Inner(3): on open soil and soil along rock in desert scrub, with or without shade [690]. Mead(1): component of soil crust at base of wall, N-facing [1004]. River(2): component of soil crust at base of limestone wall, N-facing and partly shaded [603], on exposed soil over sandstone outcrop above beach [240].

Crossidium squamiferum (Viviani) Juratzka: Infrequent+, 400–2100 m. Inner(5): on soil over limestone and sandstone rock, without shade [821]. Mead(1): on N-facing limestone outcrop [1015a]. River(2): on sandy soil over rock above the beach and usually lacking shade [688].

*Didymodon australasiae (Hooker & Greville) R. H. Zander: Infrequent+, 600–1400 m. Inner(4): on seeping soil over vertical wall, partly shaded [604b], component of soil crust in desert [593], on soil over sandstone and limestone rock, often shaded [568]. River(2): component of soil crust on dry, sloping soil above beach [683b], on moist soil surrounded by diabasic rocks with filtered light [573b].

Didymodon brachyphyllus (Sullivant) R. H. Zander: Infrequent+, 700–2500 m. NRim(2): on sandstone boulders and outcrops in direct sun or partly shaded [1092b]. SRim(1): on soil over limestone rock lacking shade in *Pinus ponderosa* forest [795]. Inner(4): on sandy soil bordering streamlet [498c], on intermittent seeping rock in mixed-conifer forest [1093], on sandstone cliff faces and walls usually in direct sun [990]. Notes: this likely species was cited in Clover & Jotter (1944), but the historic collection(s) has not been verified. [*D. trifarius* (Hedw.) Brid.]

**Didymodon fallax* (Hedwig) R. H. Zander: Rare+, 500–1400 m. Inner(1): Miner's Spring off of Grand View Trail, at base of Redwall Limestone wall on moist soil [804]. River(3): CRM 196.1, river right, riverside on wet vertical face of muddy bank below the high-water mark with filtered light [704], Warm Springs, on bank of river below high-water mark [658a], Ledges, in vicinity of CRM 151, in seepage area on wet rock partly shaded by rock overhangs and on wet rock bordering cascades [619]. Notes: This species is known throughout most of North America and has been collected from adjacent states with the exception of Nevada.

**Didymodon nevadensis* R. H. Zander: Infrequent+, 500–2400 m. NRim(2): on sandstone rocks [1230]. Inner(2): on travertine and sandstone, exposed or partly shaded [237c], in soil crust on exposed N-facing slope [594]. Mead(1): component of soil crust below cliffs and on limestone, mostly N-facing [1005].

River(4): <10 m from the river on sandy shore below rocks, NW-facing [636b], on soil below dibasic outcrop, NE-facing and partly shaded [581]. Notes: Known previously from British Columbia and five US states (CO, NV, NM, NB, TX), this record bridges the gap in distribution between Nevada and New Mexico.

Didymodon nicholsonii Culmann: Rare#, 700–2400 m. Inner(1): North Kaibab Trail, on soil shaded by overhanging rock [1098b]. River(1): fan of Forester Canyon, on moist N-facing sandy bank 3 m from the river's edge [543]. Notes: Restricted to a portion of western North America, this collection is the first for the American Southwest.

Didymodon rigidulus var. **icmadophilus** (Schimper ex Müll. Hal.) R. H. Zander: Infrequent+, 700–2700 m. NRim(1): on small rock with filtered light over a SW-facing, 30° slope [127b]. Inner(4): component of soil crust on bare gravely soil in open woodland [923], on dry sandy soil over sloping rock, N-facing [227b], on moist sandy soil at base of rocks in dry spring channel [647b]. River(1): on sandy bank above beach beneath *Baccharis* sp. [646]. Notes: This record continues to fill the scattered distribution of this species in North America.

Didymodon rigidulus Hedwig var. *rigidulus*: Infrequent+, 400–1300 m. Inner(4): on soil beneath rock overhang and on soil over sandstone rock [246a], on dry sandy soil bordering streamlet, open to shaded [498d], exposed on limestone cliff face [243]. River(5): above beach on soil over limestone and sandstone rock, open or partly shaded [68a7, 734a], component of soil crust in partial shade of *Acacia* sp., *Grindelia nuda*, and *Larrea tridentata* [715].

Didymodon tectorum (Müll. Hal.) K. Saito: Rare#, 2000 m. Inner(1): Bright Angel Trail, trailside on dry soil along crevice of rock slab at the base of a steep N-facing slope, partly-shaded, 1 m above ground [190a]. Notes: Known previously from Colorado, Kansas, Maryland, and New Mexico, this record extends the western distributional limit of this species in North America.

Didymodon tophaceus (Bridel) Lisa: Infrequent+, 500–1400 m. Inner(3): on moist bank of spring streamlet [IH ns 9/9/1940], at base of Redwall Limestone wall on moist soil in vicinity of spring [805], on S-facing Bright Angel Shale at mouth of tributary [GR: 7308]. River(4): on a moist sandy bank 3 m from the river, N-facing and open [805], on moist soil of seeps and springs [540b, 640], on travertine wall below the high-water mark of the river [661]. Marble(1): at spring on unknown substratum [LES ns 10-May-02]. [*Husnotiella pringlei* (Card.) Grout]

Didymodon vinealis (Bridel) R. H. Zander: Common+, 500–2500 m. NRim(5): frequent on soil in crevices of sandstone and limestone rock [90], rare on seeping soil over rock in full shade [305, 1071], on decaying log in mixed-conifer forest [1041]. Inner(7): common on limestone and sandstone outcrops, often with soil, usually N-facing and shaded [421, 203], frequent on soil shaded by overhanging rock ledges or shrubs [1098], on vertical rock wall behind cascade, partly shaded [538]. Mead(1): in moist soil crust below cliff on gentle N-facing slope, near calcareous seep deposits [1006]. River(4): above beach and N-facing on shaded sandy soil at base of diabasic cliffs [581b], small rocks [548], and between pebbles [651]. Notes: This species was not reported by Haring (1946), but she had collected it incidentally with *Tortula obtusifolia* [IH: 3706].

Eucladium verticillatum (Bridel) Bruch & Schimper: Common+, 500–1500 m. Inner(7): frequent at seeps on shaded, dripping calcareous rock faces [558, 800], frequent at springs on rocks submerged in pools and along streamlets [1117]. River(8): common on dripping rock at springs and seeps, often partly shaded and N-facing [485, 620], on seeping travertine wall below the high-water mark of the CO River [665]. Notes: This species was reported by Clover & Jotter (1944).

*Gymnostomum aeruginosum Smith: Rare#, 700–2500 m. NRim(1): North Kaibab Trail above the rim, on sandstone rock in mixed-conifer forest [1226]. Inner(2): Kanab Canyon, within 1 mi of CO River, on seeping soil over vertical wall, partly shaded [605], Grandview Trail, on soil and rock partly shaded beneath the overhang of a large boulder [832].

**Gymnostomum calcareum Nees & Hornschuch: Rare#, 700–2400 m. NRim(1): Cliff Spring, on wet limestone rock [JS: 5446]. River(2): Elves' Chasm, below falls on moist sandy bank of streamlet [500], Grand View Trail at Miner's Spring, on moist red clay below large boulders, NW-facing and shaded [813]. Inner(1): 1/4 mi up trail from Honga Rapids, river left, on moist sandy soil below rocks in dry spring channel [648]. Notes: This species has been historically synonymized with the cosmopolitan G. aeruginosum, but recently material from California confirmed the distinction between the two taxa. To date, the only legitimate specimens of *G. calcareum* exist for California, Missouri, North Carolina, and Mexico. This record marks the first report for the Southwestern US.

**Gyroweisia tenuis (Schrader ex Hedwig) Schimper: Rare-, 700 m. River(1): 1 mile above Forster Canyon along the Colorado River, on seeping moist soil [560]. Notes: This species has a scattered and limited distribution in North America. This record extends its southwestern range.

Hymenostylium recurvirostrum var. *recurvirostrum* (Hedwig) Dixon: Infrequent+, 900–2400 m. Inner(4): on dripping rock at seeps and springs, often covered in calcareous deposits [122, GR: 6753]. River(1): spring on moist basic wall, open and E-facing [GR: 6685]. Notes: This species was reported in Clover and Jotter (1944). [*Gymnostomum recurvirostrum* Hedwig, an illegal name for *Gymnostomum recurvirostre* Hedw.]

*Microbryum starckeanum (Hedwig) R. H. Zander: Rare-, 700 m. Inner(1): Elves' Chasm, along streamlet from main waterfall on loose soil beside rock, fully shaded [521d].

Pleurochaete luteola (Bescherelle) Thériot: Infrequent+, 500–1300 m. Inner(5): on soil over rock at base of limestone and quartzite cliffs [GR: 4139b, 8388a]. River(4): above beach on moist and shaded soil along rock bases [494, 706], on dry, but ephemerally seeping Mauve Limestone ledge, E-facing and open [612]. Notes: Reported by Clover and Jotter (1944).

Pseudocrossidium crinitum (Schultz) R. H. Zander: Rare#, 400–2100 m. SRim(1): section of Arizona Trail near Grand Canyon Village on limestone rock in Pinus ponderosa forest [1228]. Inner(1): Havasu Canyon, at the intersection of Beaver Creek and Havasu Creek, on dry soil and soil over sandstone rock [247]. River(2): Three Springs Rapid, CRM 215.2, River left, in cove formed by Tapeats Sandstone, on dry sandy soil over rock at base of vertical wall, partly shaded [734d], at the fan of Forester Canyon, on moist sandy bank 3 m from the river margin, N-facing and open [540a]. Notes: Reported by Clover and Jotter (1944). [*Tortula aurea* Bartr.]

Pterygoneurum lamellatum (Lindberg) Juratzka: Rare#, 400–2100 m. NRim(1): North Kaibab Trail, on dry soil in crevices of constructed limestone rock wall, N-facing and exposed [390b]. SRim(1): Bright Angel Trail, trailside on dry sandy soil over limestone slab, open [188a]. Inner(2): section of Arizona Trail near Grand Canyon Village, component of roadside soil crust at base of grass tuft in open *Pinus ponderosa* forest on partly shaded gravely soil [918], Rim Trail, on flat ground in open pinyon-juniper woodland, on soil free of litter [790b].

Pterygoneurum ovatum (Hedwig) Dixon: Rare-, 1800 m. Inner(1): Dripping Springs, on sandstone rock [IH ns 9/7/1940].

Pterygoneurum subsessile var. *subsessile* (Bridel) Juratzka: Rare-, 2100 m. SRim(1): Rim Trail, on flat ground in open pinyon-juniper woodland, on soil in a clearing without pine needles, [790f].

Syntrichia caninervis Mitten: Common+, 500–2400 m. NRim(1): component of soil crust surrounded by grasses in open *Pinus ponderosa* forest [870]. SRim(2): rare in open forests and along the rim on gravely or sandy soil and as a component of soil crust [850]. Inner(8): frequent on soil over limestone and sandstone rock, in shaded or open situations [389], rare component of soil crusts [898a], on N-facing basalt outcrop in open desert [GR: 6690]. Mead(1): in moist soil crust below cliff on N-facing 15°slope [1003]. River(8): frequent on sandy soil and soil over limestone rock usually without shade [609], infrequent above beach as a component of soil crust in open desert [708].

Syntrichia laevipila Bridel: Rare-, 1300 m. Inner(2): North Kaibab Trail in vicinity of Cottonwood Campground, partly shaded on base of *Quercus* sp. [1127b], North Kaibab Trail ½ mi up from Cottonwood Campground, partly shaded in oak thicket on base of Quercus sp. [1132].

Syntrichia montana Nees: Rare-, 1800–2200 m. SRim(1): Grandview Trail, on soil over bark at base of *Juniperus* sp. [836]. Inner(2): Bright Angel Trail, on concrete of constructed limestone rock wall, W-facing and partly shaded [180], Bright Angel Trail, trailside on vertical limestone wall, NE-facing and partly shaded [232].

Syntrichia norvegica F. Weber: Common+, 1900–2600 m. NRim(7): frequent on soil over limestone and sandstone rock [964], infrequent directly on limestone and sandstone rock [108], on soil over *Pinus ponderosa* root [309]. SRim(2): on base of Juniperus sp. with filtered light [752], on soil at base of *Artemisia tridentata* and along limestone rock [909]. Inner(3): frequent on soil over limestone or sandstone rock in sunny or shaded situations [413a], rare directly on sandstone rock [1210], on soil over base of *Pinus ponderosa* [1036].

Syntrichia papillosissima (Coppey) Loeske: Rare-, 2600 m. NRim(1): roadside in vicinity of North Kaibab trailhead, on base of moist bole with filtered light, W-facing [260].

Syntrichia ruralis (Hedwig) F. Weber & D. Mohr: Abundant+, 500–2700 m. NRim(>15): common directly on calcareous rock or above thin layer of soil over rock, in shaded or open situations [100], frequent on soil abutting trees and shrubs or amongst grasses, usually shaded [960], on soil over base of

Artemisia tridentata [276]. SRim(>10): common on dry soil along rock bases or with coniferous litter in open woodlands along the rim [746], frequent on soil over limestone and sandstone rock along the rim [927], infrequent on bases of *Juniperus* sp. [846],. Inner(>15): common on exposed and shaded soil, often along edges of rocks or rarely with pine litter beneath conifers [1136], common directly on limestone rock or with a thin layer of soil over rock, usually lacking shade [419], rare on decaying wood [1023], rare on soil over bases of conifers [344], rare component of soil crust [592]. Mead(1): on log and N-facing, moist sandy soil at base of grasses, and on N side of *Quercus gambelii* [1014c]. River(9): frequent above the beach on dry sandy soil and soil between rocks, commonly without shade [718], on ephemerally seeping wall of Mauve Limestone, NE-facing [611]. [*Tortula ruralis* (Hedw.) Smith]

Tortella alpicola Dixon: Rare-, 1800 m. Inner(1): Northwest of the saddle between North Rim and Juno Temple, substratum unknown [GR: 7021c].

Tortula acaulon (Withering) R. H. Zander: Infrequent-, 2100–2400 m. SRim(4): on exposed, gravely soil in open woodlands [748, 790a], component of soil crust, partly shaded in *Pinus ponderosa* forest [794]. Inner(1): on exposed sandstone outcrop [1204], on open sandy and gravely slope, S-facing [380].

Tortula atrovirens (Smith) Lindberg: Infrequent+, 500–2200 m. SRim(1): on limestone rock in *Pinus ponderosa* forest [1231]. Inner(3): on limestone cliff, W-facing and open [243c], on soil over limestone ledge at base of N-facing wall, partly shaded [597], on soil beneath rock overhang, partly shaded [244b], component of soil crust on moist bank of tributary beneath Acacia and *Larrea tridentata* [716]. River(3): at base of rock on beach sand, exposed [636a], above the beach on soil over exposed rocky slopes [702, 720]. Notes: Reported by Haring (1946), but misidentified; intended specimens may have been lost, but those remaining were *Tortula obtusifolia* [IH: 3704]. Also reported by Clover and Jotter (1944). [*Desmatodon convolutus* (Brid.) Grout]

Tortula hoppeana (Schultz) Ochyra: Rare-, 2500 m. NRim(1): North Kaibab Trail, on highly textured rock at an inverted slope beneath limestone outcrop overhang, partly shaded and E-facing [331].

Tortula inermis (Bridel) Montagne: Common+, 400–2400 m. NRim(1): on outcrop without shade [116c]. SRim(1): on sandy soil in crevice of limestone wall, fully shaded [167]. Inner(10): frequent in rock crevices, partly to fully shaded [192a], frequent on soil shaded by rock walls and overhangs [ ], rare directly on sandstone and limestone rock [209, 1232]. River(3): frequent above high-water mark on dry sand abutting rocks and over rock, partly shaded or exposed [573, 730]. Notes: Reported by Clover and Jotter (1944).

Tortula lanceola R. H. Zander: Rare+, 500–2100 m. SRim(1): Rim Trail, on limestone cliff in pinyon-juniper woodland [935c]. Inner(1): river left 1/4 mi up foot path from Colorado River at Honga Rapids, on exposed moist and sandy soil abutting rocks in a dry spring channel [647]. River(1): Mouth of Parashant Canyon, component of soil crust over rock slab, partly shaded by rock overhang [711].

Tortula mucronifolia Schwägrichen: Infrequent+, 2000–2600 m. NRim(3): on shaded soil and soil over rock [967c], on exposed boulder [479a]. SRim(1): on soil beneath rock overhang, N-facing and fully shaded [933]. Inner(4): on soil over sandstone rock [986d], on gravely soil fully shaded beneath roots of *Quercus gambelii* [379], on log in advanced decay, N-facing [1023], on limestone boulder,

N-facing [200b].

Tortula muralis Hedwig: Infrequent#, 2200–2500 m. NRim(3): on limestone rock in mixed conifer forest [1224]. SRim(1): on soil over limestone rock [925]. Inner(1): on limestone rock at edge of rim, highly exposed [350].

Tortula obtusifolia (Schwägrichen) Mathieu: Common+, 2100–2600 m. NRim(3): common on limestone outcrops, exposed or partly shaded [315], rare on soil over rock [863], rare on sandstone rock [984]. Inner(7): frequent on calcareous rock or with a thin layer of soil, usually shaded [986], on ephemerally seeping rock [1095b], on sandy soil beneath sandstone overhang, fully shaded [1098a]. [*Desmatodon obtusifolius* (Schwäegr.) Jur.]

Trichostomum planifolium (Dixon) R. H. Zander: Rare-, 700 m. Inner(1): Kanab Canyon off Colorado River, on dry steep bank over limestone rock at base of Mauve Limestone wall, partly shaded and N-facing [599c]. Notes: This species is known in North America only from the southwestern US. This record in conjunction with a record from John Spence (UT) completes the distribution of the species in all states within this region. This identification is tentative because sporophytes were lacking and the plant was immature

Trichostomum tenuirostre (Hooker & Taylor) Lindberg: Rare-, 400 m. River(1): Above Three Springs Rapid at CRM 215.0, in cove formed by Tapeats Sandstone, in dry crevice, fully shaded [731a].

Weissia controversa Hedwig: Rare#, 1700–2500 m. Inner(2): Grandview Trail, on soil and rock beneath overhang of boulder, partly shaded [832b], North Kaibab Trail, on sandy, gravely slope below *Acer grandidentatum*, fully shaded and E-facing [335].

Weissia ligulifolia (E. B. Bartram) Grout: Common+, 500–2100 m. SRim(1): on soil in open woods [IH ns 8/18/1940]. Inner(7): common on shaded soil abutting rocks and beneath overhangs [613a], in crevice of pegmatite cliff [738a], bordering streamlet on sandy soil [502]. Mead(1): in dry tributary on moist soil beneath rock overhang, partly shaded [1017]. River(4): frequent on shaded soil and limestone rock [614, 698], component of soil crust beneath shrub on a dry, W-facing slope [728], in crevice of dry rock slab on beach, open and E-facing [691]. [W. andrewsii Bartr.]

Pterigynandraceae

Pterigynandrum filiforme Hedwig: Rare-, 2500 m. NRim(1): Basin Spring [JS: 5905]. Notes: Three specimens so named were collected by Haring, but had only *Brachytheciastrum collinum* or *Pseudoleskeella tectorum* in their packets upon examination [IH: 3713, 3725, 3727].

Splachnobryaceae

Splachnobryum obtusum (Bridel) Müller Hal.: Rare#, 400–500 m. Inner(1): along Cave Creek just upstream of Columbine Falls, substratum unknown [GR: 8491]. River(1): Warm Springs, riverside below the high-water mark on moist travertine deposits [653].

Thuidiaceae

Abietinella abietina (Hedwig) M. Fleischer: Rare-, 1600 m. Inner(1): North Kaibab Trail along the offshoot to Dripping Springs, on shaded, dry rock [IH ns 9/1/1940]. [*Thuidium abietinum* (Hedw.) Schimp.]

Timmiaceae

Timmia megapolitana subsp. *bavarica* (Hessler) Brassard: Common+, 2000–2600 m. NRim(11): common on shaded soil abutting outcrops and beneath rock overhangs [1045a], infrequent on shaded limestone rock or soil over rock [121, 306], on ephemerally seeping limestone outcrop, fully shaded and SE-facing [1071c]. SRim(2): rare in limestone rock crevices near rim [162]. Inner(2): frequent on calcareous rock [355] or with a thin layer of soil [991a], on sandy soil abutting roots of *Quercus gambelii* [348], on log in mixed-conifer forest [1042]. [*Timmia bavarica* Hessl.]

Marchantiophyta (Liverworts)

Aneuraceae

*Aneura pinguis (L.) Dumort: Rare-, 2400 m. NRim(1): Cliff Spring, on thin layer of moist soil over limestone rock, shaded [JS: 5444]. Notes: Previously known from the western US, Canada, and Europe, this record marks the species first occurrence in the American Southwest.

Aytoniaceae

**Asterella gracilis (F. Weber) Underwood: Rare-, 2500 m. NRim(1): Basin Spring on moist soil abutting sandstone boulders [JS: 5903].

*Mannia fragrans (Balb.) Frye & L. Clark: Rare-, 900 m. Marble(1): Keystone Spring, on dry soil of slope in proximity of spring [JS: 5313].

*Reboulia hemisphaerica (L.) Raddi: Rare#, 600–1500 m. Inner(1): Bright Angel Trail, trailside on soil below boulder, partly-shaded [33]. River(1): above Deubendorff, CRM 131.9 river left, on moist soil bordering and sheltered by diabasic rocks, filtered light [574].

Cephaloziellaceae

*Cephaloziella divaricata (Roth.) Warnst.: Rare+, 2500–2600 m. NRim(4): Cape Final Trail, on large *Pinus ponderosa* log in intermediate decay, N-facing [1052b], W of Harvey Meadow, along foot trail in coniferous forested gulley recently disturbed by fire, on burnt log [107], North Kaibab Trail, in forested drainage on 35° slope along the moist lower side of a burnt log, N-facing and open [289], Robber's Roost, on woody debris in advanced decay over a 20° slope, N-facing and partly shaded, 2 cm above the ground, [432].

Geocalycaceae

* *Chiloscyphus polyanthos* (L.) *Corda* var. *rivularis* (Schrad.) Nees: Rare-, 2400 m. NRim(1): Cliff Springs, on thin layer of soil over limestone rock, fully shaded [JS: 5469].

Jubulaceae

*Frullania inflata Gottsche: Rare-, 2500 m. NRim(1): Widforss Trail, on large limestone outcrop in coniferous forested drainage < 15 m from the rim, fully shaded by rock overhangs [944a].

Jungermanniaceae

*Tritomaria exsectiformis (Bridel) Loeske: Rare#, 2400–2500 m. NRim(1): Robber's Roost spring, substratum unknown [GR: 7700]. Inner(1): downstream of

Kanabownits Spring, in small meadow growing within a cushion of *Ceratodon purpureus* [GR: 8870].

Marchantiaceae

Marchantia polymorpha L. Rare-, 1600–1800 m. Inner(2): E side of upper Bright Angel Creek at hanging garden, substratum unknown [GR: 7288], Angel Spring in Bright Angel Canyon, substratum unknown [GR: 8608].

Ricciaceae

Riccia glauca L.: Rare-, 2700 m. NRim(1): within 3 mi of Little Park Lake, NE of N. Rim entrance station, abutting the edge of a log on moist soil bordering a dried pond, filtered light provided by sedges [132a].

Targioniaceae

***Targionia* sp. nov. A. T. Whittemore in ed.: Infrequent#, 700–2100 m. Inner(4): Elves' Chasm, on silty soil bordering streamlet from waterfall, fully shaded by boulder overhang [497], Boucher Trail, on soil beneath rock overhang, NE-facing and fully shaded [824], Miner's Spring off Grandview Trail, on moist sand abutting large boulders, NW-facing and partly shaded [812], South Kaibab Trail, on shaded soil below sandstone rock [886]. River(1): 1 mi S of Forster Canyon, at river high-water mark and abutting rocks on moist soil, in shade of boulder [554]. Notes: This specimen represents an undescribed taxon.

*****

3.3.5 Catalog of Excluded Taxa

The following 26 unaccepted taxa were reported in the literature by Clover and Jotter (1944), Haring (1946), or Brian (2000), or were present in the Grand Canyon Herbarium database. These taxa have been designated obsolete, misidentified, or unconfirmed. For each listed species, the current accepted nomenclature precedes any outdated names used by Haring, which follow in brackets. Additional information for all historic collections can be acquired from the Grand Canyon Herbarium.

*****

Amblystegium juratzkanum Schimper var. *giganteum* (Grout) Grout: This variety is no longer accepted and has been reduced to the species *Amblystegium serpens* (Hedw.) Bruch [IH: 2337, 3732].

Atrichum undulatum (Hedwig) P. Beauvois: All collections under this name were *A. selwynii*.

Barbula unguiculata Hedwig: The single specimen so named was *Didymodon tophaceus* [IH ns 9/9/1940].

Coscinodon calyptratus (Drummond) C. E. O. Jensen [*Grimmia calyptrata* (Hook.) C.E.O. Jensen ex Kindb.]: This species was reported by Haring, but all examined collections were *Grimmia orbicularis, Grimmia alpestris*, or *G. pulvinata* [e.g. IH: 3773, 3774].

Ceratodon purpureus (Hedwig) Bridel var. *xanthopus* (Sullivant) E. G. Britton: This variety is no longer accepted and these specimens are thus reduced to *Ceratodon purpureus* (Hedw.) Brid. subsp. *purpureus*.

Didymodon luridus Sprengel [D. trifarius (Hedw.) Brid.]: This species was reported by Clover and Jotter (1944), but does not occur in North America. The specimen(s) has not been located for verification.

Didymodon rigidulus var. *subulatus* (Thériot & Bartram) R. H. Zander [*D. mexicanus* Besch. var. *subulatus* Ter. & Bartr.]: This species was reported by Hawbecker (1936), and although likely to occur in GRCA, has not been located for verification.

Grimmia apocarpa Hedwig var. *pulvinata* (Hedw.) G. Jones: Intended specimens may have been inadvertently displaced; the only remaining plants in these packets were *Schistidium atrichum* and *Ceratodon purpureus* [IH: 3751, 3762].

Grimmia decipiens (Schultz) Lindberg: Specimen so named was *G. orbicularis* [IH ns 9/9/1940].

Grimmia montana Bruch & Schimp.: This species was reported by Hawbecker (1936). Although the record for this common acidic rock moss is not unlikely in western North America, the specimen has not been located for verification.

Grimmia pilifera P. Beauvois: This species is reported in Hawbecker (1936), but the specimen has not been located for verification. The record is unlikely, as this species is rare in western North America and has not been otherwise reported for northern Arizona.

Grimmia trichophylla Greven: Reported by Clover and Jotter (1944), this specimen has not been located for verification. It is likely to occur in GRCA and has been reported for Arizona.

Hypnum pallescens (Hedwig) P. Beauvois [*Hypnum reptile* Michx.]: This species was reported by Hawbecker (1936), but has not been located for verification. It is perhaps a valid record, but the species is infrequent in western North America.

Imbribryum gemmiparum (De Notaris) Spence [*Bryum gemmiparum* De Not.]: This specimen will be examined, but the species is unlikely [IH ns 9/7/1940 GRCA 51640].

Leptodictyum riparium (Hedwig) var. *brachyphyllum* (Cardot & Thériot): This is one of many erroneously described varieties of the species, which are now thought to be ecotypes (FNA eds. 2007+). This record is thereby reduced to *Leptodictyum riparium* (Hedwig) Warnstorf. A specimen was reported by Haring (1946), but has not been located for verification.

Philonotis capillaris C. Hartman: This species was reported by Clover and Jotter (1944), but has not been verified. This species is unlikely to occur in GRCA because it is largely restricted to coastal habitats from California to Alaska.

Pleurochaete squarrosa (Bridel) Lindberg: Specimens under this name were *P. luteola* (Besch.) Thériot [IH ns 10/9/1944].

Ptychostomum lonchocaulon (Müll. Hal.) J. R. Spence [*Bryum cirratum* Hoppe & Hornsch.]: This specimen has not been located for verification, although it was reported by Haring (1946) and is likely to occur in GRCA.

Ptychostomum pallens (Swartz) J. R. Spence [*Bryum pallens* Sw.]: This specimen is unlikely and will be examined by a specialist [IH ns 8/18/1940; GRCA 51644].

Racomitrium heterostichum subsp. *sudeticum* (Funck) Dixon [*Racomitrium heterostichum* (Hedw.) Brid. var. *sudeticum* (Funck) Jones]: The specimen so named was *G. orbicularis* [LS: 3707].

Rosulabryum capillare (Hedwig) J. R. Spence [*Bryum capillare* Hedw.]: This specimen is deemed unlikely and will be examined [IH: 3612].

Schistidium apocarpum Hedwig Bruch & Schimper [*G. apocarpa* Hedw., *G. apocarpa* Hedw. var. *atrofusca* (Schimp.) Husnot, *G. apocarpa* Hedw. var. *conferta* (Funck.) Spreng.]: Specimens so named were *Grimmia orbicularis, S. dupretii, S. confertum,* or *S. atrichum.*

Schistidium strictum (Turner) Loeske ex Mårtensson [*G. apocarpa* Hedw. var. *gracilis* (Schleich.) Web. & Mohr]: The specimen so named was *G. orbicularis* [LS ns 10/13/1944].

Scleropodium cespitans (Wilson ex Müll. Hal.) L. F. Koch var. *sublaeve* (Renauld & Cardot) Wijk & Margad.: This species was reported in Brian (2000) for a specimen previously named *Myurella tenerrima.* The collector and location of this specimen is unknown.

Syntrichia obtusissima (Müll. Hal.) R. H. Zander [*Tortula obtusissima* (Müll. Hal.) Mitten]: Reported by Clover and Jotter (1944). Although likely to occur in GRCA and reported for AZ, this species has not yet been verified for GRCA.

Tortula cernua (Huebener) Lindberg: Collected by Rose Collom in 1941 [RC: 1182] this specimen was not included in Haring's checklists for Grand Canyon (1941 and 1946). Specimen has not been located for verification and may be missing. This species is likely to occur in GRCA, as it has been reported for Arizona and occurs commonly on limestone.

*****

3.4 Discussion

3.4.1 Distribution of bryophytes in Grand Canyon National Park

Bryophytes occur along the entire elevational gradient of GRCA, from the cool reaches of North Rim to the hot desert environment of the Inner Canyon (fig. 4). They are found in all biotic communities of the canyon, growing on a variety of microhabitats. This comes as no surprise because bryophytes are collectively a ubiquitous group of plants with broad environmental tolerance and colonization patterns linked strongly to microhabitats types that occur around the globe (Mishler and Oliver 2009).

In fact, bryophytes occur on all continents and the majority of species display impressive global distribution patterns; a smaller percentage of species are locally or regionally restricted (Frahm 2008, Schofield 1984, Schofield and Crum 1972). Reflecting this trend, the bryoflora of GRCA resembles that of western North America at large, and the majority of species in the park have broad distributions throughout North America. Specifically, GRCA shares 123 of its 155 taxa (79%) with Canada, and 68 (44%) with Mexico (FNA eds. 2007+; Appendix C). Only eight taxa have populations restricted to North America, some of which are rare (See 3.4.7 *Rare species in GRCA at local, regional, and global scales*).

Furthermore, the predominant bryophyte families and growth forms found in GRCA closely reflect those characteristic of other dry regions in North America. The proportion of acrocarpous mosses (115; 74%) greatly outweighs that of pleurocarpous mosses (29; 19%) and hepatics (11; 7%), a typical population demographic in arid floras, as the cushion growth form of acrocarpous mosses facilitates water retention capacity (fig. 6; Stark 2004, Stark and Castetter 1987, Schofield 1981, Zotz et al. 2000). Two extremely xeric families, Pottiaceae and Grimmiaceae, are the most frequent and species-rich (Bowers et al. 1976, Magill 1976, Haring 1961, Stark et al. 2001; fig. 7).

Bryophyte abundance is extremely low in GRCA, limited by the heat and aridity of the region (Nash et al. 1977). Springs, seeps, and waterfalls are the only habitats where extensive bryophyte carpets occur (figs. 10 and 11), but the careful observer will find quarter-sized clumps scattered beneath shrubs, within biotic soil crust, along the crevices of rocks, on trees bases, and along the crevices of logs (fig. 12). Many bryophytes find refuge in microhabitats where moisture retention is higher and temperatures are lower, or shade is available for longer periods of the day than in the surrounding environment (Longton 1988). Such sheltered microhabitats in GRCA include north-facing slopes and rock faces and the bases of shrubs, trees, and logs. Other bryophytes, such as *Syntrichia caninervis* and *Grimmia pulvinata* (fig. 13), are adapted to extreme desiccation and high levels of light; such species are commonly found on exposed rock surfaces or are components of soil crust at hot, open sites (fig. 1; Bewley 1979, Belnap and Lange 2003, Zotz et al. 2000).

3.4.2 Diversity of bryophytes in Grand Canyon National Park

3.4.2.1 Diversity comparison. Despite the extensive altitudinal relief present in GRCA, bryophyte richness (155 taxa) is considerably lower than that found in temperate or tropical areas. In a Colombian tropical rainforest, one of the most biologically diverse ecosystems in the

Figure 10. Riparian mosses are diverse in Grand Canyon NP. (GRCA). Springs, waterfalls, and seeps support the most prolific bryophyte communities in GRCA. In total, 88 bryophyte species have been collected in moist wetland or riparian environments in GRCA, but only about half of these species (45) are restricted to aquatic or semi-aquatic habitat (Roaring Springs, North Kaibab Trail).

Figure 11. Seep mosses. Bryophytes commonly inhabit ephemeral seeps. **Left top** and **bottom**: dry cushions of *Didymodon brachyphyllus* tolerate an arid period, which occurs frequently on these sandstone walls along the North Kaibab Trail. **Top right**: *Didymodon tophaceus* is a common seep moss that forms thick cushions on seeping rocks. **Bottom right**: *Ptychostomum pseudotriquetrum* is common on moist soil, often growing near seeps. (Photos top and bottom right courtesy of the Western New Mexico University Department of Natural Sciences & the Dale A. Zimmerman Herbarium).

Figure 12. Bryophyte log colonists are infrequent in Grand Canyon NP (GRCA). **Left**: Bryophytes colonize downed wood infrequently in GRCA. Twenty-five species have been collected on this substrate, few of which are wood specialists. When present, these corticolous bryophytes typically form small cushions embedded within bark or wood crevices where shade and porous surfaces increase their water-holding capacity. **Center**: Wet cushions of *Syntrichia ruralis* and *Grimmia pulvinata* situated in the crevice of a decaying log along the same trail. **Right**: A dry, dormant mat of *Ceratodon purpureus* growing with lichen on a decaying log, Arizona Trail, South Rim.

Figure 13. Two common rock mosses: *Grimmia pulvinata* and *Grimmia alpestris*. Rocks support at least 95 different species in Grand Canyon NP. **Left:** Dry cushions of *Grimmia pulvinata* on an exposed limestone rock demonstrate this species' ability to tolerate extreme conditions (Arizona Trail, South Rim). **Right:** Hydrated cushions of *Grimmia alpestris*, a species slightly less tolerant of aridity, are shown here beneath shaded mixed conifer forest on a sandy-limestone rock (Ken Patrick Trail, North Rim).

world, Churchill (1991) reported 900 bryophyte species distributed along a 3,300 m elevational gradient. The alpine and subalpine zones of Maine's Mount Katahdin, which cover an elevational relief of 700 m, support a bryoflora of 130 species (Miller 2009). Nevertheless, the bryoflora of GRCA now represents a proportion of the Arizona flora (~34%, 155/450 species) comparable to that of vascular plants (~31%) and lichens (~21%; Bates et al. 2010, Boykin and Nash 1995, SEINET, and J. R. Spence et al. unpublished data).

As predicted, GRCA has been shown to support a rich bryoflora compared to other areas in the American Southwest. Two areas have been adequately surveyed to justify a floristic comparison—Big Bend National Park and Grand Canyon-Parsashant National Monument. The historic flora of Big Bend National Park in the Chihuahuan Desert region of Texas includes 112 taxa which inhabited the park's floodplains, canyons, desert, and mountainous terrain (Magill 1976). This park currently shares 29% (45 species) of its bryoflora with GRCA, of which half are represented by Pottiaceae (18), Bryaceae (5), and Grimmiaceae (4). Despite near equivalent elevation gradients (~2000 m), similar climatic extremes, and comparable desert, canyon, spring, and river ecosystems, the bryoflora of Big Bend may support fewer mesic species than that of GRCA. A probable explanation for this disparity

is the limited amount of mesic habitat in Big Bend, where flat, arid lowlands are more prevalent and high-elevation habitat is restricted to mountain tops. In contrast, shaded cliff walls and extensive high-elevation forest occurs in much of GRCA, offering bryophytes many mesic opportunities for colonization in mesic microenvironments.

The most recent floristic assessment of bryophytes in the American Southwest was that of the Grand Canyon-Parashant National Monument (GCPNM), which borders GRCA to the northwest. Stark & Brinda (2011) reported 110 taxa for this neighboring monument, which supports a similar bryoflora to that of GRCA. At present, the two parks share 60 taxa. Presumably, this floristic similarity reflects not only geographic proximity, but also similar canyon topographies, geologies, habitats, and microclimates. The two floras may converge with future collecting, however, the GCPNM sits 450 m lower than the North Rim and this may preclude the occurrence of several high-elevation species found in GRCA, such as *Grimmia caespiticia* and *Distichium capillaceum* (FNA eds. 2007+). Notably, GRCA has two species that were excluded from the accepted flora of the GCPNM (*Amblystegium serpens* and *Tortula hoppeana*), but which likely reside there.

It follows that many of the 40 taxa exclusive to the GCPNM will presumably be found in GRCA, a region that overlaps and exceeds the diversity of large and fine-scale habitat in the monument. Currently, GCPNM confirms the regional occurrence of five species listed in the Catalog of Excluded Taxa (*Imbribryum gemmiparum, Rosulabryum capillare, Barbula unguiculata, Coscinodon calyptrata,* and *Grimmia montana*); if Grand Canyon holds the majority of taxa found in GCPNM, then the bryoflora of GRCA may feasibly exceed 180 species.

3.4.2.2 Hot spots of bryophyte diversity in GRCA.
Determining areas of high bryophyte richness can only be done in a qualitative sense using floristic data. Nonetheless, the North Rim, South Rim, Inner Canyon, and Colorado River collection regions were sufficiently surveyed, relative to their inherent habitat heterogeneity, to warrant such a comparison. The greatest numbers of bryophytes have been reported for the North Rim and Inner Canyon regions (93 and 105 taxa, respectively), and the largest number of unique species restricted to a particular collection region (36) was found on the North Rim (table 1). Collection intensity in the North Rim and Inner Canyon regions was approximately two and three times greater than for the South Rim and Colorado River regions, respectively. This disparity in field time may explain part of the trend, but three other factors are likely at play. First, the North Rim should support high bryophyte richness, while excluding some species favoring arid climates because it is the largest contiguous mesic region in the park. As such, it offers a diversity of mesic habitats favorable to most bryophytes (fig. 14). Second, the Inner Canyon should also hold a large number of bryophytes based on geographic extent. It is the largest collection region and as such, contains broad environmental continua along an approximately 1,900 m elevation gradient. Thus it encapsulates most of the large and fine scale environmental variation present in the park. Lastly, the highly unique bryoflora on the North Rim supports the positive relationship between elevation and richness commonly observed for bryophytes, although this relationship is often non-linear and has been shown to vary with scale and by ecosystem (e.g. Frahm & Ohlemüller 2001, Nash et al. 1977, Rahbek 2005, Stark & Castetter 1987).

3.4.3 Common species and typical habitats of bryophytes in the six collection regions of Grand Canyon National Park

3.4.3.1 Bryophyte niches in Grand Canyon National Park. The eight bryophytes classified as locally abundant (>20 localities; *Brachytheciastrum collinum, Ceratodon purpureus, Gemmabryum caespiticium, Gemmabryum kunzei, Grimmia alpestris* (fig. 13), *Grimmia orbicularis, Pseudoleskeella tectorum,* and *Syntrichia ruralis*) display relatively broad local environ-

Figure 14. Rock mosses of the North Rim. **Left:** The mesic mixed conifer forest of the North Rim harbors relatively high diversity and abundance of bryophytes (and lichens) on many rocks. **Right:** Rocks in exposed situations typically harbor only one or two species of *Grimmia*, a desiccation-tolerant genus comprising mostly rock specialists (Widforss Trail, North Rim).

A  B

C D

Figure 15. Bryophytes with broad niches. Nine common species display exceptionally broad environmental tolerance having been collected across a mile-long elevation gradient from the lower reaches of the Inner Canyon to the high-elevation forest of the North Rim: **A**. *Bryum lanatum*, **B**. *Gemmabryum kunzei* **C**. *Gemmabryum caespiticium* **D**. *Grimmia anodon* **E**. *Grimmia pulvinata*, **F**. *Syntrichia caninervis*, and **G, H**. *Weissia ligulifolia*. Not shown are *Syntrichia ruralis* and *Tortula inermis* (See fig. 8). (Photos C & G courtesy of the Western New Mexico University Department of Natural Sciences & the Dale A. Zimmerman Herbarium. All others courtesy of John Brinda.)

E F

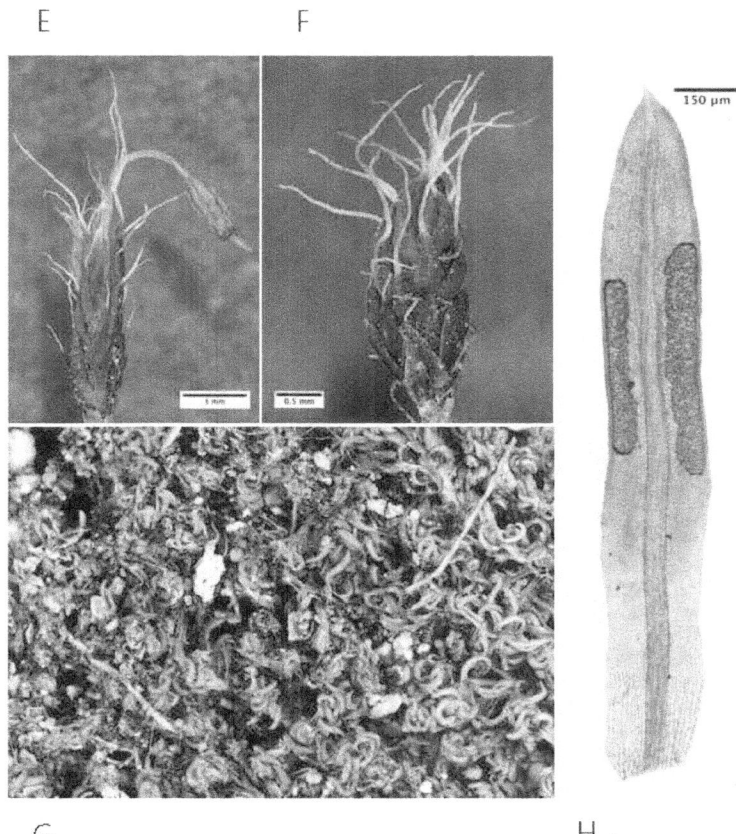

G H

mental tolerance. With the exception of *Grimmia orbicularis*, a desert rock moss, all occur on several substrata in the North Rim, South Rim and Inner Canyon regions (table 3). Of these eight species, *Gemmabryum kunzei*, *Gemmabryum caespiticium*, and *Syntrichia ruralis* have been collected along the entire elevation gradient, as have six other locally common (10–20 localities) generalists—*Bryum lanatum*, *Grimmia anodon*, *Grimmia pulvinata*, *Syntrichia caninervis*, *Tortula inermis*, and *Weissia ligulifolia* (fig. 15).

These species represent the most species-rich families in the flora—Pottiaceae, Grimmiaceae, and Bryaceae. Presumably, however, all species have optima where they are most abundant. Furthermore, most bryophyte species are sensitive to differing climatic regimes and to the type, texture, acidity, and porosity of their substrata (e.g. Birks et al. 1998, Cleavitt 2001, Ponzetti et al. 2007). Consequently, most taxa either occur within narrower altitudinal ranges or display some level of substratum-specificity, or both. Few species are restricted to one substratum, however. For example, although 88 species have been reported from moist, emergent, or aquatic microhabitats associated with springs, seeps, waterfalls, streams and ponds, only about half appear restricted to these riparian and wetland areas in the canyon (e.g. *Hygroamblystegium varium*, *Leptodictyum riparium*, *Mannia fragrans*, *Philonotis fontana*, *Philonotis marchia*, *Brachythecium frigidum*).

3.4.3.2 Bryophytes and their habitats in the North Rim collection region.

Bryophytes restricted to high-elevation habitats have been found on the North Rim and along the upper reaches of the Inner Canyon below the Kaibab Plateau. Of the 36 species found exclusively in the North Rim region (above the rim), 5 are liverworts (of the 11 total liverworts reported), 11 are pleurocarpous mosses, and the remaining 10 are acrocarpous mosses. Based on collection frequency, generalists inhabiting soil, wood, tree bases, and rock on North Rim include *Ceratodon purpureus*, *Syntrichia ruralis*, *Pseudoleskeella tectorum* (fig. 16), *Dicranoweisia crispula*, *Brachytheciastrum collinum* and *Brachythecium fendleri*. Species common to calcareous limestone and sandstone rocks include *Grimmia alpestris*, *Grimmia anodon*, *Pseudoleskeella tectorum*, *Brachythecium collinum*, and *Ceratodon purpureus*. On dry soil, *Brachytheciastrum collinum*, *Ceratodon purpureus*, and *Polytrichum juniperinum* are common species. Bryophytes occur infrequently on trees in arid regions, but seemed more common in this collection region (personal observation). These epiphytes were found close to the ground (<0.1 m) where bark moisture is higher (Billings and Drew 1938). The majority of epiphyte collections are from *Populus tremuloides* and *Pseudotsuga menziesii*; typical assemblages on these tree bases include *Dicranoweisia crispula* and *Pseudoleskeella tectorum*. Bryophytes have not been collected on most conifer species,

Figure 16. *Pseudoleskeella tectorum* is one of the most abundant and common pleurocarpous mosses in Grand Canyon NP, occurring across the entire elevation gradient (500–2700 m). It has been collected repeatedly on downed wood (**right**) and calcareous rock (**left**) throughout the canyon.

such as *Pinus ponderosa* and *Picea* spp., whose bark is likely too acidic and dry (Billings & Drew 1938). In the North Rim region, bryophytes have been frequently collected on downed wood, which supports assemblages like those of trees with the addition of *Ceratodon purpureus*. One bryophyte, *Dicranoweisia crispula*, has been collected on burnt wood as well here (fig. 17). Soil crust was rarely sampled on North Rim, but typical species include *Ceratodon purpureus* and *Gemmabryum caespiticium*.

3.4.3.3 Bryophytes and their habitats in the South Rim collection region.

Observed richness in the South Rim region (43 taxa) is approximately half that reported for the North Rim and Inner Canyon regions. The South Rim is situated nearly 400 m lower in elevation than the North Rim, encompasses only 250 m of altitudinal relief, and is dominated by two open-canopy communities with sparse understories that provide little shade (Merkle 1952 & 1962). The combination of these factors is the likely cause for a much reduced bryoflora here. Additionally, little of the South Rim flora is unique to the collection region. Approximately 85% (38 species) of taxa reported also occur within the Inner Canyon, suggesting that microhabitat within the Inner Canyon may not significantly differ from that on the South Rim. The limited distribution of the five singleton species exclusive to this region may be a consequence of rarity rather than an implication of unique habitat on the South Rim.

Relative to the North Rim region, bryophytes on the South Rim appear considerably less abundant and are easily overlooked (personal observation). Nonetheless, a suite of hospitable microhabitats exist where bryophytes can survive. *Ceratodon purpureus* is the most conspicuous species and forms large, dark green cushions on soil in the ponderosa pine forest (fig. 18; personal observation). *Grimmia anodon* was the most frequently collected species on dry limestone and sandstone rocks in exposed or partly shaded situations. Soil

Figure 17. *Dicranoweisia crispula* is one of few bryophytes adapted to grow on burnt logs, but is also found on downed wood and rock in Grand Canyon NP (Widforss Trail, North Rim).

Figure 18. *Ceratodon purpureus* is a common bryophyte on the North and the South Rim. **Left**: It has been collected frequently on soil between pine needles in the ponderosa pine forest (Arizona Trail, South Rim). **Right**: This species is easily recognized with abundant sporophytes, which are typically tall with dark red, cylindric capsules. (Photo courtesy of John Brinda)

crust communities were infrequently collected, but taxa observed at more than one locality include *Bryum argenteum*, *Bryum lanatum*, *Gemmabryum caespiticium*, *Didymodon rigidulus* var. *icmadophilus*, and *Syntrichia caninervis*. Few collections were made on trees or dead wood in this region, presumably because the xeric conditions of these exposed substrata are too severe to frequently support bryophytes. Nonethe-

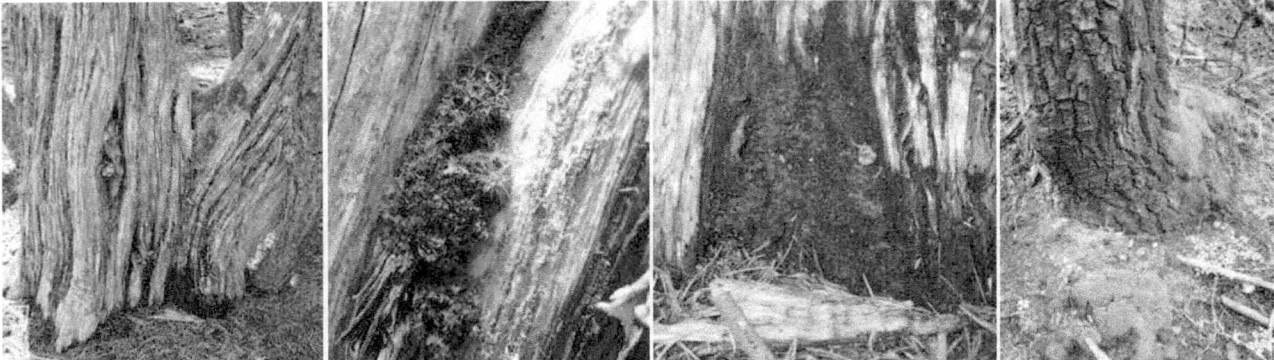

Figure 19. Bryophytes occur infrequently on trees in GRCA. **Left**: Epiphytic bryophytes are rare on the South Rim, but most typically colonize Juniper trunk bases and crevices presumably where humidity levels are higher. **Center left:** *Syntrichia ruralis* is a common epiphyte growing here on the base of a Juniper (Arizona Trail, South Rim). ***Center right*** - *Syntrichia ruralis*, in the crevice of Juniper bark. **Right:** Epiphytic bryophytes are more frequent on the North Rim; *Ceratodon purpureus* and *Hypnum revolutum* form an extensive carpet over the base of an aspen tree (Widforss Trail, North Rim).

less, observed corticolous species were usually *S. ruralis* and *Pseudoleskeella tectorum*, which were collected almost exclusively on the bases of *Juniperus osteosperma* (fig. 19). The stringy, layered, and grooved bark of this tree presumably has a higher water-holding capacity than other coniferous species (e.g. *Pinus ponderosa, Pinus edulis*) (Billings & Drew 1938). The three observed colonists on downed wood were *Syntrichia ruralis, Pseudoleskeella tectorum*, and *Orthotrichum alpestre*.

3.4.3.4 Bryophytes and their habitats in the Inner Canyon collection region.

High-elevation sites within the Inner Canyon region support many species that have been reported on the North Rim, while lower elevation sites support many species also found in the Colorado River region where the climate is also hot and dry. Consequently, only 16 taxa out of 105 are unique to the Inner Canyon region. Dry bryophyte habitat within the lower reaches of the Inner Canyon (below 1900 m), is largely restricted to rock, open soil, soil over rock or along rock crevices, and beneath vegetation. The walls of the Inner Canyon offer open and shaded habitat over sloping outcrops, vertical cliff faces, exposed bedrock, and tiered ledges (personal observation). Disturbance here is high, and bryophytes appear to colonize areas sheltered from erosion, rock falls, and landslides (personal observation). Such protected microhabitats include the crevices of rocks, the ledges beneath

overhangs, and the margins of tree and shrub bases. Shade-tolerant desert bryophytes are commonly associated with shrubs, but many thrive in direct sunlight (Thompson et al. 2005). In the Inner Canyon, bryophytes typical of dry rock and soil over rock include *Grimmia orbicularis, Grimmia anodon, Grimmia pulvinata, Crossidium squamiferum, Gemmabryum kunzei*, and *Tortula inermis*.

Along the Tonto Plateau and within the lower reaches of perennial washes, extensive mats of soil crust persist, often in a dormant state throughout much of the year. Only during summer monsoons and winter precipitation are the tiny plants wet long enough to increase their biomass (Stark 2004). Otherwise, the sandy soil dries quickly after short rain showers or night dew. Soil crust and dry soil communities typically comprise combinations of *Gemmabryum kunzei, Crossidium aberrans, Didymodon rigidulus* var. *rigidulus, Syntrichia ruralis*, and *Syntrichia caninervis*. Both downed wood and trees are rare substrata in the lower canyon. Bryophytes were collected on tree bases at only 4 sites below 1,900 m. The epiphytes were actually four generalists (*Pseudoleskeella tectorum, Brachythecium fendleri, Syntrichia ruralis* and *Hypnum revolutum*), a desert moss (*Crossidium crassinervium*), and a species restricted to tree bark (*Syntrichia laevipila*). The common generalist, *Syntrichia ruralis*, was the only species recorded on downed wood. This collection was made on Grandview Trail, a highly vegetated and shaded trail.

3.4.3.5 Bryophytes and their habitats in the Colorado River collection region.

Although the local climate of the Colorado River region is hotter and drier than the upper reaches of the Inner Canyon, the two regions share markedly similar floras. The habitats and species characteristic of the lower Inner Canyon accurately describe that of the dry, rocky slopes along the Colorado River corridor. For this reason, I will focus next on intermittently inundated habitats below the river's high water line. Here, colonization of bryophytes is sparse when not associated with springs or travertine deposits (personal observation). Six taxa were locally restricted to the corridor of the Colorado River. Four of these are either facultative or obligate riparian species associated with springs and seeps (*Fissidens fontanus, Fontinalis hypnoides, Entosthodon* sp., *Gyroweisia tenuis*). The other two species are found as small, bright green cushions on sandy and alluvial soil (*Funaria hygrometrica* var. *calvescens* and *Trichostomum tenuirostre*; table 3). Perhaps bryophytes can survive in these areas where erosion from the river is minimized, particularly in eddies and along gentle-sloping sandbars where water is relatively calm (Schmidt et al. 1993). Many taxa found on these banks are otherwise associated with springs or seeps (*Gemmabryum valparaisense, Plagiobryoides vinosula, Fissidens obtusifolius, Barbula bolleana, Barbula indica, Didymodon fallax, Didymodon nicholsonii, Didymodon tophaceus*, and *Splachnobryum obtusum*), while others are adapted to sandy desert habitats (*Crossidium crassinervium, Didymodon nevadensis, Didymodon rigidulus* var. *icmadophilus, Pseudocrossidium crinitum*, and *Pleurochaete luteola*). Occasionally, bryophytes occur on muddy banks in between the stems of marsh vegetation. The presence of these riparian vascular plants may provide a more stable habitat less prone to erosion during flood events. A thalloid liverwort species of *Targionia* was also collected in

this riverside margin, but material was not sufficient for species determination. Additional riverside habitat includes travertine at the river margin. Travertine supports species found at springs and seeps throughout the canyon, and will be discussed in section 3.4.4.

3.4.3.6 Bryophytes and their habitats in the Lake Mead and Marble Canyon collection regions.

Collecting in these two regions amounted to less than three field days, and thus data is insufficient to characterize communities. Nonetheless, the ecotype of these two regions is predominantly desert scrubland; therefore the species established here will likely include those ascribed to the lower reaches of the Inner Canyon. The desert surrounding Lake Mead supports at least 20 species, mostly representative of Pottiaceae and Grimmiaceae. One thalloid liverwort, *Mannia fragrans*, and three spring-associated species (*Conardia compacta, Rhynchostegium aquaticum*, and *Didymodon tophaceus*) have been reported for Marble Canyon.

3.4.4 Common bryophyte species of riparian and wetland habitat in Grand Canyon National Park

Springs, seeps, waterfalls, ponds, and perennial streamlets constitute the variation in aquatic and semi-aquatic habitat available to bryophytes in GRCA, with the exception of the Colorado River. Resident bryophytes have scattered distributions that mirror the stochastic appearance of riparian and wetland habitat across the landscape of GRCA. Springs and seeps create micro-climates that maintain higher levels of moisture, shade, and humidity than the surrounding canyon (Spence 2008), consequently diversity at these mesic sites can be high, although this parameter was not estimated. Collectively, 88 species were found in wetland and riparian habitats in GRCA, second only to the diversity observed on dry rock habitat, which enumerated 95 species (fig. 9). Interestingly, only about half the species reported at these mesic sites require such continual moist conditions.

Figure 20. *Cratoneuron filicinum* is a showy pleurocarpous moss, one of 45 species in Grand Canyon NP that are obligate colonists of semi-aquatic or aquatic habitat.

Obligate aquatic species found frequently in the flowing water of springs, streamlets, and waterfalls, and attached to submerged rock include *Hygroamblystegium varium* and *Rhynchostegium aquaticum*. A variety of species have been infrequently collected on travertine deposits, either along the Colorado River or at springs and seeps. Several of these species are generalists (*Gemmabryum caespiticium, Grimmia orbicularis, Didymodon nevadensis*), while others are dependent on highly mesic or semi-aquatic habitat (*Rhynchostegium aquaticum, Plagiobryoides vinosula, Barbula bolleana, Didymodon tophaceus, Eucladium verticillatum*, and *Splachnobryum obtusum*).

Species typically collected on rock or moist soil surrounding seeps include *Hymenostylium recurvirostrum, Hygroamblystegium varium, Gemmabryum valparaisense, Eucladium verticillatum, Conardia compacta, Rhynchostegium aquaticum, Plagiobryoides vinosula, Didymodon tophaceus*, and *Barbula bolleana*. Many species have been collected along stream banks. The following species favor such mesic habitats (*Philonotis marchia, Oxyrrhynchium hians, Rhynchostegium aquaticum, Gemmabryum valparaisense, Ptychostomum turbinatum, Cratoneuron filicinum* (fig. 20), *Pohlia wahlenbergii, Barbula bolleana, Didymodon tophaceus, Eucladium verticillatum, Gymnostomum calcareum*).

Notably, two liverwort species, *Targionia* sp. and *Tritomaria exsectiformis* have also been collected in this habitat.

Lastly, ponds are a rare habitat in GRCA, but the following species have been found (often between sedges) along the moist banks of several ephemeral ponds fed by winter snow melt: *Dichelyma uncinatum, Pohlia camptotrachela, Riccia glauca, Sciuro-hypnum plumosum, Gemmabryum kunzei*, and *Ceratodon purpureus*.

3.4.5 New bryophyte species to the state of Arizona

Given the limited amount of bryophyte collecting that has been completed in Arizona over the past 50 years, it is not surprising that this floristic inventory has added 28 species to the state's bryoflora (table 2). Notably, five of these species have been recently reported from the GCPNM as well (Stark & Brinda 2011). These state records include three pleurocarpous mosses, 22 acrocarpous mosses, and two thalloid liverworts. The liverwort is an undescribed species of *Targionia* found on moist soil bordering ephemeral or perennial streams. Additionally, one acrocarpous moss is an undescribed species of *Grimmia* found on sandstone rock in the Inner Canyon (treatment in progress). GRCA extends the southernmost limit of ten species in North America, and marks the first report of ten species (some of the same species) in the American Southwest (defined here to include Arizona and New Mexico; table 2). Five of these species (*Grimmia caespiticia, Schistidium atrichum, Schistidium confertum, Pohlia camptotrachela*) have distributions throughout western North America, excluding Mexico. These state records extend the southern limits of these taxa in western North America.

3.4.5.1 Range extensions for several restricted species. Five species in the Pottiaceae, one in the Hypnaceae, and one in the Bryaceae have restricted distributions either globally or within North America (table 2). A summary follows based on distributions cited in

the Bryophyte Flora of North America (FNA eds. 2007+). Scattered throughout northern North America, the southern distribution of *Gyroweisia tenuis* has been dramatically extended from its previous location in Nebraska. The occurrence of *Gymnostomum calcareum* in Arizona marks a significant range extension from its limited distribution in the US. Previously, this moss was reported from California, Missouri, and North Carolina. The same can be said of *Hypnum cupressiforme*, a predominantly circumboreal species with a disjunct population in New Zealand. Largely restricted to higher latitudes this species has been previously reported in the US for only three states (CO, NM, and ND). *Didymodon nevadensis* is known only from British Columbia and five mid-western and western US states (NB, NM, CO, NV, TX), therefore its occurrence and frequency of collection (9 sites) in GRCA suggests it may have a broader distribution in arid regions throughout the West. Aside from its Asian distribution, *Didymodon tectorum* was known previously from only four states (CO, NM, KS, and MD) and this GRCA record bolsters its western extent in the US.

Lastly, although rarely reported on soil and rock in Eurasia, California and Nevada, the account of *Gemmabryum badium* in Arizona is likely to be followed by sightings in other western states as this species has been commonly mistaken for *Grimmia caespiticium*. However, the two taxa have been recently and explicitly differentiated in the literature (FNA eds. 2007+).

Few of these record taxa were collected from more than two sites in the canyon and none were found at more than nine sites. Therefore, insufficient data exists to describe the distributions of these species in GRCA or to determine their habitat specificity here. The majority (20) of taxa new to the state were collected at least once from the North Rim and of these, 9 were found only in this collection region. However, only *Grimmia caespiticium* is restricted to high-elevation habitat, while the remaining taxa are expected to be found at lower elevations (FNA eds. 2007+). Approximately half of these species new to Arizona were collected from riparian or wetland habitat (and often other habitats as well), while the other half occurred on dry substrata, most commonly rocks, suggesting that there remains undiscovered bryophyte diversity in both wet and dry habitats in GRCA and Arizona at large.

3.4.6 Distribution of desert bryophytes in Grand Canyon National Park.

Grand Canyon is located where the four major deserts of North America converge. Although comprehensive bryofloras for these deserts are lacking, Belnap and Lang (2003) provided a qualitative summary for these desert bryophytes. They listed several "common" species characteristic of each desert, based on a qualitative assessment reflecting their extensive field experience and collections. Fully aware of the limitations of my data, I was curious to explore whether bryophyte distributions in GRCA mirror the convergence pattern observed for vascular plants, in which species characteristic of each desert occur together in the lower reaches of the canyon (Phillips et al. 1987). The results presented next are tenuous trends, based on the frequencies and localities of bryophyte collections made below 2,100 m in the park.

The floristic records suggest that the convergence pattern may be present in GRCA, as 12 of the 15 listed species thought to characterize the four North American deserts have been found in the arid reaches of the park (fig. 21). The map illustrates a spatial "convergence" in so far as characteristic species from each desert co-occur in the Inner Canyon region. More definitively, these records suggest that the bryoflora of the lower inner canyon most closely resembles that of the nearby Mojave Desert. All six characteristic species (*Crossidium crassinervium, Didymodon rigidulus, Didymodon australasiae, Microbryum*

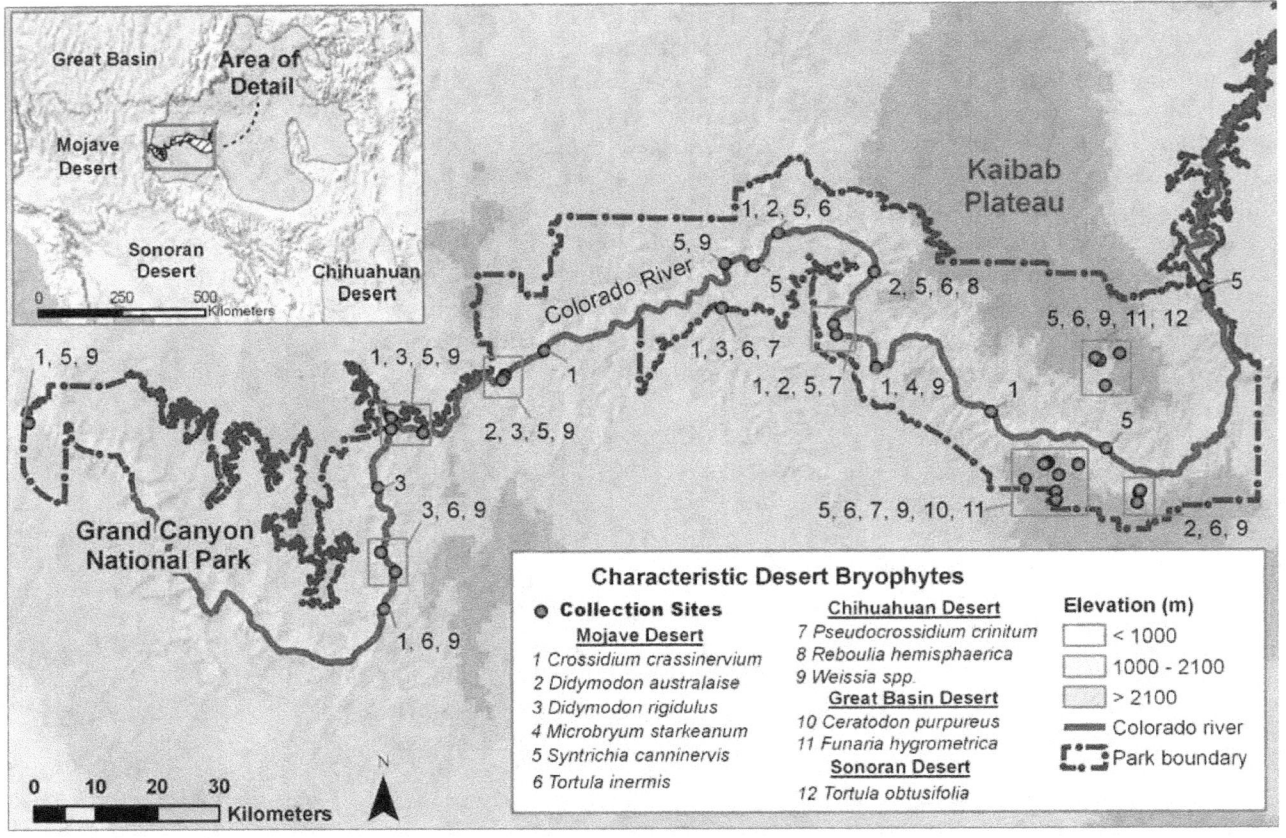

Figure 21. The distribution of twelve bryophyte species within the lower Inner Canyon (below 2,100 m) is shown. These species are thought to characterize one of the four North American deserts (inset). This data suggests that bryophytes characteristic of the Mojave Desert are most frequent in the desert habitat of Grand Canyon NP.

starckeanum, Syntrichia caninervis, and *Tortula inermis*) for this desert have been documented in the Inner Canyon, and most occur multiple times throughout this desert environment (Belnap & Lange 2003; fig. 21). The Chihuahuan Desert bryoflora is much less represented in GRCA, but three of the four potential indicator species (*Pseudocrossidium crinitum, Weissia* spp., *Reboulia*

hemisphaerica) of this desert have been collected from at least two localities. Notable is the broad distribution of *Weissia ligulifolia*, which occurs from Lake Mead in the far west, to Marble Canyon in the east. However, Belnap & Lange (2003) did not specify a species for the genus, *Weissia*; the actual characteristic species may not be *W. ligulifolia*. Lastly, the Great Basin and Sonoran

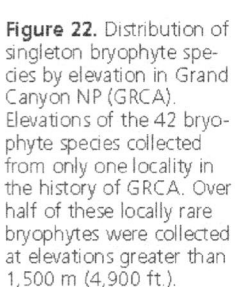

Figure 22. Distribution of singleton bryophyte species by elevation in Grand Canyon NP (GRCA). Elevations of the 42 bryophyte species collected from only one locality in the history of GRCA. Over half of these locally rare bryophytes were collected at elevations greater than 1,500 m (4,900 ft.).

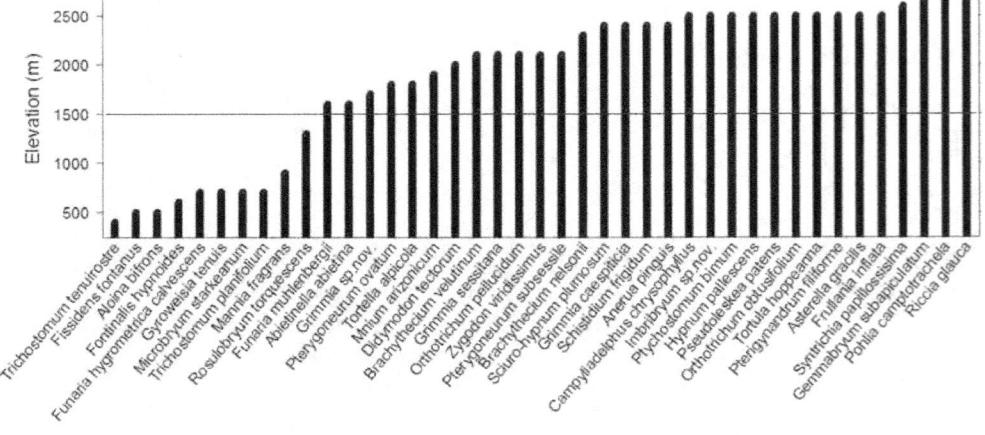

Deserts are hardly represented, with fewer than 4 relevant collections each, but Belnap and Lange (2003) listed few potential indicator species for these two deserts. Specifically, two of the three Great Basin Desert species (*Ceratodon purpureus* and *Funaria hygrometrica*) have been collected, and only one of the three Sonoran Desert species (*Tortula obtusifolia*) has been found, making this latter desert the least represented in GRCA. Future collecting and plot-based sampling are required to substantiate the presence of a significant pattern, as well as the existence of significant indicator species for each of the North American deserts.

3.4.7 Rare species in Grand Canyon National Park at local, regional, and global scales

Bryophytes are capable of long-distance dispersal via spores, but constraints to successful colonization exist, such as spore size and production (which effect dispersal distances), sexual reproductive frequency or absence, dispersal efficacy of asexual propagules, ecological tolerance, substratum specificity, and competitive vigor (Magill 2009, Frahm 2008). Occasionally, such limitations to dispersal, amongst other factors, lead to endemism at various scales (Schofield 1992, Schofield & Crum 1972). However, some globally distributed species may be rare regionally or locally and warrant monitoring. The designation of rare bryophytes, in practice, has been based on collection frequency and the putative vulnerability of a species' habitat; unfortunately, such assessments are frequently limited by inadequate distributional data (Cleavitt 2005). Species in the American Southwest have been placed, perhaps prematurely, into these categories, only later to be found at additional locations (Stark 2004, FNA eds. 2007+). It can be argued, however, that a conservative approach is best, before it is too late for remedial measures (Hallingbäck and Tan 2010). The threat of extinction is real. Current red lists indicate extinction rates of bryophytes range from 2–4%, and are primarily correlated with habitat loss (Hallingbäck & Tan 2010).

In GRCA, several bryophytes are classified as either regionally or locally rare. Conserving their populations in GRCA requires that their preferred habitats are understood and protected from unnatural disturbances (see section 3.4.8.).

3.4.7.1 Locally rare bryophytes. Rare (<5 localities) and infrequent (5–10 localities) taxa in GRCA total 94, of which 43 are reported from a single locality (fig. 21; appendix D). The remaining 51 taxa were found at fewer than 5 localities. Figure 22 shows that approximately half of the singleton species were collected on the North Rim. These taxa may remain locally rare, even as collecting continues—the North Rim region was intensely sampled and no additional localities were discovered. However, as was mentioned above, the regional and global populations of most rarely collected taxa in the park are not threatened. While some of these species may appear rare at the regional scale (i.e. new to Arizona), collection bias is likely to blame for their depauperate circumscriptions in the American West. It is possible that some of these species are broadly distributed in appropriate ecotypes throughout Arizona, but several taxa that have previously been classified as regionally and globally rare warrant protection until their conservation status is proven otherwise.

3.4.7.2 Regionally and globally rare bryophytes. The distributions of several species denoted globally "rare" or "of conservation concern" are expanding in recent years as collecting in the Southwest continues (FNA eds. 2007+); GRCA holds three such species: *Didymodon nevadensis*, *Crossidium seriatum*, and *Grimmia moxleyi* (table 5). *Didymodon nevadensis* was documented as a rare Pottiaceous moss restricted to gypsum formations in the Mohave Desert (Stark 2004), but since then has been ascribed to a broader distribution on soil and limestone in British Colombia and four western states, plus Nebraska (FNA eds. 2007+). This nuanced species, easily confused with two other Pottiaceous mosses, was collected from 8 distinct localities in GRCA. It was also reported

Table 5. Species of conservation concern reported to occur in Grand Canyon NP (GRCA). The global distribution, GRCA collection regions, elevation range in GRCA, and the known habitat of each species are listed.

Species	Distribution	Collection regions; (elevation, ft)	Known habitat
Globally rare			
Didymodon nevadensis[a]	British Colombia, Nebraska, Colorado, Nevada, New Mexico, Texas, GRCA	Inner Canyon; Colorado River; Lake Mead; (1700–8000)	gypsum; limestone; sandstone; travertine; dry soil as component of biotic crust; soil over limestone
Crossidium seriatum[b]	British Colombia, Mexico, Europe, Arizona, California, Nevada, and New Mexico, GRCA	Inner Canyon; Colorado River; Lake Mead; (1400–2400)	dry soil as component of biotic crust; open, dry soil; dry soil over sandstone; along dry washes on sandy soil or rocks
Endemic to Southwestern North America			
Grimmia moxleyi[b]	Arizona, California, Nevada, and northern Mexico, GRCA	South Rim; Inner Canyon, Colorado River, Lake Mead (1600–6900)	dry acidic rock; on soil over sandstone rock with biotic crust
Gemmabryum badium[a]	California, Nevada, GRCA	North Rim; Inner Canyon (5600–8200)	dry soil or rock, dry sandstone
Rare in the interior mountains of the American Southwest			
Grimmia sessitana[b]	high-elevation sites throughout Western North America	South Rim (6900)	exposed or sheltered on moist, acidic granite and sandstone

[a] species new to Arizona
[b] species new to GRCA

for GCPNM (Stark & Brinda 2011).

Crossidium seriatum has a broad global distribution for a rare species, with reports in British Colombia, Mexico, Europe, Arizona, California, Nevada, and New Mexico (FNA eds. 2007+). Scattered throughout the hot deserts of North America (Stark 2004), this Pottiaceous moss was collected on dry soil and within soil crust at 6 distinct localities broadly distributed across GRCA, and was also found in the GCPNM.

Limited to acidic rocks in the American Southwest, *Grimmia moxleyi* is of conservation concern, known only from Arizona, California, Nevada, and northern Mexico (FNA eds. 2007+). However, this rock moss was collected in GRCA at three sites differing markedly in their elevation and ecology.

Although not identified to species (sterile condition not diagnostic), several collections of *Entosthodon* have been made in GRCA. The genus *Entosthodon*

includes four rare species endemic to western North America, some of which are known from fewer than five localities (*E. planoconvexus* Bartr., *E. sonorae* Card., *E. tucsonii* Bart., and *E. wigginsii* Steere).

Lastly, a locally rare species, *Grimmia sessitana* was found at one location on the North Rim, is broadly distributed throughout western North America, but is limited to high-elevation sites (table 5). Very rare in the interior mountains of the American Southwest, it is the least xerophytic species of *Grimmia* in the continental flora (FNA eds. 2007+).

3.4.8 Vulnerable bryophyte habitats and implications for management

Habitat protection is the most important strategy in the maintenance of bryophyte diversity and the conservation of rare species (Hallingbäck & Tan 2010). Vulnerable habitats for bryophytes in GRCA include soil crust and riparian areas.

3.4.8.1 Soil crust habitat. Bryophytes are an important component of many soil crust communities. These delicate communities facilitate many ecosystem services in aridlands and warrant protection in their own right (Belnap & Lange 2003). Preventing unnatural disturbance is critical, as remedial measures are not promising for soil crusts, whose recovery from surface degradation is slow to non-existent in arid regions (Belnap 1993). Our understanding of soil crust dynamics is far from complete, but research has shown that this fragile layer is negatively impacted by recreational trampling, livestock grazing, invasive grasses, and intense fires (Belnap 2003, Ponzetti et al. 2007, Belnap & Lange 2003). The negative effects from several of these disturbances have already been empirically documented in GRCA. In the pinyon-juniper woodland on the South Rim, sites historically grazed and those that experienced trespass grazing (e.g. broken fences along the GRCA border) had ~50% less soil crust cover than ungrazed sites (Beymer & Klopatek 1992). Another study demonstrated that minimal trampling by hikers can destroy soil crust structure along trails in the Inner Canyon (Cole 1991). During my time collecting bryophytes on the Colorado River, I noticed the trampling of soil crusts above beaches, where rafting groups (including my own) frequently establish camp sites.

Outside of GRCA, several aridland studies have suggested that fire management can help maintain the diversity and abundance of soil crusts, although across different ecosystems, the outcomes of interactions between nonnative grasses, fire, and soil crust differ (Ponzetti et al. 2007, Eldridge & Bradstock 1994, Greene et al. 1990). For example, in the Chihuahuan Desert, the presence of native grasses was shown to mediate the negative effects of fire on soil crusts. Conversely, invasive grasses were shown to increase fire intensity to lethal magnitudes, killing the crusts by eliminating open areas where they could otherwise avoid severe flames (Johansen

et al. 1984).

3.4.8.2 Riparian habitats. Riparian and wetland habitats in GRCA are also vulnerable to disturbance that can negatively impact bryophytes. Under many environmental conditions, grazing has been shown to reduce the abundance and diversity of plants in riparian and wetland habitats (e.g. Debano et al. 2003, Skartvedt 2000); resident bryophytes are surely impacted by the trampling of hooves and the removal of riparian vegetation that creates microhabitat conditions important to many species. Additionally, I have observed on the North Rim, several ponds and streams with banks partially degraded by grazing animals, presumably elk or bison. Furthermore, the Inner Canyon supports waterfalls and springs that are frequented by hikers in need of water or seeking recreation. Small bryophyte species growing on banks or exposed rock surfaces may be threatened on sites that are highly trafficked. Fortunately, though, many bryophytes are sheltered from this impact in microhabitats, including the crevices and holes of rock walls and boulders, which surround many seeps, streams, and waterfalls.

3.4.8.3 Implications for management. Managing bryophyte diversity in GRCA does not necessarily require that a resident bryologist perform yearly inventories of these abstruse plants. The most important aspect of any management plan seeking to conserve bryophyte biodiversity is to protect and monitor habitat quality (Cleavitt 2005), knowing that species dependent on these habitats will simultaneously be protected if conditions in and around the habitat remain relatively unaltered. The factors highlighted in this section have important implications for managing bryophyte habitat susceptible to unnatural disturbance. Specifically, a management plan involving bryophytes in GRCA should consider

1. suppressing invasive grass populations

2. reducing elk and bison populations and/or their access to riparian and

wetland areas

3. enforcing "leave-no-trace" practices for park visitors and rafters

4. increasing soil crust signage and the inclusion of bryophytes in outreach programs and educational pamphlets for visitors.

3.4.9 Summary of the bryoflora of Grand Canyon National Park

Grand Canyon National Park holds the richest known bryoflora currently ascribed to any region in the American Southwest. The modern collections associated with this study have more than tripled the flora's size. I surmise that diversity in GRCA may potentially exceed 180 species, given the floristic variation of the neighboring Grand Canyon-Parashant National Monument. Areas that warrant further bryological exploration include the Inner Canyon, Marble Canyon, and the western section of the North Rim; dry, low-elevation areas here resemble conditions in the Parashant, and likely hold species currently exclusive to the monument.

Despite the arid and semi-arid climate of GRCA, its rich bryoflora is likely maintained by the broad spectrum of vegetation communities, climatic regimes, geologic formations, and varied topography that span the canyon's mile-high elevation gradient. Although bryophytes have low abundance in most areas, they are pervasive, often occurring in microhabitats that offer protection from direct sun and erosion. Many locally rare species have been collected on the North Rim, over one third of the flora appears restricted to riparian or wetland habitat and several species of conservation concern have been found on soil crusts and rocks. Collectively, these findings illustrate the importance of GRCA as an oasis for conserving aridland bryophytes in the American Southwest, a region threatened broadly by human impacts and habitat loss.

4 Rock bryophyte ecology in the forests of Grand Canyon National Park

4.1 Objectives

There were four main research objectives for this ecological investigation, which sampled rock bryophyte communities along trail corridors throughout the pinyon-juniper, ponderosa pine, and mixed conifer forests of GRCA.

1. Estimate the bryophyte parameters of richness, abundance, evenness, and diversity across and within the three forest types.

2. Identify locally dominant, rare, and forest indicator species.

3. Estimate the degree to which forest type can explain changes in bryophyte responses, and then examine whether site-level environmental variables (elevation, rock type, aspect, slope, PDIR, and shade cover) can account for additional variation in species richness and total percent cover.

4. Determine if species community composition differs by forest type and whether any site-level environmental variables can explain additional variation. In concert these findings may substantiate the use of a simple forest-scaled conservation plan for monitoring the diversity dynamics of rock bryophytes in GRCA.

4.2 Methods

4.2.1 Sampling sites in the forests of Grand Canyon National Park

The study region was located in the canyon's eastern section and included portions of the Kaibab and Coconino Plateaus, as well as below-rim terrain on four trails (fig. 23.). The Kaibab Plateau is located on the North Rim of the canyon (~2,400 m) and supports both mixed conifer and ponderosa pine forest distributed across sloping valleys (table 6). The Coconino Plateau forms the South Rim, approximately 300 m lower in elevation than the North Rim, and is covered with pinyon-juniper and ponderosa pine forests (Merkle 1952).

The open pinyon-juniper woodland is dominant along the rim and experiences high disturbance relative to the ponderosa pine stands that generally occur away from the rim. The pinyon-juniper woodland is the most prevalent below-rim forest type and can hardly be called a forest here due to its low density along the steep, erosive walls of the Inner Canyon (Merkle 1952). Pure stands of *Pinus ponderosa* generally occur above 2,200 m, and the tall, open canopy of this forest provides enough light and shade to foster a diverse understory of grasses and annual herbs (Merkle 1962; table 6).

Both plateaus are capped by the Kaibab Formation, a highly variable stratum of porous limestone, sandstone, and chert deposited in the Permian (McKee 1938). In addition to this formation, sites below the rim bisected sedimentary rocks of the Toroweap, Coconino Sandstone, Hermit Shale, and Supai Formations. These strata form a broad sequence of ledges and cliffs that include cliff-forming sandstones and limestones, and slope-forming shales (White 1929, Breed & Roat 1976, McKee 1933). Climatic variation found among the forests of GRCA is summarized by two weather stations on the North and South Rims (fig. 3; WRCC 2011). Mean annual precipitation on the North and South Rims is 515 mm (25 in) and 450 mm (18 in), respectively (WRCC 2011). Winter temperatures average -2° C on the North Rim and 0° C on the South Rim, while mean summer temperatures on the North and South Rims are 15° C and 18° C, respectively (WRCC 2011).

4.2.2 Bryophyte sampling

4.2.2.1 Sites. I implemented a generalized random tessellation stratified design along approximately 13 m (8 mi) of trail distributed across the three forest types. Over 140 waypoints were generated along corridor trails defined by the GRCA GIS Trails dataset (Stevens & Olsen 2004). Along each trail, waypoints

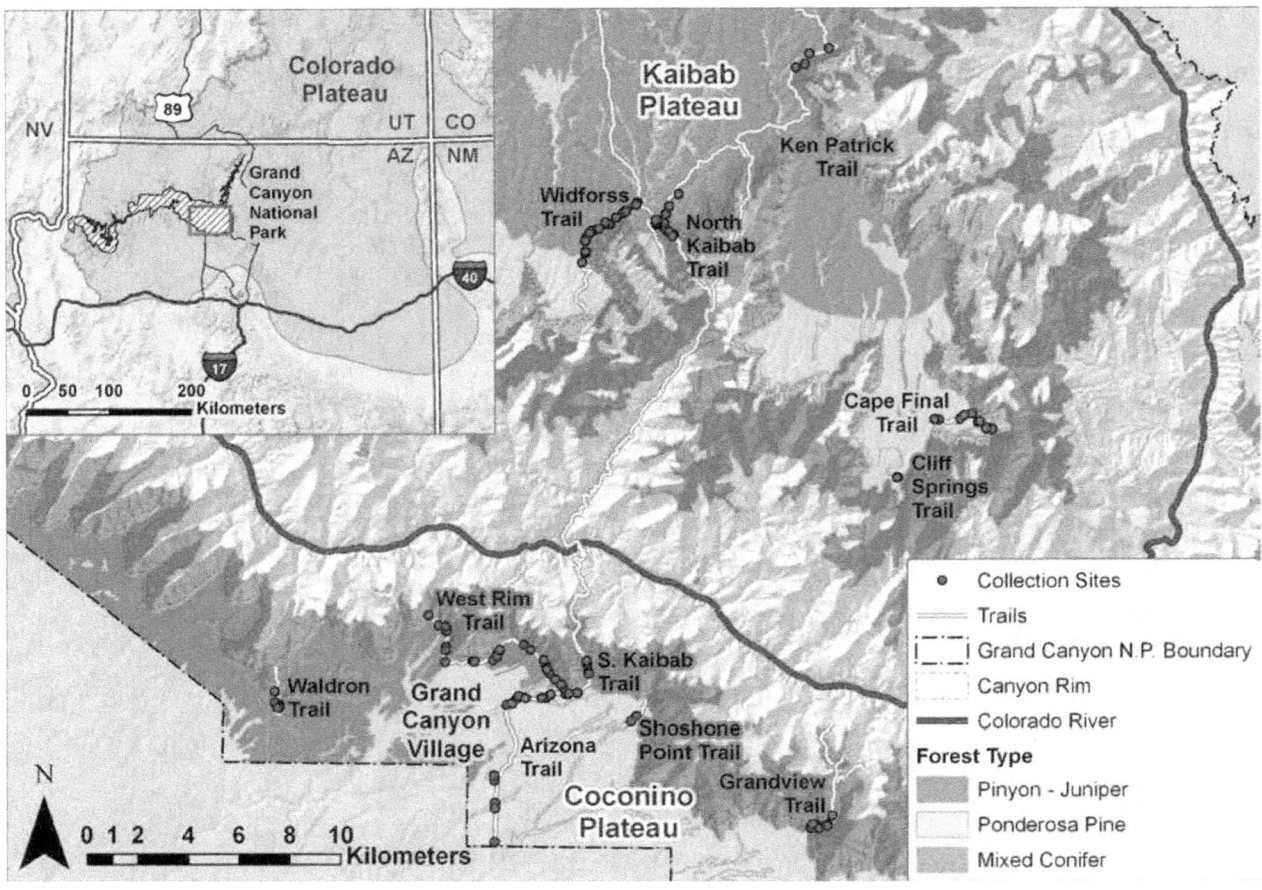

Figure 23. Sampling sites in the forests of Grand Canyon NP (GRCA). Sites (104) sampled along trail corridors, stratified by forest type. The three high-elevation forests of GRCA are pinyon-juniper woodland, ponderosa pine forest, and mixed conifer forest.

numbers 1 through 140 were sampled preferentially unless a particular site (1) could not be distinguished on the GPS from a nearby site, (2) contained rocks inaccessible or uncolonized by bryophytes, (3) appeared recently disturbed by construction or fire, or (4) lacked dry rock substrata.

Between March 2008 and September 2009, I sampled 104 of these sites along 12 trails that spanned 1000 m (~3330 ft.) of vertical relief (fig. 23). Three rocks were randomly selected at a site in one of two ways. If few large rocks were present, then the three rocks closest to the site waypoint were sampled, but care was taken to exclude rocks clearly disturbed by hikers. If the site had abundant rock habitat available, then a direction was randomly chosen on a calculator (0°–360°) and the first rock encountered along the directional vector from the waypoint was sampled. This

procedure was repeated in different directions with a 15 m maximum radius until three such rocks were found. In addition to bearing bryophytes, sampled rocks were at least 1 m from the trail and large enough to fill the quadrat.

4.2.2.2 Quadrat sampling. A nearly one-dimensional quadrat, 100 cm × 1 cm (fig. 24), was used to sample rock bryophytes. I chose this non-conventional technique because longer quadrats have been shown to maximize species capture in sparse vegetation communities, presumably because long quadrats traverse more of the microhabitat present on many substrata (Mitchell & Hughes 1995). Further supporting this choice is the fact that, when using the traditional Braun-Blanquet scale, highly biased estimates of species cover are common in sparse vegetation communities

Table 6. Characteristics of pinyon-juniper, ponderosa pine, and mixed conifer forests in Grand Canyon N.P.
(Compiled from Merkle 1954, Merkle 1962, White & Vankat 1993, and Pearson 1920.

Variable	Pinyon-Juniper	Ponderosa pine	Mixed conifer
Canopy	*Pinus edulis, Juniperus osteosperma, J. scopulorum, J. utahensis*	*Pinus ponderosa*	*Abies concolor & lasiocarpa, Pinus ponderosa, Pseudotsuga menziesii, Picea pungens & engelmannii, Populus tremuloides*
Common understory species in GRCA	rabbit brush, fern bush, broomweed, Arizona fescue, blue grama grass	sagebrush, rabbitbrush, clif-frose, Gambel oak, Arizona fescue, squirrel tail, junegrass	manzanita, locust, rose, barberry, pine dropseed, mountain muhly
Elevation m (ft.)	1900–2200 (6500–7300)	<2500 (7000–8300)	>2500 (>8300)
Canopy closure	None	Lacking closure or partly closed	Nearly closed
Mean summer temperature	55°F	49°F	44–46°F
Summer evaporation from water surface	42 in.	27 in.	16–6 in.
Distribution in GRCA	South Rim; Inner Canyon; narrow margin along the edge of the North Rim	South Rim	North

Figure 24. Randomized sampling of rock bryophytes in Grand Canyon NP (GRCA). Bryophyte abundance and richness were estimated using a 100 × 1 cm transect randomly oriented on three rocks at each of 104 sites along trail corridors in the forests of GRCA. Bryophyte percent cover was estimated to the nearest 1 cm².

(Lévesque 1996). There are two other advantages to using this type of quadrat on dry rock habitat in arid regions: (1) It rarely under- or over-estimates species cover because resident bryophytes commonly grow in circular clumps (fig. 25), allowing a nearly 1-dimensional quadrat to accurately estimate the cover of individual clumps. (2). This method enabled the length of each clump to be recorded and linked to a corresponding voucher, an essential step because few of these small and nuanced species could be identified in the field. After vouchers were determined in the lab, the length of all clumps for each species could be summed per quadrat; this length multiplied by the 1 cm width of the tape measure and divided by 100 cm² gave the species' percent cover.

The middle of the quadrat was positioned on the center of a selected rock, orientated in a randomly chosen direction (0–360°), and then rotated if necessary to keep the entire quadrat on the rock or to avoid vascular vegetation or soil patches intersecting the length of the transect for more than 2 cm.

Figure 25. Rock moss cushions. The cushion-forming growth habit of many rock mosses is an adaptation to aridity, which reduces exposure of tissues to harmful UV radiation and maximizes the water-holding capacity of the colony (Zotz et al. 2000). *Grimmia anodon* (dark cushions) is one of the most common and abundant acrocarpous mosses found on calcareous rock throughout Grand Canyon NP. It can often be identified in the field with a hand lens when mature sporophytes (opened capsules) are present. Its capsules lack a peristome, resembling empty tea cups after spores are released (See fig. 15).

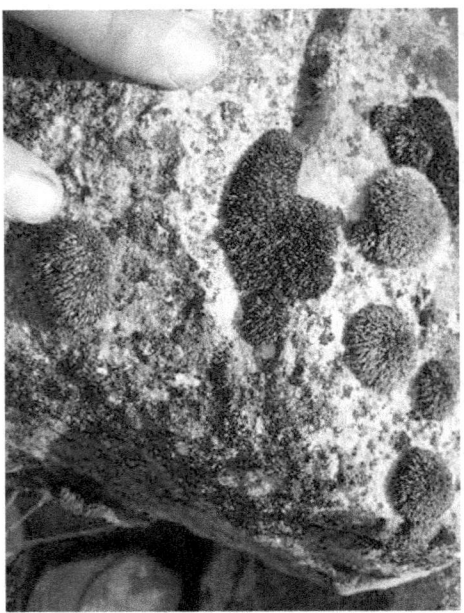

4.2.2.3 Voucher specimens. Rare taxa collected as vouchers for this study were curated as part of the floristic collection and are housed at the Grand Canyon Herbarium. Nomenclature follows the Bryophyte Flora of North America (FNA eds. 2007+). Questionable specimens were sent to specialists for determination. If a voucher contained a fragment of another species not distinguished in the field, this concomitant species was assigned a cover of one percent. *Orthotrichum* specimens could often not be determined without the presence of capsules and thus were classified into two groups based on leaf stratosity. Double-stratose species were either *O. cupulatum* or *O. hallii*, while one-stratose species may have been *O. pumilum* or *O. pellucidum*, two one-stratose species recorded previously in GRCA, although other possibilities exist (FNA eds. 2007+).

4.2.2.4 Environmental variables. At each site, forest type, UTM coordinates, elevation, and aspect of the overall topography were recorded. For each rock sampled, the underlying slope was measured with a clinometer, but if the rock was a large formation, the slope measured was that of the rock itself. The shade cover provided by surrounding canopy and understory vegetation and/ or nearby rocks was measured 0.5 m above each sampled rock using a hemi-spherical densitometer. Rock type was recorded for each subsample as either limestone (porous, not sandy), sandstone (nonporous & sandy), or chert (smooth, nonporous, & not sandy). This coarse classification system was based largely on texture due to the prevalence of limestone-sandstone intermediates that were impossible to characterize in the field. Since the number of sampled chert rocks was very low (10/312), a variable for this rock type was unnecessary. As the absence of limestone implied the presence of sandstone at the majority of sites, I created a discrete site-scaled variable that will be called "percent limestone" to represent this limestone-sandstone gradient. Because three rocks were sampled at each site, the variable has three values: 0/3 (3 sandstone), 1/3 (1 limestone and 2 sandstone), 2/3 (2 limestone and 1 sandstone), and 1 (3 limestone).

Aspect data were transformed into a linear measure, which can be interpreted as a heat load index. Specifically, aspect was transformed to folded aspect, a scale that ranges from 0 (the coolest Northeast-facing slopes) to one (the warmest Southwest-facing slopes) by the formula:

Folded aspect = 180° - [aspect° – 180°]

The composite variable, potential annual direct incident radiation, (PDIR), was calculated to estimate the yearly load of solar radiation on a site based on its latitude, aspect, and slope (Mc-Cune and Keon 2002)

4.3 Data Analysis

4.3.1 Bryophyte response parameter estimates

Unless otherwise noted, all analyses were performed in R using the base (R Development Core Team 2011), vegan (Øksanen et al. 2010), and labdsv (Roberts 2010) packages. Site-level bryophyte parameters were estimated as the average response across three rocks (i.e. subsamples). Therefore, site-level species richness was the mean number of species captured across three rocks. Similarly, the site-level abundance of a species was its average percent cover ($cm^2/100\ cm^2$) across three rocks, and total bryophyte abundance at a site was estimated as the average total cover across three rocks.

Diversity was estimated from these measurements using the Simpson diversity index, which calculates the probability that two randomly selected bryophytes on a rock will be different species:

$$Diversity\ = 1 - \sum_{i=1}^{s} p_i^2$$

where p_i is the relative abundance of species i and S is species richness of the rock. The index ranges from 0 to 1, with 0 and 1 representing perfectly homogenous and perfectly heterogeneous communities, respectively (Simpson 1949).

Evenness was calculated using the Shannon-Weiner Index (H'):

$$H' = -\sum_{i=1}^{s} p_i\ log\ (p_i)$$

where p_i and S are as above. This index measures the equability of the community and has an undefined range dependent on the number of species in the sample and therefore is reported for each forest type (Whittaker 1972).

Beta diversity (β_w), an estimate of species turnover, was calculated among sites for each forest as

$$\beta_w = \frac{\gamma}{\alpha} - 1$$

where γ = gamma diversity (i.e. the total number of species found across each forest) and α = mean alpha diversity (species richness) at sites (Whittaker 1972). This index can be interpreted as an estimation of the number of distinct assemblages across rocks sampled per forest.

4.3.2 Predicting univariate bryophyte responses with forest type and site-level variables

All six univariate responses (bryophyte species richness, family richness, total cover, diversity, and evenness) violated assumptions of normality by forest type and could not be normalized by a transformation. I therefore took a nonparametric approach to test for mean differences by forest. Each response was modeled using Euclidean distances, with forest type employed as the fixed main factor in a one-way permutational multivariate analysis of variance (PERMANOVA) (Anderson 2001). The significance of each pseudo-F-ratio (identical to an ANOVA F-ratio when Euclidean distance is used with one variable) was tested using 9,999 permutations of the raw data under the reduced model. The resulting family of six P-values was adjusted with Holm's (1979) non-conservative correction factor. When significance was found, PERMANOVA and Holm's (1979) correction factor were also used for pairwise comparison tests ($P < 0.05$). Notably, as with ANOVA, PERMANOVA is sensitive to differences in the variance of responses among groups and will report significant results if these differ, even when means do not (Anderson 2001). In order to test for homogeneity of variance among forest types, I employed the Fligner-Killeen median test because it is the most robust against departures from normality (Conover et al. 1981).

Subsequently, sequential (Type I) sums of squares PERMANOVA was used in order to explore the potential influence of site-level environmental variables on richness and total cover. These two models employed elevation, percent limestone, slope, aspect, PDIR, and shade cover as covariates, and interactions were tested. Covariates were entered into the model in order of importance, with the exception of elevation, which was placed as the first covariate in each model in order to assess whether forest type had encapsulated the indirect effect of elevation on the bryophyte community. Notably, units of feet were used for elevation because the increased resolution of this measurement significantly modeled a higher proportion of variation than did elevation in meters. Insignificant terms were removed before running final models.

4.3.3 Indicator species analysis by forest type

After confirming bryophyte compositional differences by forest type, Indicator Species Analysis (ISA) was used to quantify the affinity of each species to a particular forest type (Dufrene and Legendre 1997). Forest indicator values (IVs) are calculated as the product of each species' relative abundance and relative frequency in the respective forest. This product is then multiplied by 100 so that IVs range from 0 to 100. An IV of 100 signifies a species that occurs 100% of the tiime in one forest type and is thus a perfect indicator of that forest. For example, if both the relative abundance and relative frequency of a species in the pinyon-juniper forest is 0.50, then its IV is 25 ($0.5 \times 0.5 \times 100$). The ecological significance of IVs below 25 are questionable (Dufrene and Legendre 1997), however statistical significance is assessed by a probability distribution of the IVs created with a Monte Carlo permutation method in which sites are randomly shuffled across forest groups. Consequently, the p-value ($P < 0.05$) for a particular species' IV is the probability of randomly obtaining an IV ≥ the observed IV (i.e. the proportion of times that the randomized data yields an IV ≥ observed IV from the real data).

4.3.4 Revealing patterns in composition: NMS ordination

Non-metric multidimensional scaling (NMS) ordination was used to detect multivariate patterns in community composition and analyze their relationship to univariate bryophyte responses (richness, cover) and environmental variables including forest type and continuous site-level variables (elevation, percent limestone, aspect, shade cover, PDIR, slope; Kruskal 1964). Unlike traditional ordination methods (e.g. principle components analysis, correspondence analysis, canonical correspondence analysis, or detrended correspondence analysis), NMS is a robust method for multivariate community data because it lacks the assumptions of normally distributed species data and linear relationships among species abundances, and also handles the presence of many zeros (i.e. species absences) in the data (McCune and Grace 2002).

4.3.4.1 Preparing the community matrix. Abundances were relativized and rare species and outlier sites were removed from the species × site matrix before running the ordination. Rare species were defined for each forest as those which occurred in <5% of sites. This required the removal of 24 species (16 retained) and effectively reduced noise in the dimensionality of species space, enhancing the ability of the ordination to detect major gradients in composition (McCune & Grace 2002).

Multivariate outlier analysis (PC-ORD 5.0) recommended the removal of two sites (#s 103 & 88), which had an average distance from all other sites greater than 2 standard deviations from the grand mean. Outlier sites effect stress (a measure of the lack of fit between the NMS ordination and the raw data) and can structure spurious gradients in the ordination (McCune and Grace 2002). Compositional dissimilarity in the resulting species matrix (102 sites × 16 species) was represented using the Bray-Curtis (semi-metric Sørensen) distance measure (Faith et al. 1987). This semi-metric measure performs better for ecological analyses than metric distance measures (i.e. Euclidean) because it tends to linearize the relationship between species composition and environmental gradients and does not assign correlative power to the joint absence of species, which usually represents shortcomings in sampling (McCune & Grace 2002). Lastly, total bryophyte cover across all sites varied moderately (coefficient of variation = 80.8), indicating that a relativization by total site abundance would moderately reduce the overwhelming influence of dominant species on the extracted gradients simply by decreasing the abundance disparity between dominant and rare species (McCune and Grace 2001).

4.3.4.2 NMS parameters. The Slow-and-Thorough autopilot setting was used in PC-ORD 5.0 (McCune and Mefford 1999) with the following parameters: 400 maximum iterations; 40 runs with the real data each from a random starting configuration; 50 randomized runs for the Monte Carlo test; and 500 iterations for the final solution. To assess the reliability of the ordination, I examined the final stress, instability, approximate coefficient of determination, and the results of a Monte Carlo permutation test. The permutation test determines if the ordination has extracted stronger gradients (i.e. axes) than are expected by chance. The associated p-value is the proportion of runs with randomized data producing stress values less than or equal to that of the final ordination. The approximate coefficient of determination (R^2) is the proportion of variation in the original Bray-Curtis distance matrix that is represented by Euclidean distance in the final ordination space.

4.3.4.3 Environmental and biological relationships with community composition. Sites plotted in the ordination were coded by forest type to reveal the presence of patterns in community composition among and within forests. Environmental vectors were joint-plotted to illustrate the strength (length) and sign (direction) of their relationship to each axis. Lastly, the ordination was rigidly rotated 22° in order to maximize the linear relationship between axis 2 and percent limestone (the variable with the strongest correlation to an axis). This facilitated an ecological interpretation of compositional change along axis 2 by creating axis scores that represented a strong relationship between rock type and community composition.

4.3.5 Predicting composition with forest type and site-level variables

The flexibility of PERMANOVA is critical to analyzing multivariate ecological datasets that notoriously fail to meet the strict assumptions of multivariate normality and homogeneity of variance in species' responses (Anderson 2001). Therefore, a covariate PERMANOVA with sequential (Type 1) sums of squares was used in a multivariate application to test for compositional differences among forest types and for exploring the ability of site-level variables to account for additional variation in composition, given that forest type and elevation were included first in the model. The model-fitting procedure was the same as in Section 4.3.2. For this model, Bray-Curtis distances were used in the required distance matrix and P-values were calculated using 9,999 permutations of the raw data.

As mentioned in section 4.3.2., PERMANOVA is sensitive to non-equal variances, however, detecting such differences in community composition is ecologically meaningful. Therefore, I tested for homogeneity of multivariate dispersion among forest groups using a dissimilarity-based multivariate analogue to Levene's test called PERMDISP2. This test can only be performed on non-relativized abundance data (Anderson 2006, Anderson et al. 2006), thus it was applied to the raw dataset only. P-values were calculated by permuting model residuals, a process robust to skewed and zero-inflated data (Anderson 2006). To assess variation in the relativized community matrix, I used a graphical method with the NMS ordination, which plots a 95% confidence ellipse around the centroid of each forest (i.e. the mean compositional distance between all sites in the respective forest; McCune and Grace 2002).

4.3.6 Predicting dominant species distributions

The distributions of dominant moss species along environmental gradients are nonlinear and therefore methods of nonparametric regression were employed as an exploratory tool for modeling these abundance responses. Specifically, generalized additive models (GAMs) were used in the R package, mgcv (Wood 2004, 2011) to elucidate the complex relationships between two dominant bryophyte species and elevation. GAMs were chosen over more traditional generalized linear models (GLMs) because the latter are not capable of modeling skewed (not symmetrical) bell curves or multi-modal curves typical of species distributions along environmental gradients (Yee & Mitchell 1991). A GAM uses unknown smoothing functions (instead of linear functions) that fit a nonparametric curve to local sections of the data, but requires greater numbers of degrees of freedom (d.f.) to increase model fit than does parametric regression (Yee & Mitchell 1991). All three models utilized the Gaussian distribution with the identity link function and a thin plate regression splines base (i.e. basis function) (R function gam{mgcv}). The maximum number of d.f. allowed for each smoothing function (term) was set at a minimum in order to reduce the costly use of smoothing functions on the d.f. available for assessing model fit. Additionally,

the parameter k was tested at different levels to minimize the resulting model deviance, an approximate measure of model fit similar to residual sums of squares, and to avoid over-fitting or negative, nonsensical fitted values.

I used nonparametric smoothing spline functions to explore the nonlinear relationships of three dominant species to ordination axis 2. Under this method, a model is parameterized with the smoothing parameter, lambda (λ), which controls the degree of model fit (Chambers and Hastie 1992). Because the primary purpose in this model-fitting process was exploration of ecological patterns and not prediction, cross-validation was not reported. This method was preferentially employed over a GAM because it produced better-fitting curves.

4.4 Results

4.4.1 Rock bryophyte abundance and diversity across the forests

<u>4.4.1.1 Floristic richness.</u> Plot sampling in the pinyon-juniper, ponderosa pine, and mixed conifer forests of GRCA captured 39 moss and 1 liverwort species growing on rock, or a thin layer of soil over rock (table 7). These species encompassed 11 families and 19 genera. The four most abundant (measured by percent cover) and frequently captured families were Pottiaceae, Grimmiaceae, Orthotricaceae, and Leskeaceae (fig. 26). The desert moss family, Pottiaceae, was the most diverse (6 genera, 15 species) and the rock moss family, Grimmiaceae, was the most abundant, with its major genus, *Grimmia*, the most species rich (10 species). One species of *Grimmia* was determined new to science with the help of a specialist and will be described in a future publication.

<u>4.4.1.2 Richness, abundance and diversity.</u> Mean site-level species richness on rocks was 3 ($\pm$ SE 0.2) and ranged from 0–9 species, with 50% of sites supporting between 2 and 4 species. Although an outlier, the site with nine

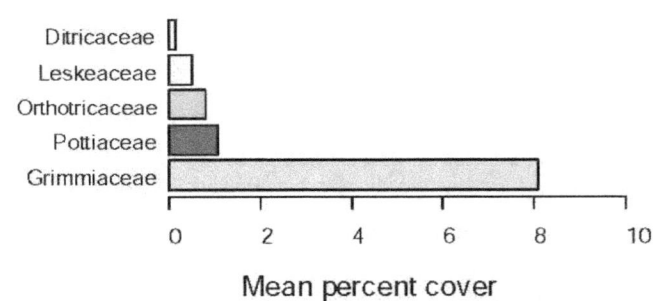

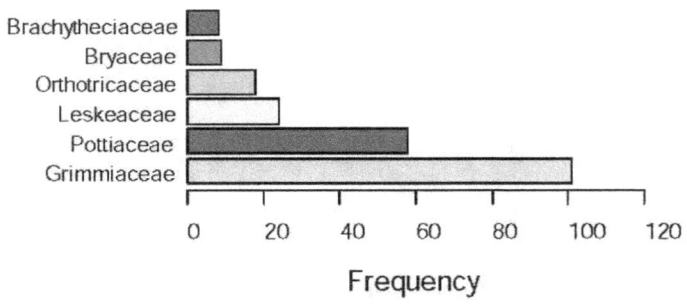

Figure 26. Mean percent cover and frequency of dominant bryophyte families growing on rocks across the mixed conifer, ponderosa pine, and pinyon-juniper forests of Grand Canyon N.P. **Top**: Mean percent cover of abundant (mean covers >0.1%) bryophyte families sampled on rocks. **Bottom**: Frequency of occurrence for common (at least 5 sites out of 104) bryophyte families sampled on rocks. Colors are conserved across figures.

Table 7. Frequency and mean percent cover of rock bryophyte species by forest type in Grand Canyon NP (GRCA). Abundance (percent cover) and occurrence frequency of rock bryophyte species (39 mosses & 1 liverwort) found in 104 sites across the forests of GRCA. Species frequency is expressed as the proportion of sites in which a species occurred out of the total number of sites in each forest type. Species mean percent cover is listed for each forest. The absence of a species in a forest is indicated by a dash (-). PJ = pinyon-juniper woodland, PON = ponderosa pine forest, and MC = mixed conifer forest. * = singleton species found at only 1 site. Species new to the state are denoted with a + following their names.

Species	Frequency (%)			Mean cover (%)		
	PJ	PON	MC	PJ	PON	MC
Brachytheciastrum collinum	-	0.03	0.16	-	0.01(0)	0.26(0.14)
Brachytheciastrum fendleri*	-	-	0.03	-	-	0.01(0.01)
Brachytheciastrum velutinum*+	-	0.03	-	-	0.05(0.01)	-
Ceratodon purpureus	-	-	0.13	-	-	0.48(0.42)
Crossidium aberrans*	0.02	-	-	0.01(0.01)	-	-
Crossidium squamiferum*	0.02	-	-	0.02(0.02)	-	-
Dicranoweisia crispula	-	-	0.06	-	-	0.25(0.21)
Didymodon nevadensis	0.02	0.07	0.06	0.01(0.01)	0.21(0.03)	0.33(0.31)
Didymodon vinealis	0.05	-	-	0.04(0.03)	-	-
Encalypta vulgaris*	-	0.03	-	-	0.21(0.04)	-
Frullania inflata*	-	-	0.03	-	-	0.07(0.07)
Funaria sp.*	-	-	0.03	-	-	0.01(0.01)
Gemmabryum caespiticium	0.02	0.07	0.16	0.01(0.01)	0.02(0)	0.15(0.07)
Gemmabryum kunzei*	0.02	-	-	0.01(0.01)	-	-
Grimmia alpestris	0.09	0.34	0.66	0.43(0.25)	7.83(0.42)	5.26(1.07)
Grimmia anodon	0.93	0.59	0.47	4.44(0.5)	3(0.15)	1.24(0.35)
Grimmia longirostris*	-	0.03	-	-	0.06(0.01)	-
Grimmia ovalis	0.05	0.03	-	0.02(0.02)	0.11(0.02)	-
Grimmia plagiopodia	0.26	0.38	0.28	0.21(0.06)	0.74(0.06)	1.28(0.52)
Grimmia pulvinata	0.05	0.07	0.06	0.08(0.07)	0.09(0.01)	0.17(0.16)
Grimmia sp. nov.*+	0.02	-	-	0.02(0.02)	-	-
Gymnostomum aeruginosum*	-	-	0.03	-	-	0.03(0.03)
Orthotrichum obtusifolium*+	-	-	0.03	-	-	0.07(0.07)
Orthotrichum spp. (1-stratose)	0.02	-	0.03	0.02(0.02)	-	0.17(0.17)
Orthotrichum spp. (2-stratose)	0.14	0.1	0.25	0.34(0.19)	0.1(0.01)	1.79(0.65)
Pottiaceae sp.*	-	0.03	-	-	0.07(0.01)	-
Pseudocrossidium crinitum*	-	0.03	-	-	0.01(0)	-
Pseudoleskeella tectorum	0.23	0.1	0.34	0.31(0.16)	0.1(0.01)	1.11(0.4)
Rosulabryum flaccidum*	-	-	0.03	-	-	0.01(0.01)
Schistidium atrichum	-	-	0.19	-	-	0.24(0.14)
Schistidium confertum	-	-	0.09	-	-	0.27(0.18)
Schistidium papillosum*	-	0.03	-	-	0.01(0)	-
Syntrichia norvegica	0.05	0.1	0.22	0.02(0.02)	0.08(0.01)	0.26(0.13)

Table 7. *continued*

Species	Frequency (%)			Mean cover (%)		
	PJ	PON	MC	PJ	PON	MC
Syntrichia ruralis	0.44	0.38	0.41	0.49(0.15)	0.43(0.02)	0.9(0.29)
*Tortula atrovirens**	-	0.03	-	-	0.01(0)	-
Tortula inermis	-	-	0.06	-	-	0.17(0.15)
Tortula muralis	0.02	0.07	0.06	0.01(0.01)	0.08(0.01)	0.24(0.23)
*Tortula obtusifolia**	-	0.03	-	-	0.05(0.01)	-
*Weissia ligulifolia**	-	0.03	-	-	0.02(0)	-
Zygodon viridissimus+*	-	-	0.03	-	-	0.01(0.01)

species was retained in analysis because it accurately represented a prolific community on the North Kaibab Trail at 2,490 m. On average, sampling captured 2 (± SE 0.11) families per site and site-level family richness ranged from 0–6. Mean site-level total cover on rocks was 10% (± SE 0.8%) and ranged from 0–37%. The zero-site occurred along the Arizona Trail on the South Rim at 2,100 m, while the most prolific site occurred on the Cape Final Trail on the North Rim at 2,430 m. Mean site-level diversity (Simpson index) was 0.34 (± SE 0.03), which means there is a 34% chance, on average, that two bryophytes randomly selected from a site will be different species. Beta diversity (species turnover) across the forests was relatively high (14) suggesting that 14 distinct bryophyte assemblages occur on rocks throughout the forests of GRCA. Mean community evenness was 0.6 ± SE 0.05.

4.4.2 Dominant, rare and indicator species

Throughout all three forest types, 11 of the 40 captured bryophytes (~28%) were relatively common, occurring at more than 5 of the 104 sites (fig. 27). The moss, *Grimmia alpestris*, was the most abundant species on rocks and had a mean cover of 4 % (± SE 0.8). It was also very common (38/104 sites), third in frequency to *Syntrichia ruralis* and *Grimmia anodon*, the latter of which occurred at 72 sites and had the second largest mean cover (3% ± SE 0.03). Other relatively common species were *Grim-mia plagiopodia, Syntrichia ruralis,* and *Pseudoleskeella tectorum,* each of which was found at greater than 20 sites (fig. 27). Locally rare singleton species totaled 20 (50%) and most occurred in the mixed conifer forest (table 7).

Indicator species analysis determined eight species to be significant (p <0.05) indicators of the mixed conifer forest, of which *Pseudoleskeella tectorum, Grimmia alpestris,* and *Orthotrichum* spp. were the strongest (table 8). However, *Grimmia alpestris* also displayed a strong affinity for the ponderosa pine forest (IV = 20) and there were no other significant indicator species for this forest type. *Grimmia anodon* was the sole indicator of the pinyon-juniper woodland and the strongest of all indicator species (IV = 48). Although each forest had several unique species, all occurred infrequently and in low enough abundance that they were not significant indicator species (Dufrene & Legendre 1997) with the exception of *Ceratodon purpureus, Schistidium atrichum,* and *S. confertum,* weak indicators of the mixed conifer forest. Thirteen species were exclusive to the mixed conifer forest, including the sole captured liverwort (*Frullania inflata*), while two species were restricted to the ponderosa pine forest (*Tortula obtusifolia, Weissia ligulifolia*) and five were found only in the pinyon-juniper woodland (*Crossidium aberrans* and *squamiferum, Didymodon vinealis, Gemmabryum kunzei, Grimmia* sp. nov.; table 7).

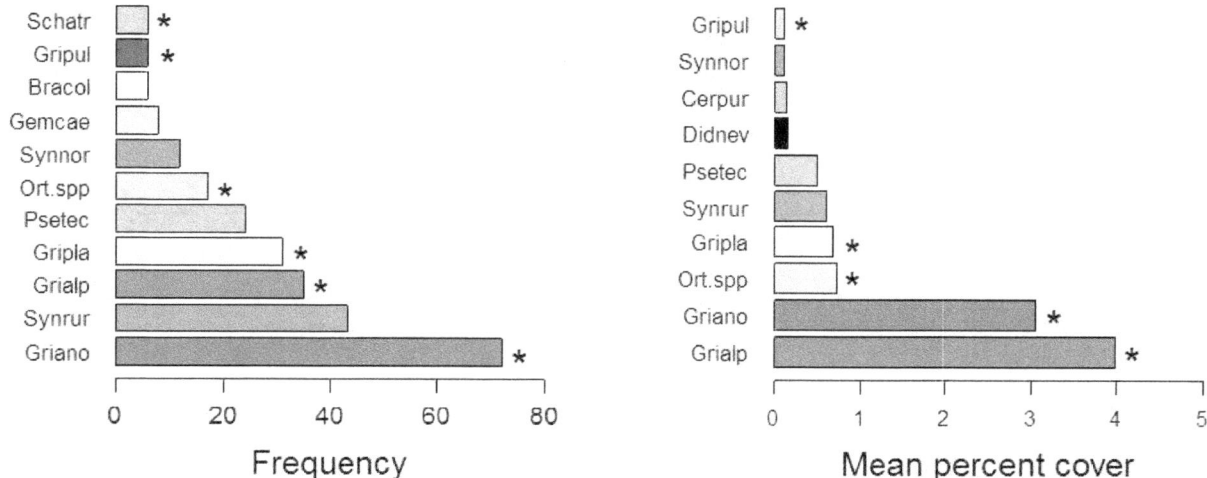

Figure 27. Frequency and abundance (mean percent cover) of dominant bryophyte species sampled on rocks across the pinyon-juniper, ponderosa pine, and mixed conifer forests in Grand Canyon NP. **Left**: Frequency (number of occurrences) of species found at more than 5 out of 104 sites. **Right**: Mean percent cover of abundant species (means >0.1%). Scientific names are abbreviated using the first three letters of the genus and species. Species are color-coded and colors are conserved across figures. *Ort* spp. includes *Orthotrichum cupulatum* and *O. hallii*, which could not be differentiated when sterile. An asterisk (*) denotes obligate rock species.

Table 8. Indicator species of the forests in Grand Canyon NP. Results from Indicator Species Analysis testing the significance of 40 bryophytes captured in sampling in the pinyon-juniper woodland (PJ), ponderosa pine forest (PON), and mixed conifer forest (MC). Significant (P <0.05) indicator species are reported with their indicator values. The ecological significance of indicator values below 25 is questionable (Dufrene & Legendre 1997).

| | Indicator value | | |
Species	PJ	PON	MC
Orthotrichum spp.	2	0	20
Brachytheciastrum collinum	0	0	15
Ceratodon purpureus	0	0	13
Gemmabryum caespiticium	0	1	13
Grimmia alpestris	0	20	25
Grimmia anodon	48	20	7
Pseudoleskeella tectorum	5	1	25
Schistidium atrichum	0	0	16
Schistidium confertum	0	0	9

4.4.3 Comparing richness, abundance, and diversity by forest type

Mean rock bryophyte species richness, family richness, diversity, total cover, and evenness did not differ significantly in all three forests, as hypothesized, but one of the three forest types differed significantly in each case, although the pattern was not consistent across responses (Univariate PERMANOVAs; table 9, fig. 28). Forest type was able to account for 10–19% of observed variation in any one response.

4.4.3.1 Mean species and family richness.

Variance of species richness did not differ significantly among forest types (Fligner-Killeen median test: $\chi^2 = 3.1$, P = 0.211). Pairwise comparisons indicated no difference in mean species richness between the pinyon-juniper and ponderosa pine forest, but both of these forests were less rich than the mixed conifer forest (table 9). Forest type accounted for 13% of variation in bryophyte species richness and the covariate slope explained an additional

Table 9. Mean rock bryophyte community statistics in the forests of Grand Canyon NP. One-way PERMANOVA results for bryophyte species responses on rocks in the three forests (d.f. = 103). Means and (standard error) are calculated from 43, 29, & 32 sites sampled in the pinyon-juniper (PJ), ponderosa (PON), & mixed conifer (MC) forests, respectively. Holm's family-wise P-values indicate significant differences among forests. Letters denote significantly different means from pairwise comparison tests (PERMANOVA) using Holm's error rate adjustment (see section 4.4.2.). Also reported by forest is gamma diversity (the total number of species captured per forest), beta diversity (species turnover), and the number of unique species.

Bryophyte response	All forests	PJ	PON	MC	Pseudo - F	Holm's P
Species richness	3 (0.2)	2.5 (0.1)a	2.7 (0.2)a	4.4 (0.2)b	7.6	0.003
Species total cover	10 (0.8)	6.1 (0.4)a	12.9 (-1.1)b	13.9 (-0.7)b	12.0	0.0005
Species evenness	-	0.47 (0.01)a	0.53 (0.02)a	0.89 (0.02)b	8.2	0.002
Species diversity	0.34 (0.03)	0.25 (0.02)a	0.30 (0.02)b	0.34 (0.02)b	6.5	0.006
Family richness	2.18 (0.11)	2.0 (0.1)a	1.9 (0.1)a	2.8 (0.1)b	6.0	0.006
Gamma diversity	40	18	22	25	-	-
Beta diversity	14	6.6	7.5	5.4		
Unique species	-	7	2	13	-	-

4% of variation (table 10). However, there were significant interactions between several variables (forest × slope, forest × elevation × slope), which indicates that the observed relationships between richness, elevation and slope vary depending upon the forest type. Notably, elevation, when placed as the first covariate following forest type, could not explain any further variation, and was therefore not included in the final model. Non-significant covariates included percent limestone, aspect, PDIR, and shade cover. Mean family richness mirrored the trend in species richness (table 9) and forest type accounted for 10.55% of this variation. It follows that the ratio of family-to-species richness is higher in the mixed conifer forest. Specifically, a given rock in the mixed conifer forest is expected to support four species, of which three will likely represent different families, while in the pinyon-juniper or ponderosa pine forest, rocks are expected to harbor 2–3 species, which are expected to be in the same family.

4.4.3.2 Mean total percent cover.
Mean total percent cover of bryophytes was not significantly different in the ponderosa pine and mixed conifer forests, but was greater in these two forests than in the pinyon-juniper woodland (table 9, fig. 28). Variability in total cover in the pinyon-juniper woodland was signifi-

cantly less than that in the other two forests (Fligner-Killeen median test: χ^2= 18.7, P < 0.0001; fig. 29). Forest type accounted for 19% of observed variation, and several site-level variables (elevation, percent limestone, forest × elevation, forest × percent limestone, and forest × slope) significantly explained additional variation in this response (table 10). The site-level variable that accounted for the greatest amount of variation was percent limestone (r^2 = 0.12). The implications of the interaction terms will be discussed in Section 4.5.3. With respect to total cover, elevation was able to explain an additional 6% of variation in total cover that was not encapsulated by forest type.

4.4.3.3 Mean evenness and diversity.
Gamma diversity (forest-level richness) was greatest in the mixed conifer forest (25 species) and lowest in the pinyon-juniper woodland (18 species), while beta diversity (species turnover among sites within each forest) was highest in the ponderosa pine forest (table 9). Pairwise comparisons indicated that both evenness (Shannon-Weiner Index) and diversity (Simpson Index) did not differ between the pinyon-juniper and ponderosa pine forests, but both of these forests had communities less even and diverse than the mixed conifer forest (table 9). Forest type was able to explain 14% of the variation in evenness

Table 10. PERMANOVA models of rock bryophyte richness, percent cover, and community composition in the forests of Grand Canyon NP. Results of two sequential sums of squares permutation analyses of variance (PERMANOVA) used to explore relationships between environmental variables and rock bryophyte species richness (A), total percent cover (B), and relative community composition (C), given that the fixed factor, forest type, and the covariate, elevation, were included first in each model when significant. Additional covariates tested were percent limestone, shade cover, slope, aspect, and PDIR. Significant interaction terms are included and reflect the nonrandom distribution of rock types, forest types, and topographical features within each forest type. D. Pairwise comparison tests of mean composition between forest types (PERMANOVA). Partial correlation coefficients (Partial r²) are rounded to the nearest one thousandth.

	df	MS	pseudo-F	P	Partial r²
A. Species richness					
Forest	2	20.94	9.3	0.0004	0.131
Slope	1	13.46	5.98	0.0159	0.042
Forest x slope	2	8.49	3.77	0.0268	0.053
Forest x elevation x slope	3	11.22	4.98	0.002	0.105
Error	95	2.25			0.669
Total	103	56.36			1.000
B. Total percent cover					
Forest	2	677.8	19.6	0.0001	0.191
Elevation	1	411.1	11.9	0.0009	0.058
Percent limestone	1	871.9	25.2	0.0001	0.123
Forest x elevation	2	221.5	6.4	0.0032	0.063
Forest x percent limestone	2	202.3	5.9	0.0057	0.057
Forest x slope	2	137.1	4.0	0.0114	0.058
Error	92	34.6			0.450
Total	103				1.000
C. Relative community composition					
Forest	2	2.68	15.2	0.001	0.186
Elevation	1	1.87	10.6	0.001	0.065
Percent limestone	1	3.04	17.2	0.001	0.105
Slope	1	0.46	2.6	0.045	0.016
Forest type x elevation	2	0.75	4.2	0.002	0.052
Error	94	0.18			0.576
Total	101	8.97			1.000
D. Pairwise comparisons - Community composition				Holm's P	
Pinyon-juniper vs. mixed conifer	1, 72	5.01	23.4	0.004	0.245
Pinyon-juniper vs. ponderosa	1, 68	1.68	8.5	0.004	0.111
Ponderosa vs. mixed conifer	1, 58	0.99	3.2	0.02	0.050

and 11% of the variation in diversity.

4.4.4 Comparing rock bryophyte species composition by forest type

4.4.4.1 Absolute and relative composition. Absolute rock bryophyte species composition differed significantly among forest types (PERMANOVA: $F_{2,99}$ = 8.05, P = 0.0004) and between all forest pairs (Holm's P <0.05), however this significance is due in part to unequal variability among forest communities, rather than solely to differences in forest compositional means (PERMDISP2: F = 11.02, 999 permutations, P = 0.001). Specifically, multivariate dispersion is less in the pinyon-juniper forest than in both the other forests (P <0.01). Similarly, relative bryophyte composition also differed in all three forest types and forest type accounted for ~19% of observed variation (table 10). The highly

Figure 28. Mean rock bryophyte parameters by forest type in Grand Canyon NP. Mean ± SE species richness, percent cover, diversity (Simpson Index) and evenness (Shannon-Weiner Index) on rocks in the pinyon-juniper (PJ), ponderosa (PON), and mixed conifer (MC) forests. Letters denote forest types that differed significantly for a given mean response (univariate PERMANOVAs; Holm's P <0.01). See also Table 9.

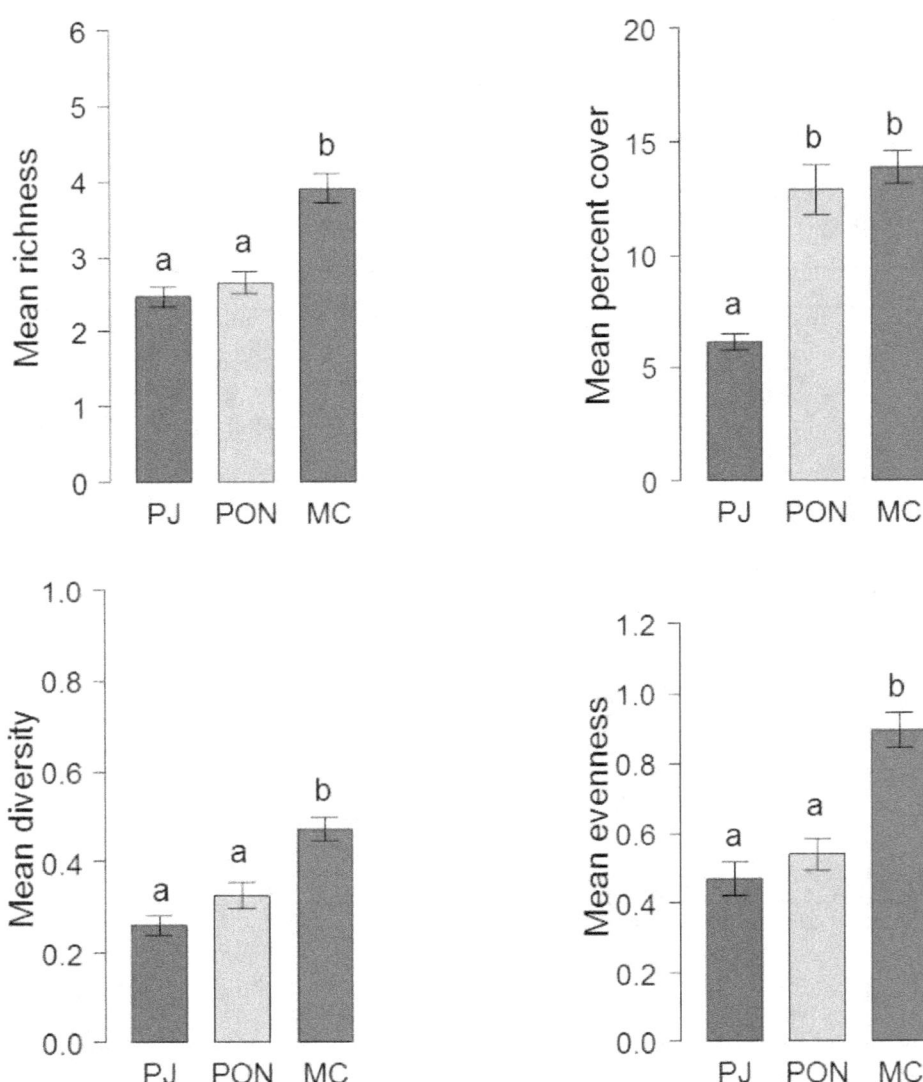

Figure 29. Boxplots of bryophyte total percent cover on rocks in the pinyon-juniper (PJ), ponderosa pine (PON), and mixed conifer (MC) forests of Grand Canyon NP. Boxes represent the interquartile range and thereby contain 50% of the observed data. Upper and lower whiskers mark extreme values not considered outliers and falling within 1.5 lengths of the box. These distributions illustrate differences in the variability of bryophyte cover by forest type. Letters denote forest types with significantly different variability in total percent cover (Fligner-Killeen median test: χ^2= 18.7, P<0.0001).

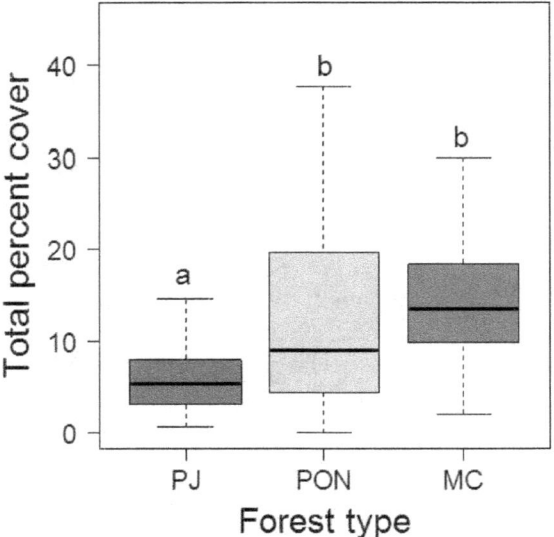

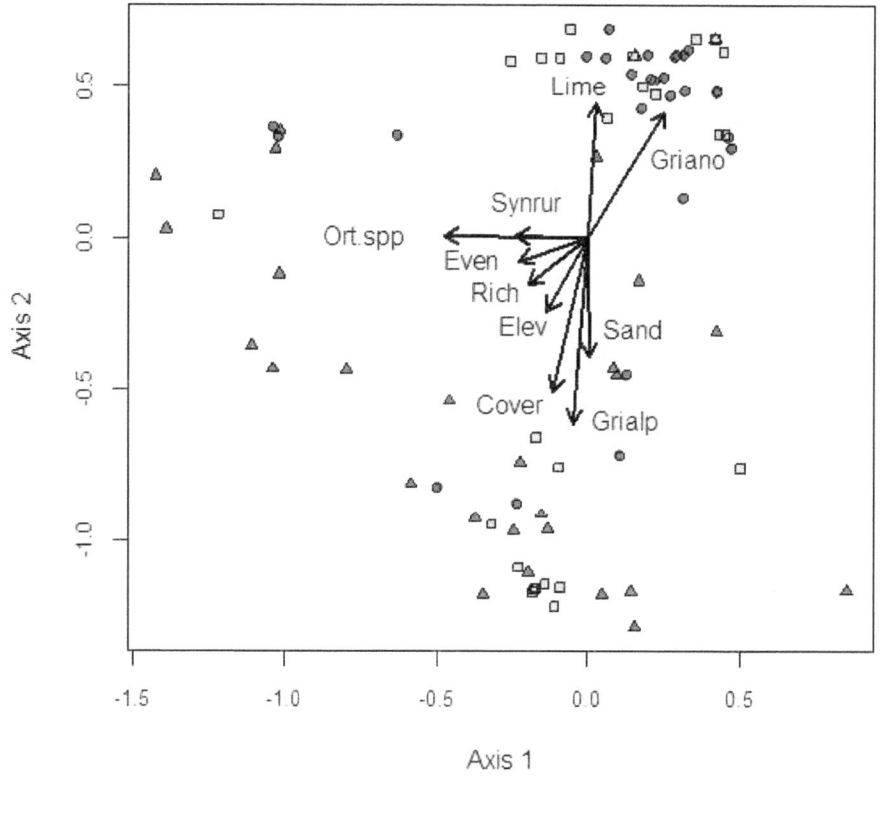

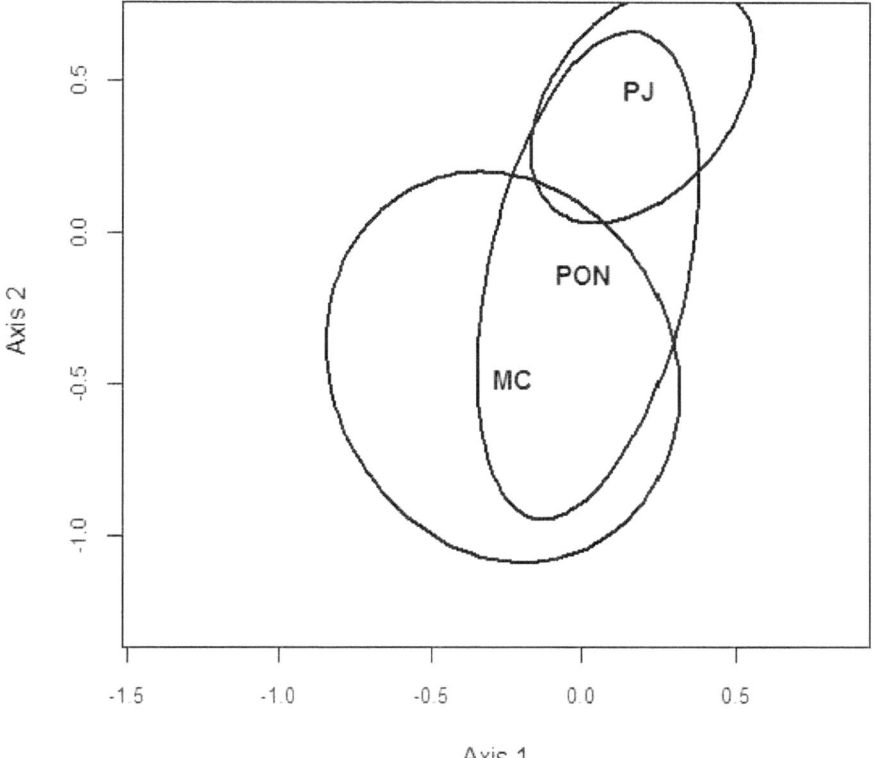

Figure 30. NMS ordination: relationship of species composition to the environment. **Top:** Two axes from a rotated three-dimensional NMS ordination of 102 sites (coded by forest) in relativized species space (low stress = 10.25 , acceptable instability = 0.001). In terms of sampled bryophyte species composition, the three forest types did not form well-defined clusters in this view of the three-dimensional ordination; despite this, mean bryophyte species composition did differ on average between all forest types (PERMANOVA; see table 10). Vectors depict relationships between species composition and environmental or community variables: *Grimmia alpestris* (Grialp), *Grimmia anodon* (Griano), *Orthotrichum* spp. (Ort spp.), *Syntrichia ruralis* (Synrur), percent limestone (Lime), percent sandstone (Sand), elevation in meters (Elev), total percent cover (Cover), species richness (Rich), evenness (Even). **Bottom:** Biplots of 95% confidence ellipses of bryophyte species composition in each forest type. The confidence ellipses suggest that bryophyte community composition varies less in the pinyon-juniper forest (PJ) than in the ponderosa pine (PON) or mixed conifer (MC) forest. Mean bryophyte composition in each forest is depicted by the centroid of each ellipse, marked with the forest abbreviations. Although the ellipses overlap, their non-overlapping centroids illustrate differences in mean composition by forest type, which were found to be significant (after relativization) by the PERMANOVA test.

significant, three-dimensional NMS ordination (Monte Carlo test; P = 0.004) successfully summarized major changes in relative rock bryophyte composition, reducing variation in the 16-species community dataset by 27.1% (fig. 30, top). Although sites within each forest overlap to differing degrees, a biplot of 95% confidence ellipses illustrates differing mean compositions in each forest, supporting the results from PERMANOVA (fig. 30, bottom). Additionally, this biplot suggests that variation in relative composition is less pronounced in the pinyon-juniper woodland than in the other two forests, as was the case with absolute composition.

4.4.4.2 Variables related to community change.

PERMANOVA revealed that several site-level variables (elevation, percent limestone, slope, and forest × elevation) could account for additional variation, given that forest type was already included in the model (table 10). Notably, again, elevation was only able to explain an additional 6% of variation, further supporting the trend seen with richness and total cover in which forest type is able to encapsulate most of the influence that elevation-related factors have on bryophytes. These multivariate patterns were visualized and explored further in ordination biplots using overlaid environmental vectors (fig. 30, top, table 11). Ordination axis 2 represented the largest gradient in community composition detected by the ordination and accounted for 31.5% of total variation. This axis is most strongly (positively) correlated with the percent of limestone

rock sampled at sites ($r^2 = 0.40$, $r = 0.63$) and the elevation of sites ($r^2 = 0.25$, $r = -0.5$). Elevation is moderately correlated to axis 1 ($r^2 = 0.12$, $r = -0.35$), which represents 21.7% of community variation. Axis 3 was not strongly correlated with any environmental variables (all $r^2 <0.12$, $|r|<0.35$; not plotted).

Axis 2 can be interpreted as a rock–elevation gradient due to its strong correlation with these two variables. Changes in the abundances of *Grimmia anodon* and *Grimmia alpestris* structure a large proportion of community variation along this axis ($r^2 = 0.37$, $r = 0.61$ & 0.55, $r = -0.74$, respectively) and appear to favor opposite ends of this gradient. Smoothing functions revealed the true nature of these species' relationships with axis 2 to be nonlinear, in contrast to that suggested by the corresponding biplot vectors (fig. 30). *Orthotrichum* spp. was strongly and negatively correlated with axis 1 ($r^2 = 0.44$, $r = 0.66$) and nonlinearly related to axis 2, displaying a unimodal distribution along axis 2 that peaks at intermediate levels of the rock – elevation gradient where the two species of *Grimmia* are less abundant. Lastly, total percent cover was strongly, negatively correlated with axis 2 ($r^2 = 0.47$, $r = -0.69$), while spe-

Table 11. Relationship of variables to gradients in community composition across the forests of Grand Canyon NP. Correlations (R^2) between NMS ordination axes and environmental and biotic variables. Variables were only reported & joint-plotted on the ordination when its $R^2 >0.2$ for at least one axis. The sign of each correlation can be seen in the ordination biplot (fig. 30). The percent of variation represented by each axis is reported as % variation.

	Axis 1	Axis 2	Axis 3
Percent limestone	0.01	0.40	0.01
Percent sandstone	0.00	0.37	0.01
Elevation	0.12	0.25	0.09
Total bryophyte percent cover	0.09	0.47	0.08
Species richness	0.22	0.17	0.03
Evenness	0.26	0.10	0.14
Grimmia anodon	0.21	0.37	0.00
Grimmia alpestris	0.04	0.55	0.22
Orthotrichum spp.	0.44	0.00	0.04
Syntrichia ruralis	0.22	0.00	0.04
% variation	21.7	31.5	19.6

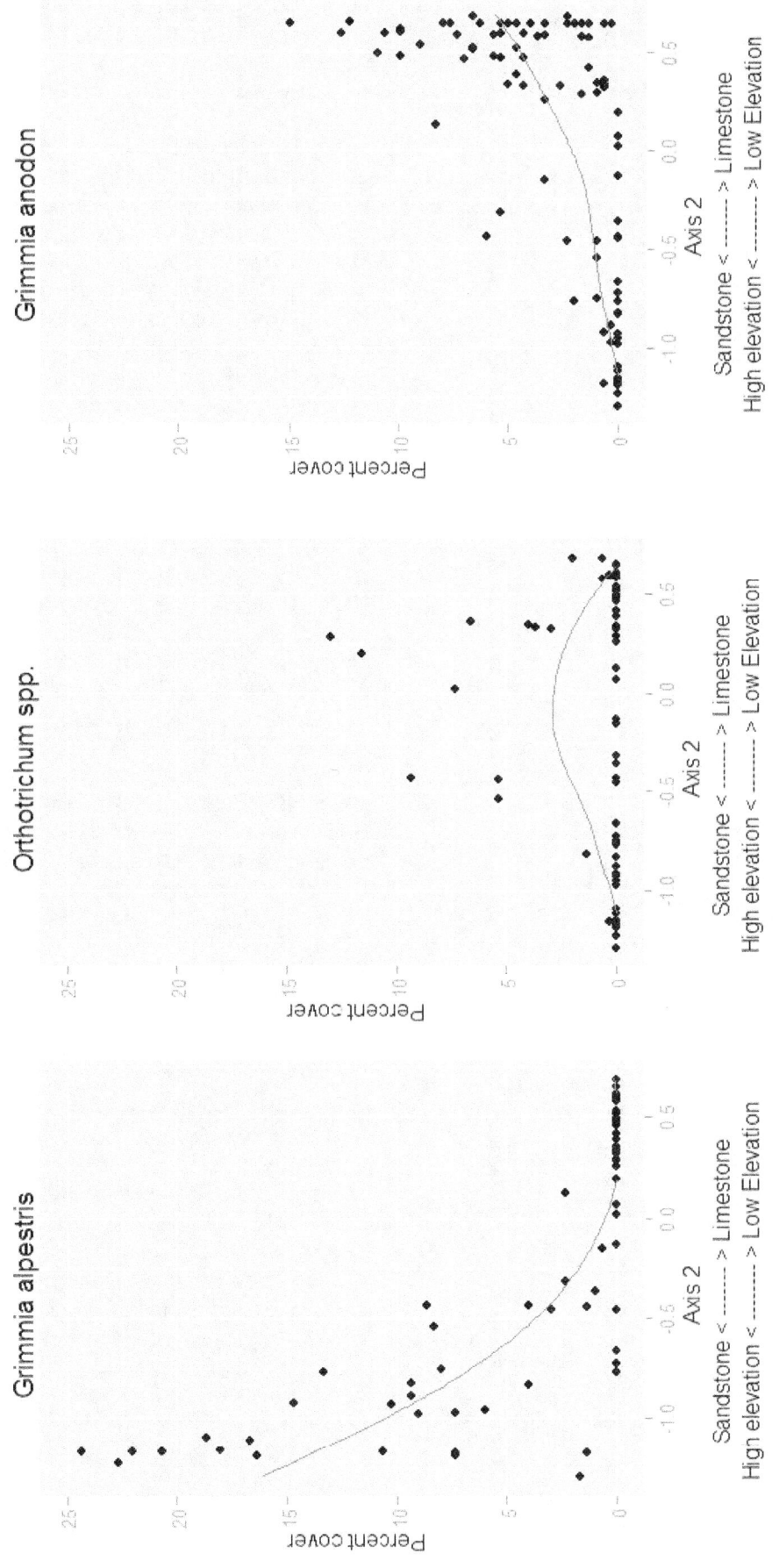

Figure 31. Response of three common bryophyte species to a rock type gradient. Nonparametric smoothing curves model the abundance of *Grimmia alpestris* ($\lambda_{256} = 0.005$), and *Grimmia anodon* ($\lambda_{a,91} = 0.005$) along NMS ordination Axis 2, which represents a gradient in rock type and elevation. The approximate gradient ranges from mostly low-elevation sites with 3 sand-stone rocks to mostly high elevation sites with 3 limestone rocks. Sites in between these limits have mostly intermediate elevations and a subset of the two rock types.

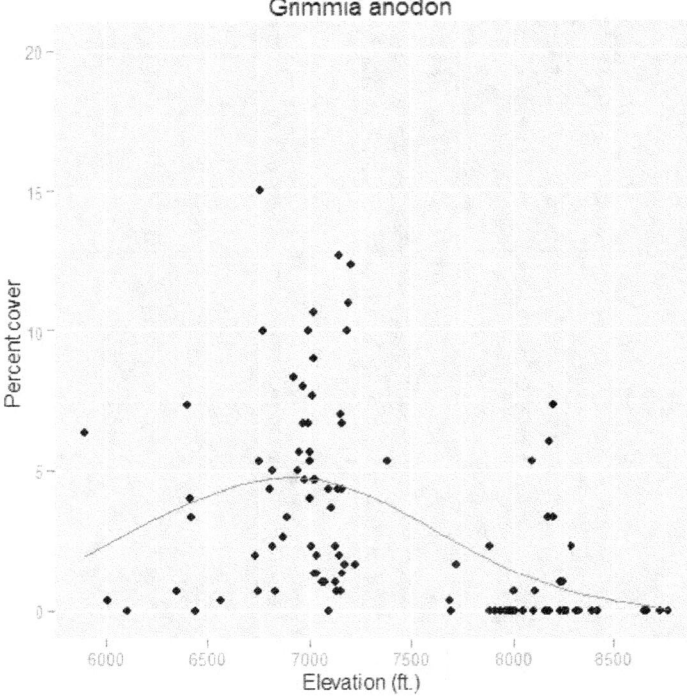

Grimmia anodon

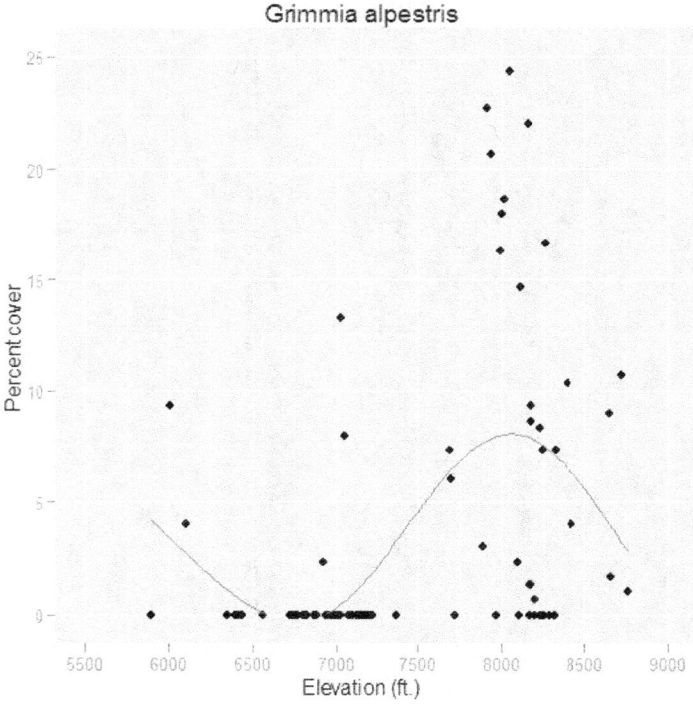

Grimmia alpestris

Figure 32. Response of two dominant rock bryophyte species to elevation across three forest types in Grand Canyon NP (GRCA). GAMs (Generalized Additive Models) of the abundance of two indicator species across the elevation gradient sampled within three forest types (pinyon-juniper, ponderosa pine, and mixed conifer) of GRCA. Fitted curves are plotted. **Top:** Abundance curve of *Grimmia anodon*, a significant indicator of the pinyon-juniper forest (Deviance explained = 25.5%, P < 0.0001). **Bottom:** Abundance curve of *Grimmia alpestris*, an indicator of both the ponderosa pine and mixed conifer forests (Deviance explained = 33.3%, P <0.0001). The artificial rise in abundance at the lower tail of this model reflects an insufficient detection rate for this species at lower elevations and likely does not imply that this species has a bimodal response to elevation. Note: Y-axes are not uniform in order to highlight the relative shape of each species' response curve to the gradient.

cies richness was moderately, negatively correlated with both axes 1 & 2 (r^2 = 0.22, r = - 0.47, and r^2 = 0.17, r = - 0.41, respectively).

Lastly, I wanted to explore how elevation may be influencing patterns in abundance of the two species most strongly correlated with compositional change, *Grimmia anodon* and G. *alpestris*. The biplot vectors suggest that a linear relationship exists between these two species and elevation (fig. 30), but research has shown that rarely do species respond in a linear fashion to environmental continua (when a sufficient portion of the gradient is sampled; McCune and Grace 2002). Generalized additive modeling (GAM), revealed the nature of these relationships to be unimodal (fig. 32). In particular, the two *Grimmia* species dominate opposite ends of the sampled elevation gradient; *Grimmia anodon* is most prolific around 7,000 ft., while the abundance of *Grimmia alpestris* reaches its maximum around 8,000 ft. It follows then, that while biplot vectors are an elegant means of revealing complex relationships between species (or species composition) and the environment, they do have one major caveat—their inability to detect nonlinear relationships.

4.5 Discussion

4.5.1 Rock Bryophyte richness and abundance in the forests of Grand Canyon National Park

4.5.1.1 Species richness. Rock bryophyte communities along trail corridors in the pinyon-juniper, ponderosa pine, and mixed conifer forests of GRCA harbor at least 40 species across the 1,000 m elevation gradient sampled. These forest bryophyte communities mirror the composition of other known aridland bryofloras which include a high proportion of acrocarpous moss species and very few liverworts (Stark & Brinda 2011, Stark & Castetter 1987, Stark & Whittemore 2000). Only four pleurocarpous moss species were captured, and all but *Pseudoleskeella tectorum* appear to be locally rare (*Brachy-*

theciastrum collinum, B. velutinum, and *B. fendleri*; table 7). The sole liverwort species captured in sampling was *Frullania inflata,* found in a cool-air drainage along the North Rim's Widforss Trail, growing prolifically over a shaded limestone outcrop and evidently flourishing in this rare, highly mesic microhabitat. In contrast, six of the eleven most abundant and frequently sampled species were obligate epilithic mosses tolerant of exposed rock faces and long periods of desiccation (FNA eds. 2007+, Proctor et al. 2007; fig. 27). *Syntrichia ruralis* and *Pseudoleskeella tectorum* were common although not abundant generalists capable of colonizing bare soil, downed wood, and tree bases, in addition to rock (see Section 3.4.3). Although plot-based sampling typically fails to capture rare species, I found three species new to the state and one species of *Grimmia* new to science, which was mentioned in section 3.3.2. (table 2). These records substantiate the need for continued collecting in Arizona and speak to the cryptic nature of rock-dwelling bryophytes in the American Southwest, the latter of which dissuades many bryologists from mastering their taxonomy.

4.5.1.2 Abundance. Overall, bryophyte abundance is low on rocks across the forests of GRCA, despite my observation that rocks harbor the most prolific communities of any dry substratum available. On average, 10% of exposed surfaces of colonized rocks were covered, but this result is not surprising in the arid Southwest where infrequent precipitation, low humidity levels, and high light intensity limits bryophyte growth (Glime 2007). In contrast, light and litter accumulation can limit the productivity of certain species in tropical and temperate closed canopy forests (e.g. Monge-Nájera 1989, Glime 2007), but in general, most bryophyte species are adapted to low light conditions and reach optimal rates of productivity in shaded habitats with sufficient water availability (Glime 2007).

A final note of caution is needed regarding the community parameters estimated in this study: their inference space is limited to the set of colonized rocks along trail corridors in the forests of GRCA. With respect to abundance, this implies that the average cover of bryophytes on all rocks in this region is much lower than the mean of 10%, and that mean abundance of most species likely approaches zero.

4.5.2 Forest-level patterns in rock bryophyte richness, abundance, and composition

Mean richness, abundance, diversity, and evenness were not significantly different between all forest types, although a significant increase in these responses was found from the lowest-elevation pinyon-juniper woodland to the highest-elevation mixed conifer forest (figs. 28, 33). A positive relationship between elevation and bryophyte diversity and productivity has been observed when humidity or precipitation is positively correlated with elevation and (usually) negatively correlated with temperature, in temperate (Austrheim 2002, Frahm 2002), tropical (Churchill 1991, Frahm and Gradstein 1991, Frahm and Ohlemüller 2001), and arid (Eldridge and Tozer 1997, Nash et al. 1977, Stark and Castetter 1987) regions. This pattern reflects the established fact that the vast majority of bryophytes favor high levels of humidity and precipitation, which are positively associated with growth rate (Proctor et al. 2007).

The multivariate response of bryophyte species composition differed in each forest (table 10), although differences were most pronounced between the pinyon-juniper and mixed conifer forests and a component of the statistical signal was likely due to greater compositional variability in the ponderosa pine and mixed conifer forests.

Collectively, these results demonstrate that forest type is a useful landscape-scale composite variable that can be used to estimate the influence of large-scale climatic gradients on bryophyte communities. Accordingly, the rock bryophyte communities within each for-

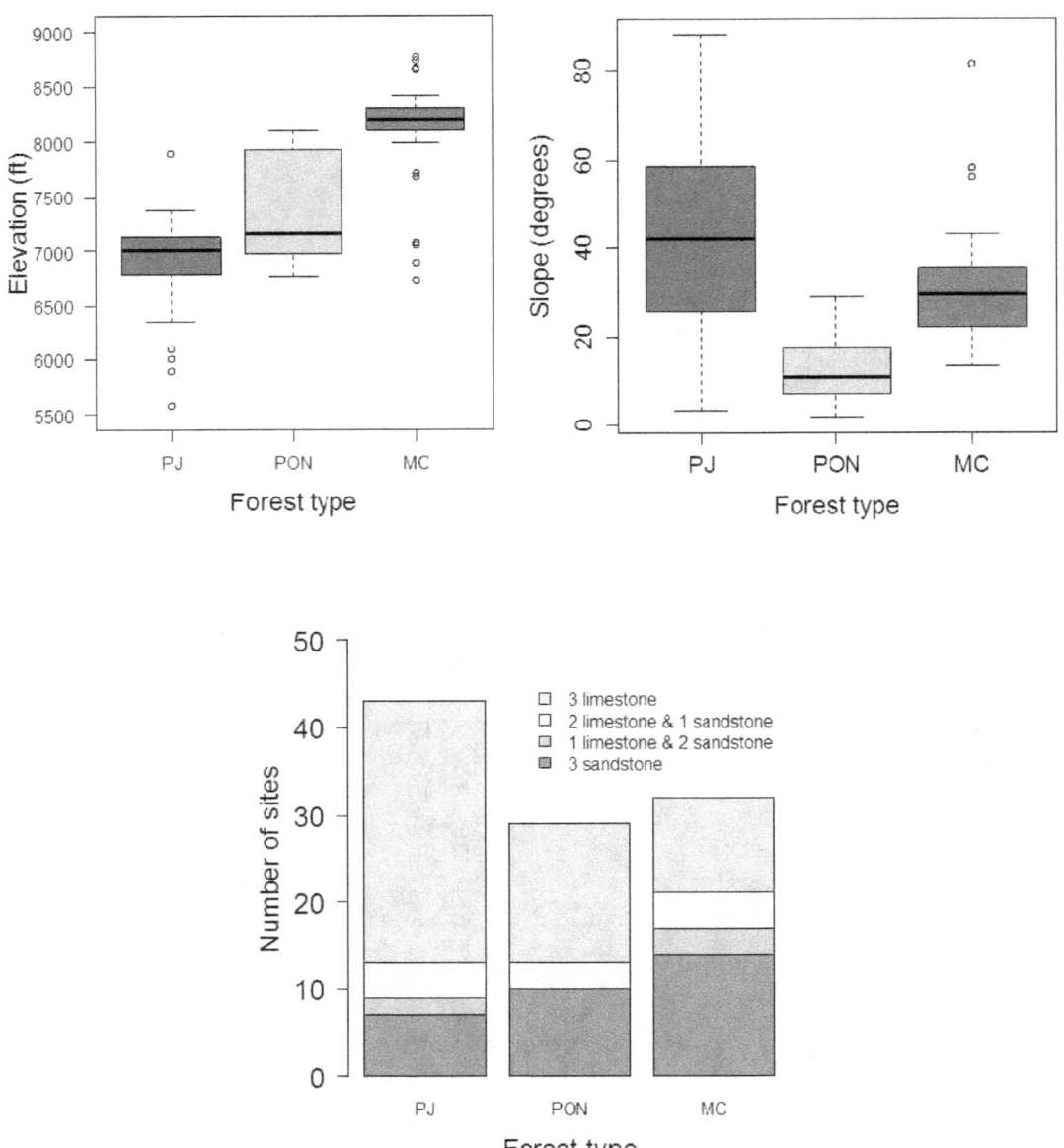

Figure 33. Depiction of nonindependent environmental variables that have significant main and interaction effects on bryophyte responses (See table 10). **Top left:** Elevational distribution of 104 sites sampled in the pinyon-juniper (PJ), ponderosa pine (PON), and mixed conifer (MC) forests. The relationship between forest type and elevation is significant (PERMANOVA: R^2 = 0.55, P = 0.0001). **Top right:** Distribution of slope measurements taken at sites in each forest type; the relationship between forest type and slope is significant (PERMANOVA: R^2 = 0.35, P = 0.0001). **Bottom:** Distribution of sampled rock types (i.e. the number of limestone and sandstone rocks sampled out of three rocks per site) by forest type; the relationship between forest type and the proportion of limestone rock sampled at a site is significant (PERMANOVA: R^2 = 0.07, P = 0.011).

est are summarized below.

4.5.2.1 Pinyon-juniper woodland.

Within the pinyon-juniper woodland, bryophyte communities are distinguished largely by their homogeneity. Rock bryophyte communities at most sites in this forest support between 1 and 2 species, and cover 4–8% of exposed

rock surfaces, dominated by the sole indicator species, *Grimmia anodon* (estimates derived from boxplots). Compared to the other two forest types, these rock bryophyte communities are much less productive and variable (fig. 30). Presumably, the desert-like climate associated with this low-elevation forest greatly limits productivity and constrains diversity. In addition, many bryophytes in the pinyon-juniper woodland establish on rocks near or just below the edge of the South Rim (e.g. West Rim Trail & South Kaibab Trail) where updrafts from the Inner Canyon create an even hotter climate (Halvorson 1972), and where evaporative water loss from bryophyte tissues must be rapid due to high winds and direct sun exposure. The majority of rock bryophytes in this forest experience direct sun for much of the day, although rock ledges, cavities, and overhangs can buffer this light intensity. Scattered *Pinus edulis* and *Juniperus osteosperma* trees provide shade for a small part of the day, but only to those rocks immediately beneath their compact, low-standing canopies. Although studies of rock bryophytes in mesic habitats have found disturbance important to maintaining diversity (e.g. gap-formation that enables recruitment of new species and prevents competitive exclusion; Slack 1997), it appears that frequent disturbance events (i.e. monsoons, erosion, and ice melt) within the rim habitat of this forest type, do not play a similar role. Although I occasionally observed gaps in established bryophyte colonies, I surmise that limitations to spore and propagule establishment are more likely the factor constraining recruitment (Wiklund and Rydin 2004) of species in this hot, dry woodland.

4.5.2.2 Ponderosa pine and mixed conifer forests. The abundance and species composition of rock bryophyte communities in the ponderosa pine and mixed conifer forests are more heterogonous than those in the pinyon-juniper woodland (figs. 28, 29, 30). Trail corridors through these forests display bryophyte communities that usually cover 5–20% of exposed rock surfaces and typically comprise 2–5 species (estimates derived from boxplots.). With the exception of composition, epilithic bryophyte assemblages in the ponderosa pine forest are difficult to delineate because they resemble those in both other forest types in terms of either abundance, richness and diversity, or indicator species. Although the strong indicator species,

Grimmia alpestris, dominates rocks in the ponderosa pine forest, it cannot effectively distinguish this forest type from the mixed conifer forest because it is also a significant indicator species in the latter (table 8). I presume the lack of differentiation between bryophyte assemblages in the ponderosa and mixed conifer forest reflects the broad environmental tolerance of the ponderosa forest, evidenced by its large elevation range in the sample (fig. 33).

Epilithic bryophyte communities in the mixed conifer forest are distinguished by higher species richness, diversity, and evenness (table 9). Additionally, 11 unique indicator species occur frequently, the strongest of which are *Orthotrichum* spp. and *Pseudoleskeella tectorum* (table 8). This significant pattern is likely explained by climate, as the majority of sites in this high-elevation forest exceed 2,400 m (8,000 ft.); the local climate is cooler, precipitation rates are higher, and evaporation rates are lower than those experienced by most sites in the ponderosa pine forest (table 6). Furthermore, the increased tree density and relatively closed canopy of this forest probably contribute to humidity levels more favorable to bryophytes (table 6; Merkle 1952, 1962).

4.5.2.3 Environmental and biotic correlates with species composition. Across the forests of GRCA, rock type and elevation seem to be the strongest environmental drivers for bryophyte community change, of the variables explored. Along these two correlated gradients, changes in composition include increasing richness and cover and transitions between dominant species (fig 30). These trends substantiate the importance of both climate and substratum to bryophytes and will be discussed further in section 4.5.3.

In most plant communities, abundant and frequent species structure major changes in composition across space, while the sporadic occurrences of rare species have little effect (McCune & Grace 2002). My results agree with this trend in that four dominant bryophyte species were highly correlated with gradients in composition across the three forests. The relative abundance of *Grimmia alpestris* appears to increase exponentially with elevation and the number of sandstone rocks sampled at a site (fig. 31). Almost in perfect opposition, the relative abundance of *Grimmia anodon* was inversely related to the rock-elevation gradient, favoring limestone rocks in the pinyon-juniper woodland at low elevations (fig. 31). *Orthotrichum* spp. was not linearly related to this rock-elevation gradient, but was found to peak in abundance at intermediate levels where elevation is moderate and sites contain a combination of both sandstone and limestone rocks. The most commonly sampled species of *Orthotrichum*, *O. hallii*, is known to favor relatively mesic and shaded, calcareous sandstone or limestone cliffs (FNA eds. 2007+, Lewinsky-Haapasaari and Norris 1998). This realized niche coupled with the species' strong relationship to axis 1, leads me to speculate that compositional change along this unexplained axis may be driven in part by a fine-scale moisture gradient (figs. 30, 31).

Current ecological theory predicts that some component of variability in bryophyte richness, abundance, and composition will be attributable to environmental and biotic filters operating at finer scales than that of forest type (Rydin 2009), and thus I have begun to explore what habitat factors may be relevant to bryophytes at the site-scale.

4.5.3 Site-level predictors of rock bryophyte responses

The distribution and abundance of bryophytes are known broadly to be a function of both large and fine-scaled environmental factors (e.g. Hattaway 1980, Mills & McDonald 2005, Økland 1994). My results suggest that at least rock type (proportion of limestone and sandstone sampled at each site) and slope (of the underlying topography) may explain additional variation in several rock bryophyte responses, independent of forest type and elevation

(table 10). This result aligns with our understanding of substratum specificity and microhabitat sensitivity displayed by many bryophyte species (Wiklund & Rydin 2004, Pharo & Beattie 2002, Sagar & Wilson 2009).

4.5.3.1 Rock type. Specifically, my results suggest that some feature differentiating limestone and sandstone rock may affect bryophyte species composition and abundance. With respect to composition, this signal certainly reflects at least a gradient of rock pH, known to determine substratum specificity in many epilithic bryophytes (Aho & Weaver 2006, Downing 1992, Nagano 1969). Although, the majority of sites (87/104) in GRCA occurred within the Kaibab Limestone Formation, the diversity of rock types within this formation is great, and ranges from calcareous limestone to acidic sandstone, including many intermediates (McKee 1938).

Clearly, *Grimmia anodon and G. alpestris*, two dominant, obligate rock mosses are responding to this pH gradient. The ecological distribution of these two species in the park aligns with their documented niches at large (FNA eds. 2007+). Specifically, the calcifuge (plant that does not grow well in lime-rich soil), *Grimmia alpestris*, appears to favor acidic sandstone at moderate to high elevations, while the calcicole (plant that thrives in lime-rich soil) *Grimmia anodon*, thrives on calcareous limestones and calcareous sandstones at lower elevations (fig. 30, 31, 32).

The NMS ordination vectors of percent cover and percent sandstone are positively correlated (i.e. both vectors are oriented in similar directions), suggesting that sandstone rocks may support higher bryophyte cover than do limestone rocks (fig. 30); this trend will be discussed in more detail in the next subsection. The observed relationship between abundance and rock type has varied by region and climate (Bates 1978, Downing 1992, Nagano 1969), and in some cases may be confounded with macro-environmental effects. One possible mechanism for lower cover on limestone rocks may be a shorter water retention period. Aho and Weaver (2006) determined the duration of water retention for nine limestone cliffs in Yellowstone National Park to be less than 2 hours, which was extremely short compared to a volcanic stone (andesite), which retained water for over 26 hours after saturation. I am not aware of a comparable study assessing the water-holding capacity of sandstone, but it likely varies greatly depending on the porosity of the bedding material.

4.5.3.2 Slope. The significant site-level variable of slope was able to explain additional variation in species richness, total cover, and composition, but the moderate significance and small partial correlation coefficient in each model suggests this signal may not be ecologically relevant (table 10). Nonetheless, slope is known to impact the duration of daily sun exposure experienced by a site. Consequently, it affects water-retention by local substrata, and in exposed situations, this effect can become more pronounced. Water retention is critical to bryophyte growth and thus it comes as no surprise that this variable has been a significant environmental correlate to bryophyte responses on many substrata in other studies (e.g. Pharo and Beattie 2002, Eldridge and Tozer 1997, Weibull and Rydin 2005).

4.5.3.3 Significant interactions between predictors. Notably, significant interaction terms exist in the PERMANOVA models of bryophyte total cover and community composition. these interaction terms suggest that the precise linear relationship between each response variable and the corresponding continuous predictor (elevation, slope, or percent limestone) depends on the forest type (table 10). However, these significant interactions are most likely an artifact of the nonrandom distribution of elevation, slope, and percent limestone among the three forest types; in other words, there was a lack of

independence between each of these continuous predictors and forest type (fig. 33), which could give rise to significant interaction terms because continuous predictor variables could not be sampled uniformly within each forest type. Therefore, I suggest that although these interaction terms were statistically significant, they most likely are not ecologically informative.

4.5.3.4 Confounded predictor variables. Seeking relationships between species responses and the environment becomes more complex in systems like Grand Canyon where many environmental variables, such as geology, topography, and biotic communities, co-vary with elevation. The NMS ordination illustrates several intercorrelated environmental variables (forest type, elevation, rock type). These environmental variables were significant predictors in modeling species richness, total cover, and composition (table 10), but their effects on these bryophyte responses are confounded. For example, the proportion of limestone rock sampled decreased with elevation from the pinyon-juniper forest to the mixed conifer forest (fig. 33), raising the question, which variable, rock type or forest type (or both), was responsible for the observed pattern in bryophyte abundance and community composition?

I began to explore this question by analyzing whether rock type correlated with bryophyte abundance, independent of elevation (selecting the variable elevation instead of forest type because the former is a more precise measure of climate). I used a subset of the data (sites with all limestone or all sandstone rocks) in a type I sequential sums of squares PERMANOVA to test the significance of the factor rock type (two levels: sandstone or limestone) on total bryophyte percent cover after subtracting the effects of the covariate, elevation. The PERMANOVA model indicated that rock type accounts for 14% of variation in total cover ($F = 18.4$, $P = 0.0001$), independent of elevation ($F = 27.4$, $R^2 = 0.21$, $P = 0.0001$) and the interaction term was not significant ($F = 0.18$, $R^2 = 0.001$, $P = 0.66$); this model suggests that rock type affects bryophyte abundance at all elevations. A future publication will employ a more complex model to disentangle the relative importance of the intercorrelated environmental variables on bryophyte responses.

4.5.3.5 Insignificant environmental variables.

At the site-scale, this study did not reveal a significant relationship between bryophyte responses and PDIR, aspect, or shade cover; however, the absence of signal at the site-scale does not preclude the possibility that these variables may be operating at finer scales, potentially at the scale of the rocks themselves. In this study, these three variables were reported at the site-scale, but measurements were taken on three individual rocks and averaged to create a site-level metric; this averaging may have cancelled effects present on individual rocks, especially considering that the slope and aspect of smaller rocks could vary greatly within one site.

Aspect, PDIR, and shade cover are presumably important to rock bryophytes in arid and exposed environments such as that found throughout much of GRCA, where their mediating effect on microclimate is likely pronounced and may override local environmental conditions determined by elevation (Berryman and McCune 2006). To my knowledge no one has examined the relationship between PDIR and rock bryophyte communities, but this variable was strongly related to lichen and bryophyte composition of soil crust communities measured at the plot scale (i.e. no averaging) in a sagebrush-steppe ecosystem within the Colombia Basin of Washington (Ponzetti et al. 2007). Lastly, both aspect and shade have been reported as significant correlates to bryophyte cover and composition and may be important to rock bryophytes in GRCA at the scae of individual rocks (e.g. Alpert 1985, Anderson et al. 1995, Bowker et al. 2006, Eldridge and Tozer 1997).

4.5.3.6 Unmeasured variables.

In addition to considerations of scale, there are certainly other biotic and abiotic variables I did not measure that may be eliciting an effect on bryophyte responses. Rock microhabitat features, recruitment limitations, species interactions, and stochasticity of dispersal are likely at play (Ingerpuu et al. 2003, Mills and McDonald 2005, Rydin 1997, Schofield 1992, Sim-Sim et al. 2011).

Considering the arid climate of GRCA, the most important of these factors may be the influence of rock features on microhabitat moisture retention and humidity within individual rocks. I observed many bryophytes appearing to capitalize on such features, including shaded overhangs, water-channeling crevices, water-retaining cavities, and cooler north-facing surfaces, however, it is notable that the two dominant species of *Grimmia* sampled are adapted to exposed rock surfaces and thus may have microdistributions less confined by these rock features (Alpert 1985).

In wetter ecosystems, rock size and within-boulder habitat diversity (Kimmerer and Driscoll 2000, Weibull and Rydin 2005), rock connectivity (Virtanen and Øksanen 2007), and rock slope and aspect (Alpert 1985, Pharo and Beattie 2002) have been significantly correlated to bryophyte richness, abundance, or composition. I hypothesize that the most important of these variables in GRCA are those which increase the water-holding capacity of small sections of rock; such microhabitat features may be critical to successful recruitment of spores and propagules in their early stages of growth and development (Wiklund and Rydin 2004).

4.5.4 Conclusions and conservation implications

I have reported that macroclimate, approximated by forest type, can explain 10–19% of variation in rock bryophyte communities throughout the pinyon-juniper, ponderosa pine, and mixed conifer forests of GRCA. Based on the large amount of variation that remains unexplained, my results allude to the possibility that the distribution and abundance of rock bryophyte communities in Grand Canyon National Park may be driven more by microhabitat and microclimatic variation than by substantial changes in local climate along a 1,000 m elevation gradient. The rock-level analyses necessary to explore such relationships are possible with data I have collected on individual rocks. These results will be presented in a future publication.

The small size and complex taxonomy of rock-dwelling bryophytes in the American Southwest pose serious challenges to diversity-minded monitoring in terms of time and available expertise. Continued research is required to clarify our understanding of how these bryophytes respond to environmental gradients at various spatial scales across arid and semiarid landscapes. Ideally, what is needed is a monitoring framework general enough for non-bryologists to employ in protected state and national parks and multi-use public lands. This study explored the potential utility of forest type to serve as the foundation for such a simple, non-mechanistic model. My results indicate that forest type can provide only part of such a meaningful plan. A more appropriate framework should incorporate microhabitat variation occurring at the scale of individual

rocks. Clearly, future bryological work in the aridlands of North America is required to expand and refine multi-scaled models that can predict the distributions and abundances of small rock-dwelling bryophytes.

4.6 Final remarks

Bryophytes are an ecologically important group of plants that contribute substantially to biodiversity and facilitate many ecosystem functions, even in arid regions where their productivity is lowest. Our continued pursuit to understand the magnitude and implication of these roles in the arid regions of North America is founded on baseline assessments of diversity and community patterns across these landscapes. To this end, the results presented herein establish such a baseline for rock-dwelling bryophytes in Grand Canyon National Park and will provide a foundation for future biogeographical comparisons, climate-change studies, and diversity monitoring in and beyond the Grand Canyon region. Furthermore, I hope this report will raise awareness about the ubiquity of aridland bryophytes and encourage National Park Service and public land agencies to more fully integrate these often overlooked plants into their management plans and outreach curricula.

5 Literature cited

Aho, K. and T. Weaver. 2006. Measuring water relations and pH of crypto-gam rock-surface environments. The Bryologist 109: 348–357.

Alpert, P. 1985. Distribution quantified by microdistribution in an assemblage of epilithic mosses. Vegetatio 64: 131–139.

Anderson, M. J. 2001. A new method for non-parametric multivariate analysis of variance. Austral Ecology 26: 32–46.

Anderson, M. J. 2006. Distance-based tests for homogeneity of multivariate dispersions. Biometrics 62: 246–253.

Anderson, D. S., R. B. Davis and J. A. Jans-sens.1995. Relationships of bryophytes and lichens to environmental gradients in Maine peatlands. Plant Ecology 120: 147–159.

Anderson, M. J., K. E. Ellingsen, and B. H. McArdle. 2006. Multivariate dispersion as a measure of beta diversity. Ecology Letters 9: 683–693.

Anderson, D. C., K. T. Harper, and R. C. Holmgren. 1982. Factors influencing development of cryptogamic soil crusts in Utah deserts. Journal of Range Management 35: 180–185.

Asada, T., B. G. Warner and A. Banner. 2003. Growth of mosses in relation to climate factors in a hyper-maritime coastal peatland in British Columbia, Canada. The Bryologist 106: 516–527.

Austrheim, G. 2002. Plant diversity patterns in a semi-natural grassland along an elevational gradient in southern Norway. Plant Ecology 161: 193–205.

Bartram, E. B. 1924. New mosses from southern Arizona. The Bryologist 27: 70–73.

Bartram, E. B. 1927. Some Arizona mosses not previously reported from the United States. Ibid. 30: 45–50.

Bates, J. W. 1978. The influence of metal availability on the bryophyte and macrolichen vegetation of four rock types on Skye and Rhum. Journal of Ecology 66: 457 – 482.

Bates, S. T., A. Barber, E. Gilbert, R. T. Schroeder, & T. H. Nash III. 2010. A Revised Catalog of Arizona Lichens. Canotia 6: 26–43.

Belnap, J. 1993. Recovery rates of cryp-tobiotic crusts: inoculants use and assessment methods. Great Basin Naturalist 53: 89–95.

Belnap, J. 2002. Nitrogen fixation in biological soil crusts from southeast Utah, USA. Biology and Fertility of Soils 35: 128–135.

Belnap, J. 2003. Microbes and microfauna associated with biological soil crusts. Pages 168–174. In Belnap, J. and O. L. Lange (eds.), Biological Soil Crusts: Structure, Function, and Management, 2nd Edition. Springer, New York.

Belnap, J. and O. L. Lange (eds.). 2003. Biological Soil Crusts: Structure, Function, and Management, 2nd Edition. Springer, New York.

Berryman, S.and& B. McCune. 2006. Epiphytic lichens along gradients of topography and stand structure in western Oregon, USA. Pacific Northwest Fungi 1(2): 1–37.

Bewley, J. D. 1979. Physiological aspects of desiccation tolerance. Annual Review of Plant Physiology 30: 195–238.

Beymer, R. J. and J. M. Klopatek. 1991. Potential contribution of carbon by microphytic crusts in pinyon-juniper woodlands. Arid Soil Research and Rehabilitation 5: 187–198.

Beymer, R. J. and J. M. Klopatek. 1992. Effects of grazing on cryptogamic crusts in pinyon-juniper woodlands in Grand Canyon National Park. American Midland Naturalist 127: 139–148.

Billings, W. D. and W. B. Drew. 1938. Bark factors affecting the distribution of corticolous bryophytic communities. The Bryologist 20: 302 –330.

Birks, H. J. B., E. Heegaard, H. H. Birks, and B. Jonsgard. 1998. Quantifying bryophyte environmental relationships. Pages 305–319. In J. W. Bates, N. W. Ashton, & J. G. Duckett (eds.) Bryology for the Twenty-first Century. Leeds: Maney and British Bryological Society.

Bowers, F. D., C. M. Delgadillo,and A. J. Sharp. 1976. The Mosses of Baja California. Journal of the Hattori Botanical Society 40: 397–410.

Bowker, M., J. Belnap, D. W. Davidson and H. Goldstein. 2006. Correlates of biological soil crust abundance across a continuum of spatial scales: support for a hierarchical conceptual model. Journal of Applied Ecology 43: 152–163.

Bowker, M., L. R. Stark, D. N. McLetchie and B. D. Mishler. 2000. Sex expression, skewed sex ratios, and microhabitat distribution in the dioicous desert moss Syntrichia caninervis (Pottiaceae). American Journal of Botany 87: 517–526.

Boykin, M. A. and T. H. Nash III. 1995. The lichen flora of Grand Canyon National Park, Arizona. Journal of the Arizona-Nevada Academy of Science 28: 59–69.

Breed, W. J. and E. Roat. 1976. Geology of the Grand Canyon. Museum of Northern Arizona and Grand Canyon Natural History Association. Northland Press, Flagstaff, AZ.

Brian, N. 2000. Checklist of non-vascular plants of Grand Canyon National Park, Arizona. Notulae Naturae No. 474. The Academy of Natural Sciences of Philadelphia.

Brotherson, J. D., S. R. Rushforth and J. R. Johansen. 1983. Effects of long-term grazing on cryptogam crust cover in Navajo National Monument, Arizona. Journal of Rangeland Management 35: 579–581.

Chambers, J. M. and T. J. Hastie. 1992. Statistical Models in S. Wadsworth and Brooks/Cole.

Churchill, S. P. 1991. The floristic composition and elevational distribution of Colombian mosses. The Bryologist 94: 157–167.

Cleavitt, N. 2001. Disentangling moss species limitations: the role of physiologically based substratum specificity for six species occurring on substrata with varying pH and percent organic matter. The Bryologist 104: 59–68.

Cleavitt, N. 2005. Patterns, hypotheses and processes in the biology of rare bryophytes. The Bryologist 108: 554–566.

Clover, E. U. and L. Jotter. 1944. Floristic studies in the Canyon of the Colorado and tributaries. American Midland Naturalist 32: 591–642.

Cole, D. N. 1991. Trampling disturbance and recovery of cryptogamic soil crusts in Grand Canyon National Park. Great Basin Naturalist 50: 321–325.

Conover, W. J., M. E. Johnson, and M. M. Johnson. 1981. A comparative study of tests for homogeneity of variances, with applications to the outer continental shelf bidding data. Technometrics 23: 351–361.

Corrales, A., A. Duque, J. Uribe, and V. Londoño. 2010. Abundance and diversity patterns of terrestrial bryophyte species in secondary and planted montane forests in the northern portion of the Central Cordillera of Colombia. The Bryologist 113: 8–21.

Crosby, M. R., R. E. Magill, B. Allen, and S. He. 1999. Checklist of mosses [of the world]. Missouri Botanical Garden, St. Louis, Missouri.

Damon, P. E. and B. J. Giletti. 1961. The age of the basement rocks of the Colorado Plateau and adjacent areas. Annals of the New York Academy of Science 91: 443–453.

Daubenmire, R. F. 1943. Vegetational zonation in the Rocky Mountains. Botanical Review 9: 325–393.

Debano, L. F., J. N Rinne & M. B. Baker, Jr. 2003. Management of Natural Resources in Riparian Corridors. Arizona-Nevada Academy of Science 35: 58–70.

Downing, A. J. 1992. Distribution of bryophytes on limestone in eastern Australia. The Bryologist 95: 5–14.

Dufrene, M. and P. Legendre. 1997. Species assemblages and indicator species: the need for a flexible asymmetrical approach. Ecological Monographs 67: 345–366.

Eldridge, D. J. 1998. Trampling of microphytic crusts on calcareous soils and its impact on erosion under rain-impacted flow. Catena 33: 221–239.

Eldridge, D. J. & R. A. Bradstock. 1994. The effect of time since fire on the cover and composition of soil crusts on a eucalypt shrubland soil. Cunninghamii 3: 521–527.

Eldridge, D. J. and M. E. Tozer. 1997. Environmental factors relating to the distribution of terricolous bryophytes and lichens in semi-arid eastern Australia. The Bryologist 100: 28–39.

Faith, D. P., P. R. Minchin and L. Belbin. 1987. Compositional dissimilarity as a robust measure of ecological distance. Vegetation 69: 57–68.

FNA (Flora of North America) Editorial Committee, eds. 2007+. Flora of North America North of Mexico. Vol. 27, 28, and 29. New York and Oxford.

Ford, T. D., W. J. Breed, and J. S. Mitchell. 1972. Name and age of the Upper Precambrian basalts in the eastern Grand Canyon. Geological Society of America Bulletin 83: 223–226.

Frahm, J.-P. 2002. Ecology of bryophytes along altitudinal and latitudinal gradients in Chile. Studies in austral temperate rain forest bryophytes. Tropical Bryology 21: 67–79.

Frahm, J.-P. 2008. Diversity, dispersal, and biogeography of bryophytes (mosses). Biodiversity and Conservation 17: 277 – 284.

Frahm, J.-P. and S. R. Gradstein. 1991. An altitudinal zonation of tropical rain forests using bryophytes. Journal of Biogeography 18: 669 – 678.

Frahm, J.-P. and R. Ohlemüller. 2001. Ecology of bryophytes along altitudinal and latitudinal gradients in New Zealand. Studies in austral temperate rain forest bryophytes. Tropical Bryology 20: 117 – 137.

Glime, J. M. 2007. Physiological Ecology. In Bryophyte Ecology Volume 1 Ebook. Michigan Technological University & ABLS. Available at: http://www.bryoecol.mtu.edu/. Accessed on 12/11/2011.

Greene, R. S. B., C. J. Charles, and K. C. Hodgkinson. 1990. The effects of fire on the soil in a degraded semi-arid woodland. In Cryptogam cover and physical and micromorphological properties. Australian Journal of Soil Research 28: 755 – 777.

Hallingbäck, T. and B. C. Tan. 2010. Past and present activities and future strategy of bryophyte conservation. Phytotaxa 9: 266–274.

Halvorson, W. L. 1972. Environmental influence on the pattern of plant communities along the North Rim of Grand Canyon. American Midland Naturalist 87: 222 – 235.

Haring, I. M. 1941. Mosses of the Grand Canyon National Park. The Bryologist 44: 122 – 125.

Haring, I. M. 1946. Mosses of the Grand Canyon National Park, Arizona II. The Bryologist 49: 90 – 96.

Haring, I. M. 1947. A checklist of the mosses of the state of Arizona. The Bryologist 50: 189 – 201.

Haring, I. M. 1961. A checklist of the mosses of the state of Arizona. The Bryologist 64: 222–240.

Hattaway, R. A. 1980. The calciphilous bryophytes of three limestone sinks in Eastern Tennessee. The Bryologist 83: 161–169.

Hawbecker, A. C. 1936. Check-list of plants of Grand Canyon National Park. Grand Canyon Natural History Association. Bulletin No. 6, revised edition.

Hedenas, L. 2007. Global diversity patterns among pleurocarpous mosses. The Bryologist 110: 319–331.

Hirsch, R. V., J. F. Walker, J. C. Day and R. Kallio. 1990. The influence of man on hydrologic systems. Pages 329–359. In M. G. Wolman and H. C. Riggs (eds.). Surface water hydrology. The Geology of North America. Vols 0–1. Geological Society of America, Boulder, Colorado.

Holm, S. 1979. A simple sequentially rejective multiple test procedure. Scandinavian Journal of Statistics 6: 65–70.

Howell, J. 1941. Piñon and juniper woodlands of the southwest. Joural of Forestry 39: 542–545.

Huisinga, K., L. Makarick, and K. Watters. 2006. River and Desert Plants of the Grand Canyon. Mountain Press Publishing Company, Missoula, Montana.

Huttunen, S., A. Gardiner, and M. S. Ignatov. 2007. Additional comments on the phylogeny of the Brachytheciaceae (Bryophyta). In Newton, A.E. and R. Tangney (eds.) Pleurocarpous mosses: systematics and evolution. CRC Press, Boca Raton-London-New York (Systematic Association Special Volume 71): 117–143

Huttunen, S. and M. S. Ignatov. 2004. Phylogeny of the Brachytheciaceae (Bryophyta) based on morphology and sequence level data. Cladistics 20: 151–183.

Ignatov, M. S. and S. Huttunen. 2002. Brachytheciaceae (Bryophyta)—a family of sibling genera. Arctoa 11: 245–296.

Ingerpuu, N., K. Vellak, J. Liira, and M. Pärtel. 2003. Relationships between species richness patterns in deciduous forests at the north Estonian limestone escarpment. Journal of Vegetation Science 14: 773–780.

Johansen, J. R., L. L. St. Clair, B. L. Webb, and G. T. Nebeker. 1984. Recovery patterns of cryptogamic soil crusts in desert rangelands following fire disturbance. The Bryologist 87: 238–243.

Johnson, A. B. 1978. Keys to the mosses of Arizona. MNA Research Paper 14. Museum of Northern Arizona, Flagstaff, Arizona.

Kimmerer, R. W. and M. J. Driscoll. 2000. Bryophyte species richness on insular boulder habitats: the effect of area, isolation, and microhabitat diversity. The Bryologist 103: 748–756.

Kleiner, E. F. and K. T. Harper. 1977. Soil properties in relation to cryptogamic groundcover in Canyonlands

National Park. Journal of Rangeland Management 30: 202–205.

Kammerer, J. C. 1992. Largest Rivers in the United States. Department of the Interior, United States Geological Survey. Available at: <http://pubs.water.usgs.gov/ofr87242>. Accessed on 4/15/2011.

Kruskal, J. B. 1964. Multidimensional scaling by optimizing goodness of fit to a nonmetric hypothesis. Psychometrika 29: 1–27.

Lévesque, E. 1996. Minimum area and cover-abundance scales as applied to polar desert vegetation Arctic and Alpine Research 28: 156 – 162.

Lewinsky-Haapasaari, J. and D. H. Norris. 1998. *Orthotrichum shevockii* (Orthotricaceae), a new moss species from the Southern Sierra, California. The Bryologist 101: 435–438.

Longton, R. E. 1988. Life-history strategies among bryophytes of arid regions. Journal of the Hattori Botanical Laboratory 64: 15–28.

Longton, R. E. 1992. The role of bryophytes and lichens in terrestrial ecosystems. Pages 32 – 76. In Bates, J. W. and A. M. Farmer (eds.), Bryophytes and Lichens in a Changing Environment. Clarendon Press, Oxford.

Magill, R. E. 1976. Mosses of Big Bend National Park, Texas. The Bryologist 79: 269 – 295.

McCleary, J. A. 1953. Additions to the Arizona moss flora. The Bryologist 56: 121–126.

McCleary, J. A. 1954. Notes on Arizona mosses – Pottiaceae. The Bryologist 57: 238–241.

McCleary, J. A. 1959. The bryophytes of a desert region in Arizona. The Bryologist 62: 58–62.

McCleary, J. A. 1962. The distributional studies of Arizona mosses. The

American Midland Naturalist 67: 68 – 78.

McCune, B. and J. A. Antos. 1982. Epiphyte communities in the Swan Valley, Montana. The Bryologist: 85: 1 – 12.

McCune, B. and J. B. Grace. 2002. Analysis of Ecological Communities. MjM Software Design, Glenenden Beach, Oregon.

McCune, B. and D. Keon. 2002. Equations for potential annual direct incident radiation and heat load. Journal of Vegetation Science 13: 603 – 606.

McCune, B. and M. J. Mefford. 1999. PC-ORD. Multivariate Analysis of Ecological Data, Version 4.0. MjM Software, Glenenden Beach, Oregon, USA.

McDougal, W. B. 1947a. Plants of Grand Canyon National Park Bulletin No. 10. Grand Canyon Natural History Association, Grand Canyon, Arizona.

McDougal, W. B. 1947b. Plants of Grand Canyon National Park Bulletin No. 10 Addendum to Checklist of Plants of Grand Canyon National Park. Pages 106 – 107. Grand Canyon Natural History Association, Grand Canyon, Arizona.

McDougal, W. B. 1948. Plants of Grand Canyon National Park Bulletin No. 10 Supplement, July 1948. Grand Canyon Natural History Association, Grand Canyon, AZ.

McKee, E. D. 1933. The Coconino sandstone – its history and origin. In Contributions to Palaeontology. Carnegie Institution of Washington Publication No. 440: 77 – 115.

McKee, E. D. 1936. Preliminary report on the Tonto Group of the Grand Canyon, Arizona. In Contributions to Grand Canyon Geology. Natural History Bulletin No. 5. National

Park Service, Grand Canyon National Park, Grand Canyon Natural History Association.

McKee, E. D. 1937. Researches on Paleozoic stratigraphy in western Grand Canyon. In Carnegie Institution of Washington Year Book 36: 340–343.

McKee, E. D. 1938. The environment and history of the Toroweap and Kaibab formations of northern Arizona and southern Utah, Publication No. 492. Carnegie Institution of Washington, Washington D. C.

McKee, E. D. 1982. Ancient landscapes of the Grand Canyon region: the geology of Grand Canyon, Zion, Bryce, Petrified Forest and Painted Desert. Northland Press, Flagstaff, Arizona.

McKee, E. D. and R. C. Gutschick. 1969. History of the Redwall Limestone of northern Arizona. Geological Society of America Memoirs 114.

McKee, E. D. and E. H. McKee. 1972. Pliocene uplift of the Grand Canyon region, time of drainage adjustment. Geological Society of America Bulletin 83: 1923–1932.

Merkle, J. 1952. An analysis of a pinyon-juniper community at Grand Canyon, Arizona. Ecology 33: 375-384.

Merkle, J. 1954. An analysis of the spruce-fir community of the Kaibab Plateau, Arizona. Ecology 33: 316-322.

Merkle, J. 1962. Plant communities of the Grand Canyon area, Arizona. Ecology 43: 698-711.

Miller, N. G. 2009. Lichens and bryophytes of the alpine and subalpine zones of Katahdin, Maine, III. Bryophytes. The Bryologist 112: 704–748.

Mills, S. E. and E. MacDonald. 2005. Factors influencing bryophyte assemblage at different scales in the western Canadian boreal forest. The Bryologist 108: 86–100.

Mishler, B. D. and M. J. Oliver. 2009. Annual Plant Reviews 36: 1–15. Available at: www.interscience.wiley.com.

Mitchell, W. A. and H. G. Hughes. 1995. Line Intercept, Technical Report EL-95-22, Section 6.2.5. In U.S. Army Corps of Engineers Wildlife Resources Management Manual. Washington, DC.

Moir, W. H. and J. A. Ludwig. 1979. A classification of spruce fir and mixed conifer habitat types of Arizona and New Mexico. USDA Forest Service Research Paper RM-207, Rocky Mountain Forest and Range Experiment Station, Fort Collins, Colorado.

Monge-Nájera, J. 1989. The relationship between epiphyllous liverworts with leaf characteristics and light in Monte Verde, Costa Rica. Cryptogamie: Bryologie et Lichenologie 10: 345–352.

Morgan, J. W. 2006. Bryophyte mats inhibit germination of non-native species in burnt temperate native grassland remnants. Biological Invasions 8: 159–168.

Nagano, I. 1969. Comparative studies of moss vegetation developing on the limestone, chert, and other rocks lying adjacent to each other in the Chichibu Mountain area, Central Japan. Journal of the Hattori Botanical Laboratory 32: 155–203.

Nash, T. H., S. L. White, and J. E. Marsh. 1977. Lichen and moss distribution and biomass in hot desert ecosystems. The Bryologist 80: 471–479.

NatureServe. 2010. International Ecological Classification Standard: Terrestrial Ecological Classifications. NatureServe Central Databases, Arlington, Virginia. Accessed 16 July 2010.

Noble, L. F. and J. F. Hunter. 1916. A

reconnaissance of the Achaean complex of the Granite Gorge, Grand Canyon, Arizona. United States Geological Society Professional Paper 98: 95–113.

Økland, R. H. 1994. Patterns of bryophyte associations at different spatial scales in a Norwegian boreal spruce forest. Journal of Vegetation Science 5: 127–138.

Øksanen, J., F. G. Blanchet, R. Kindt, P. Legendre, R. B. O'Hara, G. L. Simpson, P. Solymos, M. Henry H. Stevens, and H. Wagner. 2010. Vegan: Community Ecology Package. R package version 1.17-2. Available at http://CRAN.R-project.org/package=vegan.

Patraw, P. M. 1932. Preliminary Checklist of Plants of Grand Canyon National Park. U.S.D.I. National Park Service, Grand Canyon National Park Technical Bulletin No. 6.

Pearson, G. A. 1920. Factors controlling the distribution of forest types, part 1. Ecology 1: 139–159.

Pharo, E. J. and A. J. Beattie. 2002. The association between substratum variability and bryophyte and lichen diversity in eastern Australian forests. The Bryologist 105: 11–26.

Phillips, B. G., A. M. Phillips, and M. S. Bernzott. 1987. Annotated Checklist of Vascular Plants of Grand Canyon, Monograph No. 7. Grand Canyon Natural History Association.

Ponzetti, J. M., B. McCune, and D. A. Pike. 2007. Biotic soil crusts in relation to topography, cheatgrass, and fire in the Columbia Basin, Washington. The Bryologist 110: 706–722.

Proctor, M. C. F. 2009. Physiological ecology. Pages 237–263. In B. Goffinet and A. J. Shaw (eds.), Bryophyte Biology, 2nd Edition. Cambridge University Press, New York.

Proctor, M. C., M. J. Oliver, A. J. Wood, P.

Alpert, L. R. Stark, N. L. Cleavitt, and B. D. Mishler. 2007. Desiccation-tolerance in bryophytes: a review. The Bryologist 110: 595–621.

R Development Core Team. 2011. R (Version 2.10.1 and Version 2.14.1): A language and environment for statistical computing. R Foundation for Statistical Computing, Vienna, Austria. Available at http://www.R-project.org/.

Rahbek, C. 2005. The role of spatial scale and the perception of large-scale species richness patterns. Ecology Letters 8: 225–239.

Rambo, T. R. and P. S. Muir. 1998. Forest floor bryophytes of Pseudotsuga menziesii-Tsuga heterophylla stands in Oregon: influences of substratum and overstory. The Bryologist 101: 116–130.

Rasmussen, D. I. 1941. Biotic Communities of Kaibab Plateau, Arizona. Ecological Monographs 11: 229–275.

Rivera-Aguilar, V., G. Montejano, S. Rodíguez-Zaragoza, and A. Durán-Diaz. 2006. Distribution and composition of cyanobacteria, mosses, and lichens of the biological soil crusts of the Tehuacán Valley, Puebla, México. Journal of Arid Environments 67: 208–225.

Roberts, D. W. 2010. labdsv: Ordination and Multivariate Analysis for Ecology. R package version 1.4-1. Available at http://CRAN.R-project.org/package=labdsv.

Rydin, H. 1997. Competition among bryophytes. Advances in Bryology 6: 135–168.

Rydin, H. 2009. Population and community ecology of bryophytes. Pages 393–444. In B. Goffinet and A. J. Shaw (eds.), Bryophyte Biology, 2nd Edition. Cambridge University Press, New York.

Sagar, T. and P. Wilson. 2009. Niches of common bryophytes in a semi-arid landscape. The Bryologist 112: 30–41.

Schmidt, J. C., D. C. Rubin, and H. Ikeda. 1993. Flume simulation of recirculating flow and sedimentation. Water Resources Research 29: 2925–2939.

Schofield, W. B. 1981. Ecological significance of morphological characters in the moss gametophyte. Bryologist 84: 149–165.

Schofield, W. B. 1984. Bryogeography of the Pacific Coast of North America. Journal of the Hattori Botanical Laboratory 55: 35–43.

Schofield, W. B. 1992. Bryophyte distribution patterns. Pages 103–130. In J. W. Bates and A. M. Farmer (eds.). Bryophytes in a Changing Climate. Oxford, Clarendon.

Schofield, W. B. and H. A. Crum. 1972. Disjunctions in bryophytes. Annals of the Missouri Botanical Garden 59: 174–202.

Sellers, W. D. and R. H. Hill (eds.). 1974. Arizona climate, 1931–1972. University of Arizona Press, Tucson, Arizona.

SEINet (Southwest Environmental Information Network). 2011. Available at http://swbiodiversity.org/seinet/index.php.

Sim-Sim M., A. Bergamini, L. Luís, S. Fontinha, S. Martins, C. Lobo, A. C. Figueiredo, J. G. Barroso, L. G. Pedro, and M. Stech. 2011. Epiphytic bryophyte diversity on Madeira Island: Effects of tree species on bryophyte species richness and composition. The Bryologist 114: 142–154.

Simpson, E. H. 1949. Measurement of diversity. Nature 163: 688.

Skartvedt, P. H. 2000. Woody riparian vegetation patterns in the upper Mimbres watershed, southwestern New Mexico. The Southwestern Naturalist 48: 6–14.

Slack, N. G. 1997. Niche theory and practice: bryophyte studies. Advances in Bryology 6: 169–204.

Slack, N. G. 2011. The ecological value of bryophytes as indicators of climate change. Pages 3–12. In T. Zoltán, T., N.G. Slack, and L. R. Stark (eds.), Bryophyte Ecology and Climate Change. Cambridge University Press, Cambridge, United Kingdom.

Spence, J. R. 2008. Spring-supported vegetation along the Colorado River on the Colorado Plateau. Floristics, vegetation structure and environment. Pages 185–210. In Stevens, L. E. and V. J. Meretsky (eds.). Aridland springs of North America: Ecology and conservation. University of Arizona Press, Tucson.

Spence, J. R., T. A. Clark, and J. Brinda. [In preparation.] Checklist of the bryophytes of Arizona.

Stark, L. R. 2004. In Churchill, S. P. and B. O'Shea. 2004. [Symposium] Moss diversity, a global perspective. Proceedings XVI International Botanical Congress.

Stark, L. R. and J. Brinda. 2011. An Investigation of Bryophyte Diversity and Distribution on the Grand Canyon-Parashant National Monument, Final Annual Report.

Stark, L. R. and R. C. Castetter. 1987. A gradient analysis of bryophyte populations in a desert mountain range. Memoirs of the New York Botanical Garden 45: 186–197.

Stark, L. R. and A. T. Whittemore. 2000. Bryophytes from the Northern Mojave Desert. The Southwestern Naturalist 45: 226–241.

Stark, L. R., A. T. Whittemore, and B. D. Mishler. 2001. Noteworthy bryophyte records from the Mojave Desert. Madroño 49: 49–53.

Stevens, D. L. and A. R. Olsen. 2004. Spatially balanced sampling of natural resources. Journal of the American Statistical Association 99: 262–278.

Stevens, L. E., J. C. Schmidt, T. J. Ayers, and B. T. Brown. 1995. Flow regulation, geomorphology, and Colorado River marsh development in the Grand Canyon, Arizona. Ecological Applications 5: 1025–1039.

Thompson, D. B., L. R. Walker, and L. R. Stark. 2005. The influence of elevation, shrub species, and biological soil crust on fertile islands in the Mojave Desert, USA.

Turner, R. M. and M. M. Karpiscak. 1980. Recent vegetation changes along the Colorado River between Glen Canyon Dam and Lake Mead, Arizona. U.S. Geological Survey Paper No. 1132.

Turner, P. A. M. and E. J. Pharo. 2005. Influence of substratum type and forest age on bryophyte species distribution in Tasmanian mixed forest. The Bryologist 108: 67–85.

USDA [United States Department of Agriculture]. 1938. Soils of the United States. Pages 979–1001. In Soils and Men: Yearbook of Agriculture 1938. U.S. Government Printing Office, Washington, D.C.

Vanderpoorten, A. and P. Engels. 2003. Patterns of bryophyte diversity and rarity at a regional scale. Biodiversity and Conservation 12: 545–553.

Vanderpoorten, A. and B. Goffinet. 2009. Ecological significance of bryophytes. Pages 26 – 42. In Introduction to Bryophytes. Cambridge University Press, United Kingdom.

Virtanen, R. and J. Øksanen. 2007. The effects of habitat connectivity on cryptogam richness in boulder metacommunity. Biological Conservation 135: 415–422.

Warren, S. D. 2003. Biological soil crusts and hydrology in North American deserts. Pages 328–337. In Belnap, J. and O. L. Lange (eds.) Biological Soil Crusts: Structure, Function, and Management, 2nd Edition. Springer, New York.

Warren, P. L., K. L. Reichhardt, D. A. Mouat, B. T. Brown, and R. R. Johnson. 1982. Vegetation of Grand Canyon National Park. Technical Report No. 9. Cooperative National Park Resources Studies Unit. University of Arizona, Tucson.

Weibull, H. 2001. Influence of tree species on the epilithic bryoflora in deciduous forests of Sweden. Journal of Bryology 23: 55–66.

Weibull, H. and Rydin, H. 2005. Bryophyte species richness on boulders: effects area, habitat diversity and covering tree species. Biological Conservation, 122: 71–79.

White, E. 1929. Flora of the Hermit Shale, Grand Canyon, Arizona. Carnegie Institution of Washington. Publication No. 405.

White, E. and J. L. Vankat 1993. Middle and high elevation coniferous forest communities of the North Rim Region of Grand Canyon National Park, Arizona, USA. Vegetatio 109: 161–174.

Whittaker, R. H. 1967. Gradient analysis of vegetation. Biological Review 42: 207–264.

Whittaker, R. H. 1972. Evolution and measurement of species diversity. Taxon 21: 213–251.

Wieder, R. K. and D. H. Vitt. 2006. Boreal Peatland Ecology. Springer-Verlag, Berline-Heidelburg, New York.

Wiklund, K. and H. Rydin. 2004. Ecophysiological constraints on spore establishment in bryophytes. Functional Ecology 18: 907–913.

Wood, S. N. 2004. Stable and efficient multiple smoothing parameter estimation for generalized additive models. Journal of the American Statistical Association 99: 673–686.

Wood, S. N. 2011. Fast, stable restricted maximum likelihood and marginal likelihood estimation of semiparametric generalized linear models. Journal of the Royal Statistical Society (B) 73: 3–36.

Woodbury, A. M. 1947. Distribution of pigmy conifers in Utah and northeastern Arizona. Ecology 28: 113–126.

WRCC. 2011. Western Regional Climate Center: Phantom Ranch, Bright Angel, and Grand Canyon NP 2 Stations. Available at http://www. wrcc.dri.edu/. Accessed on 24 April 2011.

Yee, T. W. and N. D. Mitchell. 1991. Generalized additive models in plant ecology. Journal of Vegetation Science 2: 587–602.

Zotz, G., A. Schweikert, W. Jetz, H. Westerman. 2000. Water Relations and Carbon Gain are Closely Related to Cushion Size in the Moss Grimmia pulvinata. New Phytologist 148: 59–67.

Appendix A: Annotations for historic bryophyte specimens

The Grand Canyon National Park Museum Herbarium (GRCA Herbarium) houses 324 historic bryophyte specimens collected prior to this project. Below are 161 annotated specimens: 87 nomenclatural updates (Nomenclature), 67 new determinations (Determination), and 7 unlikely determinations awaiting review (Undetermined; see also Catalog of Excluded Taxa). Historic determinations (Historic Name) are included with each collection; additional information can be acquired from the GRCA Herbarium with reference to Catalog Numbers. Of the remaining 156 historic collections, 118 required no annotation (correct determinations presumed and nomenclature unrevised); 38 await verification, likely misidentified; and 7 were not fit for review.

Catalog number	Family	Modern name	Modern author	Annotation type	Historic name
GRCA 51655	Amblystegiaceae	Amblystegium serpens	(Hedwig) Schimper	Nomenclature	Amblystegium juratzkanum Schimp.
GRCA 51654	Amblystegiaceae	Amblystegium serpens	(Hedwig) Schimper	Nomenclature	Amblystegium juratzkanum Schimp.
GRCA 51653	Amblystegiaceae	Amblystegium serpens	(Hedwig) Schimper	Nomenclature	Amblystegium juratzkanum Schimp.
GRCA 53214	Amblystegiaceae	Conardia compacta	(Müller Hal.) H. Robinson	Nomenclature	Amblystegium compactum (Müll. Hal.) Austin
GRCA 53216	Amblystegiaceae	Conardia compacta	(Müller Hal.) H. Robinson	Nomenclature	Amblystegium compactum (Müll. Hal.) Austin
GRCA 53218	Amblystegiaceae	Conardia compacta	(Müller Hal.) H. Robinson	Nomenclature	Amblystegium compactum (Müll. Hal.) Austin
GRCA 53215	Amblystegiaceae	Conardia compacta	(Müller Hal.) H. Robinson	Nomenclature	Amblystegium compactum (Müll. Hal.) Austin
GRCA 53217	Amblystegiaceae	Conardia compacta	(Müller Hal.) H. Robinson	Nomenclature	Amblystegium compactum (Müll. Hal.) Austin
GRCA 53219	Amblystegiaceae	Conardia compacta	(Müller Hal.) H. Robinson	Nomenclature	Amblystegium compactum (Müll. Hal.) Austin
GRCA 80167	Amblystegiaceae	Hygroamblystegium varium	(Hedwig) Mönkemeyer	Nomenclature	Amblystegium noterophilum (Sull. & Lesq.) Holz.
GRCA 53212	Amblystegiaceae	Hygroamblystegium varium	(Hedwig) Mönkemeyer	Determination	Amblystegium irriguum (Hook. & Wilson) Schimp.
GRCA 53213	Amblystegiaceae	Hygroamblystegium varium	(Hedwig) Mönkemeyer	Determination	Amblystegium irriguum (Hook. & Wilson) Schimp.
GRCA 51679	Brachytheciaceae	Brachythecium collinum	(Schleicher ex. Mull. Hal.) Ignatov & Huttunen	Determination	Eurhynchium strigosum (F. Weber & D. Mohr) Schimp.
GRCA 53207	Brachytheciaceae	Brachythecium collinum	(Schleicher ex. Mull. Hal.) Ignatov & Huttunen	Determination	Ptenignandrum filiforme Hedw.
GRCA 53206	Brachytheciaceae	Brachythecium collinum	(Schleicher ex. Mull. Hal.) Ignatov & Huttunen	Determination	Scleropodium cespitans (Müll. Hal.) L.F. Koch var. sublaeve (Renauld & Cardot) Wijk & Margad.
GRCA 51676	Brachytheciaceae	Eurhynchiastrum pulchellum	(Hedwig) Ignatov & Huttunen	Nomenclature	Eurhynchium diversifolium Schimp.
GRCA 51678	Brachytheciaceae	Oxyrrhynchium hians	(Hedwig) Loeske	Nomenclature	Eurhynchium hians (Hedw.) Jaeger & Sauerb.
GRCA 51677	Brachytheciaceae	Oxyrrhynchium hians	(Hedwig) Loeske	Nomenclature	Eurhynchium hians (Hedw.) Jaeger & Sauerb.
GRCA 80183	Brachytheciaceae	Rhynchostegium aquaticum	(Hedwig) Card.	Nomenclature	Rhynchostegium riparioides (Hedw.) Card.
GRCA 51632	Bryaceae	Bryum lanatum	(Palisot de Beauvois) Bridel	Nomenclature	Bryum argenteum Hedwig var. lanatum (P. Beauv.) Hampe

Appendix A *continued*

Catalog number	Family	Modern name	Modern author	Annotation type	Historic name
GRCA 51633	Bryaceae	*Bryum lanatum*	(Palisot de Beauvois) Bridel	Nomenclature	*Bryum argenteum* Hedwig var. *lanatum* (P. Beauv.) Hampe
GRCA 51629	Bryaceae	*Bryum lanatum*	(Palisot de Beauvois) Bridel	Nomenclature	*Bryum argenteum* Hedwig var. *lanatum* (P. Beauv.) Hampe
GRCA 51628	Bryaceae	*Bryum lanatum*	(Palisot de Beauvois) Bridel	Nomenclature	*Bryum argenteum* Hedwig var. *lanatum* (P. Beauv.) Hampe
GRCA 51630	Bryaceae	*Bryum lanatum*	(Palisot de Beauvois) Bridel	Nomenclature	*Bryum argenteum* Hedwig var. *lanatum* (P. Beauv.) Hampe
GRCA 51631	Bryaceae	*Bryum lanatum*	(Palisot de Beauvois) Bridel	Nomenclature	*Bryum argenteum* Hedwig var. *lanatum* (P. Beauv.) Hampe
GRCA 51635	Bryaceae	*Bryum lanatum*	(Palisot de Beauvois) Bridel	Nomenclature	*Bryum argenteum* Hedwig var. lanatum (P. Beauv.) Hampe
GRCA 51634	Bryaceae	*Bryum lanatum*	(Palisot de Beauvois) Bridel	Nomenclature	*Bryum argenteum* Hedwig var. lanatum (P. Beauv.) Hampe
GRCA 51636	Bryaceae	*Gemmabryum caespiticium*	Hedwig	Nomenclature	*Bryum caespiticium* Hedw.
GRCA 51637	Bryaceae	*Gemmabryum caespiticium*	Hedwig	Nomenclature	*Bryum caespiticium* Hedw.
GRCA 51639	Bryaceae	*Gemmabryum caespiticium*	Hedwig	Nomenclature	*Bryum caespiticium* Hedw.
GRCA 51638	Bryaceae	*Gemmabryum caespiticium*	Hedwig	Nomenclature	*Bryum caespiticium* Hedw.
GRCA 51645	Bryaceae	*Imbribryum gemmiparum*	(De Notaris) Spence	Undetermined	*Bryum gemmiparum* De Not.
GRCA 51644	Bryaceae	*Ptychostomum pallens*	(Shwartz) Spence	Undetermined	*Bryum pallens* (Brid.) Sw.
GRCA 51642	Bryaceae	*Ptychostomum pallescens*	(Schwagrichen) Spence	Undetermined	*Bryum pallescens* Schleich. ex Schwägr.
GRCA 51643	Bryaceae	*Ptychostomum pallescens*	(Schwagrichen) Spence	Undetermined	*Bryum pallescens* Schleich. ex Schwägr.
GRCA 51646	Bryaceae	*Ptychostomum turbinatum*	(Hedwig) Spence	Nomenclature	*Bryum turbinatum* (Hedw.) Turner
GRCA 51640	Bryaceae	*Rosulobryum capillare*	(Hedwig) Spence	Undetermined	*Bryum capillare* Hedw.
GRCA 51641	Bryaceae	*Rosulobryum capillare*	(Hedwig) Spence	Undetermined	*Bryum capillare* Hedw.
GRCA 53267	Ditricaceae	*Ceratodon purpureus*	(Hedwig) Bridel	Determination	*Grimmia apocarpa* Hedw. *pulvinata* (Hedw.) G. Jones
GRCA 53266	Ditricaceae	*Ceratodon purpureus*	(Hedwig) Bridel	Determination	*Grimmia apocarpa* Hedw. *pulvinata* (Hedw.) G. Jones
GRCA 53178	Ditricaceae	*Distichium capillaceum*	(Hedwig) Bridel	Nomenclature	*Distichium capillaceum* (Hedw.) Bruch & Schimp.
GRCA 53182	Ditricaceae	*Distichium capillaceum*	(Hedwig) Bridel	Nomenclature	*Distichium capillaceum* (Hedw.) Bruch & Schimp.
GRCA 53293	Grimmiaceae	*Grimmia alpestris*	(Weber & Mohr) Schleicher	Determination	*Grimmia calyptrata* (Hook.) C.E.O. Jensen ex Kindb.
GRCA 53296	Grimmiaceae	*Grimmia alpestris*	(Weber & Mohr) Schleicher	Determination	*Grimmia calyptrata* (Hook.) C.E.O. Jensen ex Kindb.
GRCA 53280	Grimmiaceae	*Grimmia alpestris*	(Weber & Mohr) Schleicher	Determination	*Grimmia calyptrata* (Hook.) C.E.O. Jensen ex Kindb.
GRCA 53281	Grimmiaceae	*Grimmia alpestris*	(Weber & Mohr) Schleicher	Determination	*Grimmia calyptrata* (Hook.) C.E.O. Jensen ex Kindb.
GRCA 53282	Grimmiaceae	*Grimmia alpestris*	(Weber & Mohr) Schleicher	Determination	*Grimmia calyptrata* (Hook.) C.E.O. Jensen ex Kindb.
GRCA 53283	Grimmiaceae	*Grimmia alpestris*	(Weber & Mohr) Schleicher	Determination	*Grimmia calyptrata* (Hook.) C.E.O. Jensen ex Kindb.
GRCA 53277	Grimmiaceae	*Grimmia alpestris*	(Weber & Mohr) Schleicher	Determination	*Grimmia calyptrata* (Hook.) C.E.O. Jensen ex Kindb.

Appendix A *continued*

Catalog number	Family	Modern name	Modern author	Annotation type	Historic name
GRCA 53278	Grimmiaceae	*Grimmia alpestris*	(Weber & Mohr) Schleicher	Determination	*Grimmia calyptrata* (Hook.) C.E.O. Jensen ex Kindb.
GRCA 53279	Grimmiaceae	*Grimmia alpestris*	(Weber & Mohr) Schleicher	Determination	*Grimmia calyptrata* (Hook.) C.E.O. Jensen ex Kindb.
GRCA 53292	Grimmiaceae	*Grimmia alpestris*	(Weber & Mohr) Schleicher	Determination	*Grimmia calyptrata* (Hook.) C.E.O. Jensen ex Kindb.
GRCA 53294	Grimmiaceae	*Grimmia alpestris*	(Weber & Mohr) Schleicher	Determination	*Grimmia calyptrata* (Hook.) C.E.O. Jensen ex Kindb.
GRCA 53295	Grimmiaceae	*Grimmia alpestris*	(Weber & Mohr) Schleicher	Determination	*Grimmia calyptrata* (Hook.) C.E.O. Jensen ex Kindb.
GRCA 51504	Grimmiaceae	*Grimmia alpestris*	(Weber & Mohr) Schleicher	Determination	*Grimmia communtata* Hüb.
GRCA 53300	Grimmiaceae	*Grimmia alpestris*	(Weber & Mohr) Schleicher	Determination	*Grimmia communtata* Hüb.
GRCA 51510	Grimmiaceae	*Grimmia alpestris*	(Weber & Mohr) Schleicher	Determination	*Grimmia communtata* Hüb.
GRCA 51497	Grimmiaceae	*Grimmia alpestris*	(Weber & Mohr) Schleicher	Determination	*Grimmia communtata* Hüb.
GRCA 51498	Grimmiaceae	*Grimmia alpestris*	(Weber & Mohr) Schleicher	Determination	*Grimmia communtata* Hüb.
GRCA 51502	Grimmiaceae	*Grimmia alpestris*	(Weber & Mohr) Schleicher	Determination	*Grimmia communtata* Hüb.
GRCA 51500	Grimmiaceae	*Grimmia alpestris*	(Weber & Mohr) Schleicher	Determination	*Grimmia communtata* Hüb.
GRCA 53297	Grimmiaceae	*Grimmia alpestris*	(Weber & Mohr) Schleicher	Determination	*Grimmia communtata* Hüb.
GRCA 53299	Grimmiaceae	*Grimmia alpestris*	(Weber & Mohr) Schleicher	Determination	*Grimmia communtata* Hüb.
GRCA 51337	Grimmiaceae	*Grimmia alpestris*	(Weber & Mohr) Schleicher	Determination	*Grimmia* sp.
GRCA 53268	Grimmiaceae	*Grimmia anodon*	Bruch & Schimper	Determination	*Grimmia apocarpa* Hedw. var. *pulvinata* (Hedw.) G. Jones
GRCA 51515	Grimmiaceae	*Grimmia anodon*	Bruch & Schimper	Determination	*Grimmia plagiopodia* Hedw.
GRCA 51516	Grimmiaceae	*Grimmia anodon*	Bruch & Schimper	Determination	*Grimmia plagiopodia* Hedw.
GRCA 51523	Grimmiaceae	*Grimmia longirosstris*	Hooker	Determination	*Grimmia pulvinata* (Hedw.) Smith
GRCA 53275	Grimmiaceae	*Grimmia orbicularis*	Wilson	Determination	*Grimmia apocarpa* Hedw. var. *gracilis* Röhl.
GRCA 53276	Grimmiaceae	*Grimmia orbicularis*	Wilson	Determination	*Grimmia apocarpa* Hedw. var. *gracilis* Röhl.
GRCA 53288	Grimmiaceae	*Grimmia orbicularis*	Wilson	Determination	*Grimmia calyptrata* (Hook.) C.E.O. Jensen ex Kindb.
GRCA 53290	Grimmiaceae	*Grimmia orbicularis*	Wilson	Determination	*Grimmia calyptrata* (Hook.) C.E.O. Jensen ex Kindb.
GRCA 53291	Grimmiaceae	*Grimmia orbicularis*	Wilson	Determination	*Grimmia calyptrata* (Hook.) C.E.O. Jensen ex Kindb.
GRCA 53298	Grimmiaceae	*Grimmia orbicularis*	Wilson	Determination	*Grimmia communtata* Hüb.
GRCA 51512	Grimmiaceae	*Grimmia orbicularis*	Wilson	Determination	*Grimmia decipiens* Renauld & Cardot
GRCA 51532	Grimmiaceae	*Grimmia orbicularis*	Wilson	Determination	*Grimmia pulvinata* (Hedw.) Smith
GRCA 51530	Grimmiaceae	*Grimmia orbicularis*	Wilson	Determination	*Grimmia pulvinata* (Hedw.) Smith
GRCA 51535	Grimmiaceae	*Grimmia orbicularis*	Wilson	Determination	*Racomitrium heterostichum* (Hedw.) Brid.

Catalog number		Family	Modern name	Modern author	Annotation type	Historic name
GRCA	51534	Grimmiaceae	*Grimmia orbicularis*	Wilson	Determination	*Racomitrium heterostichum* (Hedw.) Brid.
GRCA	53285	Grimmiaceae	*Grimmia pulvinata*	(Hedwig) Smith	Determination	*Grimmia calyptrata* (Hook.) C.E.O. Jensen ex Kindb.
GRCA	53286	Grimmiaceae	*Grimmia pulvinata*	(Hedwig) Smith	Determination	*Grimmia calyptrata* (Hook.) C.E.O. Jensen ex Kindb.
GRCA	53287	Grimmiaceae	*Grimmia pulvinata*	(Hedwig) Smith	Determination	*Grimmia calyptrata* (Hook.) C.E.O. Jensen ex Kindb.
GRCA	53263	Grimmiaceae	*Schistidium agassizii*	Sullivant & Lesquereux	Nomenclature	*Grimmia alpicola* Hedw.
GRCA	53269	Grimmiaceae	*Schistidium atrichum*	(Turner) Loeske	Determination	*Grimmia apocarpa* var. *pulvinata* (Hedw.) G. Jones
GRCA	53270	Grimmiaceae	*Schistidium atrichum*	(Turner) Loeske	Determination	*Grimmia apocarpa* Hedw. var. *conferta* (Funck) Spreng.
GRCA	53273	Grimmiaceae	*Schistidium* cf *confertum*	(Turner) Loeske	Determination	*Grimmia apocarpa* Hedw.
GRCA	53272	Grimmiaceae	*Schistidium* cf *confertum*	(Funck) Bruch & Schimper	Determination	*Grimmia apocarpa* Hedw.
GRCA	53274	Grimmiaceae	*Schistidium confertum*	(Funck) Bruch & Schimper	Determination	*Grimmia apocarpa* Hedw. var. *atrofusca* (Schimp.) Husn.
GRCA	53284	Grimmiaceae	*Schistidium confertum*	(Funck) Bruch & Schimper	Determination	*Grimmia calyptrata* (Hook.) C.E.O. Jensen ex Kindb.
GRCA	51513	Grimmiaceae	*Schistidium confertum*	(Funck) Bruch & Schimper	Determination	*Grimmia dupretii* Thér.
GRCA	51514	Grimmiaceae	*Schistidium confertum*	(Funck) Bruch & Schimper	Determination	*Grimmia dupretii* Thér.
GRCA	53271	Grimmiaceae	*Schistidium dupretii*	(Theriot) W.A. Weber	Determination	*Grimmia apocarpa* Hedw. var. *conferta* (Funck) Spreng.
GRCA	53197	Leskeaceae	*Pseudoleskeella tectorum*	(Bridel) Brotherus	Nomenclature	*Leskea tectorum* (Funck ex Brid.) Lindb. var. *flagellifera* Best
GRCA	53202	Leskeaceae	*Pseudoleskeella tectorum*	(Bridel) Brotherus	Nomenclature	*Leskea tectorum* (Funck ex Brid.) Lindb. var. *flagellifera* Best
GRCA	53193	Leskeaceae	*Pseudoleskeella tectorum*	(Bridel) Brotherus	Nomenclature	*Leskea tectorum* (Funck ex Brid.) Lindb. var. *flagellifera* Best
GRCA	53199	Leskeaceae	*Pseudoleskeella tectorum*	(Bridel) Brotherus	Nomenclature	*Leskea tectorum* (Funck ex Brid.) Lindb. var. *flagellifera* Best
GRCA	53200	Leskeaceae	*Pseudoleskeella tectorum*	(Bridel) Brotherus	Nomenclature	*Leskea tectorum* (Funck ex Brid.) Lindb. var. *flagellifera* Best
GRCA	53195	Leskeaceae	*Pseudoleskeella tectorum*	(Bridel) Brotherus	Nomenclature	*Leskea tectorum* (Funck ex Brid.) Lindb. var. *flagellifera* Best
GRCA	53196	Leskeaceae	*Pseudoleskeella tectorum*	(Bridel) Brotherus	Nomenclature	*Leskea tectorum* (Funck ex Brid.) Lindb. var. *flagellifera* Best
GRCA	53198	Leskeaceae	*Pseudoleskeella tectorum*	(Bridel) Brotherus	Nomenclature	*Leskea tectorum* (Funck ex Brid.) Lindb. var. *flagellifera* Best
GRCA	53192	Leskeaceae	*Pseudoleskeella tectorum*	(Bridel) Brotherus	Nomenclature	*Leskea tectorum* (Funck ex Brid.) Lindb. var. *flagellifera* Best
GRCA	53194	Leskeaceae	*Pseudoleskeella tectorum*	(Bridel) Brotherus	Nomenclature	*Leskea tectorum* (Funck ex Brid.) Lindb. var. *flagellifera* Best
GRCA	53204	Leskeaceae	*Pseudoleskeella tectorum*	(Bridel) Brotherus	Nomenclature	*Leskea williamsii* Best var. *filamentosa* Best
GRCA	53205	Leskeaceae	*Pseudoleskeella tectorum*	(Bridel) Brotherus	Nomenclature	*Leskea williamsii* Best var. *filamentosa* Best
GRCA	53211	Leskeaceae	*Pseudoleskeella tectorum*	(Bridel) Brotherus	Determination	*Pterigynandrum filiforme* Hedw.
GRCA	53208	Leskeaceae	*Pseudoleskeella tectorum*	(Bridel) Brotherus	Determination	*Pterigynandrum filiforme* Hedw.
GRCA	53209	Leskeaceae	*Pseudoleskeella tectorum*	(Bridel) Brotherus	Determination	*Pterigynandrum filiforme* Hedw.

Appendix A *continued*

Catalog number	Family	Modern name	Modern author	Annotation type	Historic name
GRCA 51651	Mielichhoferiaceae	*Pohlia cruda*	(Hedwig) Lindberg	Nomenclature	*Pohlia cruda* (Hedw.) Lindb.
GRCA 51652	Mielichhoferiaceae	*Pohlia cruda*	(Hedwig) Lindberg	Nomenclature	*Pohlia cruda* (Hedw.) Lindb.
GRCA 51556	Orthotricaceae	*Orthotrichum pellucidum*	Lindberg	Determination	*Orthotrichum jamesianum* Sull.
GRCA 51557	Orthotricaceae	*Orthotrichum pellucidum*	Lindberg	Determination	*Orthotrichum jamesianum* Sull.
GRCA 53220	Polytrichaceae	*Atrichum selwynii*	Austin	Nomenclature	*Atrichum undulatum* (Hedw.) Beauv.
GRCA 51584	Pottiaceae	*Bryoerythrophyllum recurvirostrum*	(Hedwig) Chen	Determination	*Didymodon tophaceus* (Brid.) Lisa
GRCA 51567	Pottiaceae	*Didymodon tophaceus*	(Bridel) Lisa	Determination	*Barbula unguiculata* Hedw.
GRCA 51578	Pottiaceae	*Didymodon vinealis*	(Bridel) Zander	Determination	*Desmatodon obtusifolius* (Schwägr.) Schimp.
GRCA 51344	Pottiaceae	*Hymenostylium recurvirostrum*	(Hedwig) Dixon	Determination	*Bryophyta* sp.
GRCA 51585	Pottiaceae	*Hymenostylium recurvirostrum*	(Hedwig) Dixon	Nomenclature	*Gymnostomum recurvirostre* Hedw.
GRCA 51586	Pottiaceae	*Hymenostylium recurvirostrum*	(Hedwig) Dixon	Nomenclature	*Gymnostomum recurvirostre* Hedw.
GRCA 51338	Pottiaceae	*Hymenostylium recurvirostrum*	(Hedwig) Dixon	Determination	*Bryophyta* sp.
GRCA 51587	Pottiaceae	*Pleurochaete luteola*	(Bescherelle) Theriot	Determination	*Pleurochaete squarrosa* (Brid.) Lindb.
GRCA 51603	Pottiaceae	*Syntrichia ruralis*	(Hedwig) F. Weber & D. Mohr	Nomenclature	*Tortula ruralis* (Hedw.) (Hedwig) P. Gaertner, B. Meyer & Scherbius
GRCA 51618	Pottiaceae	*Syntrichia ruralis*	(Hedwig) F. Weber & D. Mohr	Nomenclature	*Tortula ruralis* (Hedw.) (Hedwig) P. Gaertner, B. Meyer & Scherbius
GRCA 51592	Pottiaceae	*Syntrichia ruralis*	(Hedwig) F. Weber & D. Mohr	Nomenclature	*Tortula ruralis* (Hedw.) (Hedwig) P. Gaertner, B. Meyer & Scherbius
GRCA 51593	Pottiaceae	*Syntrichia ruralis*	(Hedwig) F. Weber & D. Mohr	Nomenclature	*Tortula ruralis* (Hedw.) (Hedwig) P. Gaertner, B. Meyer & Scherbius
GRCA 51615	Pottiaceae	*Syntrichia ruralis*	(Hedwig) F. Weber & D. Mohr	Nomenclature	*Tortula ruralis* (Hedw.) (Hedwig) P. Gaertner, B. Meyer & Scherbius
GRCA 51617	Pottiaceae	*Syntrichia ruralis*	(Hedwig) F. Weber & D. Mohr	Nomenclature	Tortula ruralis (Hedw.) (Hedwig) P. Gaertner, B. Meyer & Scherbius
GRCA 51601	Pottiaceae	*Syntrichia ruralis*	(Hedwig) F. Weber & D. Mohr	Nomenclature	*Tortula ruralis* (Hedw.) (Hedwig) P. Gaertner, B. Meyer & Scherbius

Catalog number	Family	Modern name	Modern author	Annotation type	Historic name
GRCA 51599	Pottiaceae	*Syntrichia ruralis*	(Hedwig) F. Weber & D. Mohr	Nomenclature	*Tortula ruralis* (Hedw.) (Hedwig) P. Gaertner, B. Meyer & Scherbius
GRCA 51600	Pottiaceae	*Syntrichia ruralis*	(Hedwig) F. Weber & D. Mohr	Nomenclature	*Tortula ruralis* (Hedw.) (Hedwig) P. Gaertner, B. Meyer & Scherbius
GRCA 51614	Pottiaceae	*Syntrichia ruralis*	(Hedwig) F. Weber & D. Mohr	Nomenclature	*Tortula ruralis* (Hedw.) (Hedwig) P. Gaertner, B. Meyer & Scherbius
GRCA 51616	Pottiaceae	*Syntrichia ruralis*	(Hedwig) F. Weber & D. Mohr	Nomenclature	*Tortula ruralis* (Hedw.) (Hedwig) P. Gaertner, B. Meyer & Scherbius
GRCA 51607	Pottiaceae	*Syntrichia ruralis*	(Hedwig) F. Weber & D. Mohr	Nomenclature	*Tortula ruralis* (Hedw.) (Hedwig) P. Gaertner, B. Meyer & Scherbius
GRCA 51608	Pottiaceae	*Syntrichia ruralis*	(Hedwig) F. Weber & D. Mohr	Nomenclature	*Tortula ruralis* (Hedw.) (Hedwig) P. Gaertner, B. Meyer & Scherbius
GRCA 51609	Pottiaceae	*Syntrichia ruralis*	(Hedwig) F. Weber & D. Mohr	Nomenclature	*Tortula ruralis* (Hedw.) (Hedwig) P. Gaertner, B. Meyer & Scherbius
GRCA 51610	Pottiaceae	*Syntrichia ruralis*	(Hedwig) F. Weber & D. Mohr	Nomenclature	*Tortula ruralis* (Hedw.) (Hedwig) P. Gaertner, B. Meyer & Scherbius
GRCA 51604	Pottiaceae	*Syntrichia ruralis*	(Hedwig) F. Weber & D. Mohr	Nomenclature	*Tortula ruralis* (Hedw.) (Hedwig) P. Gaertner, B. Meyer & Scherbius
GRCA 51619	Pottiaceae	*Syntrichia ruralis*	(Hedwig) F. Weber & D. Mohr	Nomenclature	*Tortula ruralis* (Hedw.) (Hedwig) P. Gaertner, B. Meyer & Scherbius
GRCA 51602	Pottiaceae	*Syntrichia ruralis*	(Hedwig) F. Weber & D. Mohr	Nomenclature	*Tortula ruralis* (Hedw.) (Hedwig) P. Gaertner, B. Meyer & Scherbius
GRCA 51605	Pottiaceae	*Syntrichia ruralis*	(Hedwig) F. Weber & D. Mohr	Nomenclature	*Tortula ruralis* (Hedw.) (Hedwig) P. Gaertner, B. Meyer & Scherbius
GRCA 51606	Pottiaceae	*Syntrichia ruralis*	(Hedwig) F. Weber & D. Mohr	Nomenclature	*Tortula ruralis* (Hedw.) (Hedwig) P. Gaertner, B. Meyer & Scherbius
GRCA 51613	Pottiaceae	*Syntrichia ruralis*	(Hedwig) F. Weber & D. Mohr	Nomenclature	*Tortula ruralis* (Hedw.) (Hedwig) P. Gaertner, B. Meyer & Scherbius
GRCA 51612	Pottiaceae	*Syntrichia ruralis*	(Hedwig) F. Weber & D. Mohr	Nomenclature	*Tortula ruralis* (Hedw.) (Hedwig) P. Gaertner, B. Meyer & Scherbius
GRCA 51611	Pottiaceae	*Syntrichia ruralis*	(Hedwig) F. Weber & D. Mohr	Nomenclature	*Tortula ruralis* (Hedw.) (Hedwig) P. Gaertner, B. Meyer & Scherbius
GRCA 51568	Pottiaceae	*Tortula cernua*	(Huebener) Lindberg	Undetermined	*Desmatodon cernuus* (Hüb.) Bruch & Schimp.

Appendix A *continued*

Catalog number	Family	Modern name	Modern author	Annotation type	Historic name
GRCA 51569	Pottiaceae	*Tortula obtusifolia*	(Schwägrichen) Mathieu	Determination	*Desmatodon convolutus* (Brid.) Grout
GRCA 51570	Pottiaceae	*Tortula obtusifolia*	(Schwägrichen) Mathieu	Determination	*Desmatodon convolutus* (Brid.) Grout
GRCA 51577	Pottiaceae	*Tortula obtusifolia*	(Schwägrichen) Mathieu	Determination	*Desmatodon obtusifolius* (Schwägr.) Schimp.
GRCA 51579	Pottiaceae	*Tortula obtusifolia*	(Schwägrichen) Mathieu	Determination	*Desmatodon obtusifolius* (Schwägr.) Schimp.
GRCA 51583	Pottiaceae	*Tortula obtusifolia*	(Schwägrichen) Mathieu	Determination	*Husnotiella pringlei* (Cardot) Grout
GRCA 51620	Pottiaceae	*Weissia ligulifolia*	(Bartram) Grout	Nomenclature	*Weissia andrewsii* E.B. Bartram
GRCA 51621	Pottiaceae	*Weissia ligulifolia*	(Bartram) Grout	Nomenclature	*Weissia andrewsii* E.B. Bartram
GRCA 53191	Thuidiaceae	*Abietinella abietina*	(Hedwig) Fleischer	Nomenclature	*Thuidium abietinum* (Hedw.) Schimp
GRCA 51560	Timmiaceae	*Timmia megapolitana ssp. bavarica*	(Hessler) Brassard	Nomenclature	*Timmia bavarica* Hessl.
GRCA 51562	Timmiaceae	*Timmia megapolitana ssp. bavarica*	(Hessler) Brassard	Nomenclature	*Timmia bavarica* Hessl.
GRCA 51558	Timmiaceae	*Timmia megapolitana ssp. bavarica*	(Hessler) Brassard	Nomenclature	*Timmia bavarica* Hessl.
GRCA 51558	Timmiaceae	*Timmia megapolitana ssp. bavarica*	(Hessler) Brassard	Nomenclature	*Timmia bavarica* Hessl.
GRCA 51558	Timmiaceae	*Timmia megapolitana ssp. bavarica*	(Hessler) Brassard	Nomenclature	*Timmia bavarica* Hessl.
GRCA 51558	Timmiaceae	*Timmia megapolitana ssp. bavarica*	(Hessler) Brassard	Nomenclature	*Timmia bavarica* Hessl.
GRCA 51558	Timmiaceae	*Timmia megapolitana ssp. bavarica*	(Hessler) Brassard	Nomenclature	*Timmia bavarica* Hessl.
GRCA 51558	Timmiaceae	*Timmia megapolitana ssp. bavarica*	(Hessler) Brassard	Nomenclature	*Timmia bavarica* Hessl.

Record status, distribution and habitat of bryophytes (by genus) in Grand Canyon National Park

An alphabetical listing, by genus, of all bryophyte taxa known to occur in GRCA. The broad distribution of each species is indicated by its presence or absence in the five collection regions (North Rim, South Rim, Inner Canyon, Colorado River corridor, Marble Canyon, and Lake Mead vicinity) as well as in the Grand Canyon-Parashant National Monument (Parashant) and Big Bend National Park.

Species	Frequency (total localities)	New record (park/state)	Elevation (ft)	GC/Parashant NM	Big Bend NP	N. Rim	S. Rim	Inner Canyon	CO River	Marble Canyon	Lake Mead	Observed habitat
Abietinella abietina	rare (1)	-	5300					X				rock
Aloina ambigua	infreq (5)	Park	1700 - 2400					X			X	crust; soil over rock
Aloina bifrons	rare (1)	Park	1700	X							X	crust
Amblystegium serpens	infreq (4)	-	4800 - 8400		X			X				limestone; spring; moist soil
Aneura pinguis	rare (1)	Park/State	7800			X						spring on limestone
Asterella gracilis	rare (1)	Park	8400			X						spring on moist soil
Atrichum selwynii	rare (2)	Park	8300			X						soil; cwd; spring
Barbula bolleana	infreq (8)	Park	1600 - 2400					X	X			seep; riverside; emergent
Barbula convoluta var. eustegia	infreq (5)	Park/State	8000 - 8500			X		X				shaded soil; rock
Barbula indica var. indica	rare (3)	Park	1500 - 4500					X	X			seep; moist soil; riverside
Brachythecium collinum	abun (30)	-	5300 - 8900	X	X	X		X	X			limestone; cwd; soil
Brachythecium fendleri	com (20)	Park	5700 - 8400	X	X	X	X	X				rock; soil over rock; tree; cwd
Brachythecium frigidum	rare (4)	Park	2600 - 8400			X		X				spring; emergent
Brachythecium nelsonii	rare (1)	Park	7600			X						spring
Brachythecium rivulare	rare (3)	Park	2400 - 8400			X		X	X			spring; emergent
Brachythecium velutinum	rare (1)	Park	7000				X					limestone
Bryoerythrophyllum recurvirostrum	rare (3)	Park	8100 - 8500	X	X	X						soil; limestone; spring

Species	Frequency (Total localities)	New record (Park/State)	Elevation (ft)	GC/Parashant NM	Big Bend NP	N. Rim	S. Rim	Inner Canyon	CO River	Marble Canyon	Lake Mead	Observed habitat
Bryum argenteum	infreq (9)	Park	2300 – 8000	X	X	X	X	X				soil over rock; crust; shaded soil
Bryum lanatum	com (17)	-	1700 – 8500	X	X	X	X	X	X		X	soil over rock; soil; crust; roadsides
Campyliadelphus chrysophyllus	rare (1)	-	8300		X	X						unknown
Cephaloziella divaricata	rare (4)	Park	8000 – 8400		X	X						cwd; burnt cwd
Ceratodon purpureus	abun (21)	-	6000 – 8800		X	X	X	X				cwd; soil; rock; crust
Chiloscyphus polyanthos var. *rivularis*	rare (1)	Park	7800			X						spring on soil over rock
Conardia compacta	com (11)	-	3400 – 8400	X	X	X		X		X		limestone; soil over rock
Cratoneuron filicinum	rare (2)	-	7600 – 8000			X	X					spring
Crossidium aberrans	infreq (14)	Park	1400 – 7100	X	X			X	X			crust; shaded soil; streamside; soil over rock
Crossidium crassinervium var. *crassinervium*	infreq (9)	Park	1500 – 2400	X	X			X	X		X	crust; soil over rock; streamside
Crossidium seriatum	infreq (6)	Park	1400 – 2400					X	X		X	crust; soil over rock; shaded soil
Crossidium squamiferum	infreq (8)	Park	1400 – 6800	X	X			X	X		X	limestone; sandstone; dry soil
Dicranoweisia crispula	com (14)	Park	1700 – 8800	X	X	X	X	X			X	cwd; limestone; tree; sandstone
Didymodon australasiae	infreq (5)	Park	2000 – 4600	X	X			X	X			crust; rock; seep
Didymodon brachyphyllus	infreq (7)	-	2400 – 8300	X		X	X	X				limestone; rock; seep; streamside
Didymodon fallax	rare (4)	Park/State	1600 – 4500		X	X		X	X			riverside; seep; waterfall
Didymodon nevadensis	infreq (9)	Park/State	1700 – 8000	X		X		X	X		X	riverside; soil; limestone; travertine
Didymodon nicholsonii	rare (2)	Park/State	2200 – 7900	X		X		X	X			riverside; shaded soil
Didymodon rigidulus var. *icmadophilus*	infreq (6)	Park/State	2300 – 8800	X		X		X	X			crust; shaded soil; rock

Species	Frequency (Total localities)	New record (Park/State)	Elevation (ft)	GC/Para-shant NM	Big Bend NP	N. Rim	S. Rim	Inner Can-yon	CO River	Mar-ble Can-yon	Lake Mead	Observed habitat
Didymodon rigidulus var. rigidulus	infreq (9)	Park	1400 - 4200					X	X			shaded soil; rock; riverside
Didymodon tectorum	rare (1)	Park/State	6700					X				rock
Didymodon tophaceus	infreq (8)	–	1700 - 4600	X				X	X	X		streamside; seep; shale; emergent
Didymodon vinealis	com (17)	Park	1700 - 8300	X		X		X	X		X	soil over rock; shaded rock; seep; waterfall
Distichium capillaceum	rare (2)	–	8200 - 8400			X						limestone; moist soil; spring
Drepanocladus aduncus	rare (2)	Park	8200 - 8900			X						limestone; pond margin
Encalypta rhaptocarpa	infreq (4)	Park	7100 - 8200			X						rock; soil
Encalypta vulgaris	com (16)	–	6600 - 8800	X	X	X		X				soil over rock; soil
Entosthodon sp.	rare (3)	–	1700 - 1800				X		X			crust; waterfalls; soil
Eucladium verticillatum	com (15)	–	1700 - 5000					X	X			seep; spring; streamside
Eurhynchiastrum pulchellum var. pulchellum	rare (2)	–	8000 - 8300		X	X						rock; spring
Fissidens fontanus	rare (1)	Park	1700		X				X			travertine; river
Fissidens grandifrons	infreq (5)	Park	2400 - 5600					X				submerged; wet rock; spring
Fissidens obtusifolius	rare (3)	Park	1700 - 2400		X			X	X		X	travertine; riverside; wet rock
Fissidens sublimbatus	infreq (5)	–	1500 - 8500	X	X	X	X	X				soil
Fontinalis hypnoides	rare (1)	Park	1900						X			pool; spring
Frullania inflata	rare (1)	Park	8300	X		X						limestone
Funaria hygrometrica var. calvescens	rare (1)	Park	2400						X			soil
Funaria hygrometrica var. hygrometrica	infreq (9)	–	4100 - 8200	X	X	X		X				disturbed soil; limestone; soil
Funaria muhlenbergii	rare (1)	–	5300	X				X				soil
Gemmabryum badium	rare (3)	Park/State	5600 - 8200			X		X				dry soil; sandstone
Gemmabryum caespiticium	abun (25)	–	1700 - 8500			X	X	X	X			soil over rock; limestone; cwd; crust

Appendix B. *continued*

Species	Frequency (Total localities)	New record (Park/State)	Elevation (ft)	GC/Parashant NM	Big Bend NP	N. Rim	S. Rim	Inner Canyon	CO River	Marble Canyon	Lake Mead	Observed habitat
Gemmabryum kunzei	abun (21)	Park	1400 - 8800	X		X	X	X	X		X	soil over rock; soil; riverside; streamside
Gemmabryum subapicula-tum	rare (1)	Park	8800			X						pond margin on moist soil
Gemmabryum valparaisense	com (12)	Park	1600 - 7800	X		X		X	X			moist soil; riverside; spring; seep
Grimmia alpestris	abun (21)	Park	4800 - 8800	X		X	X	X				limestone; sandstone
Grimmia anodon	com (17)	-	1600 - 8800	X		X	X	X	X		X	limestone; sandstone; cwd
Grimmia caespiticia	rare (1)	Park/State	7900			X						sandstone
Grimmia longirostris	rare (4)	Park	7100 - 8800	X	X	X	X	X				limestone; chert
Grimmia moxleyi	rare (4)	Park	1600 - 6900	X				X	X		X	soil over rock; soil
Grimmia orbicularis	abun (21)	Park	1500 - 7000	X			X	X	X			limestone; sandstone; soil over rock;travertine
Grimmia ovalis	infreq (6)	Park	4100 - 7000	X	X		X	X				limestone; sandstone
Grimmia plagiopodia	com (16)	-	1700 - 8400	X		X	X	X			X	limestone; sandstone; crust
Grimmia pulvinata	com (14)	Park	1800 - 8000	X		X	X	X	X			limestone; sandstone; concrete; cwd
Grimmia sessitana	rare (1)	Park	6900				X					rock
Grimmia sp.nov	rare (1)	Park/State	5600					X				sandstone
Gymnostomum aerugino-sum	rare (3)	Park	2400 - 8200	X	X	X		X				seep; soil over rock; sandstone
Gymnostomum calcareum	rare (4)	Park/State	2300 - 7800	X		X		X	X			moist soil; streamside; spring
Gyroweisia tenuis	rare (1)	Park/State	2200						X			seep
HygroAmblystegium varium	infreq (7)	Park	3000 - 7800					X				submerged; moist soil; emergent
Hymenostylium recurvirostrum var. recurvirostrum	infreq (5)	-	2900 - 7800		X			X	X			seep; spring
Hypnum cupressiforme var. subjulaceum	rare (2)	Park/State	3400 - 8200	X	X	X		X				soil; cwd
Hypnum pallescens	rare (1)	Park.	8100			X						streamside

Appendix B. continued

Species	Frequency (Total localities)	New record (Park/State)	Elevation (ft)	GC/Parashant NM	Big Bend NP	N. Rim	S. Rim	Inner Canyon	CO River	Marble Canyon	Lake Mead	Observed habitat
Hypnum revolutum	com (15)	-	5700 - 8800	X		X		X				rock; tree; soil
Hypnum vaucheri	rare (2)	Park	6000 - 6800	X	X		X	X				rock; tree
Imbribryum sp.nov	rare (1)	Park/State	8400			X						spring
Jaffeuliobryum wrightii	rare (4)	Park	1500 - 2400	X	X			X	X			dry rock; dry soil
Leptobryum pyriforme	rare (4)	-	8000 - 8500		X	X						moist soil; spring
Leptodictyum riparium	infreq (6)	-	1900 - 2700			X			X			submerged
Iesskeella nervosa	rare (2)	Park/State	7900 - 8800			X		X				cwd; sandstone
Mannia fragrans	rare (1)	Park	3000							X		moist soil
Marchantia polymorpha	rare (2)	Park	5200 - 5800					X				spring
Microbryum starkeanum	rare (1)	Park	2400	X	X			X				streamside
Mnium arizonicum	rare (1)	Park	6400					X				seep
Orthotrichum alpestre	infreq (7)	-	1700 - 8400	X		X	X	X			X	cwd; tree; rock
Orthotrichum cupulatum	rare (4)	Park	6600 - 8400	X		X	X	X				limestone; tree
Orthotrichum hallii	infreq (9)	Park	7700 - 8300	X		X	X	X				limestone; tree; sandstone
Orthotrichum obtusifolium	rare (1)	Park	8300			X						limestone
Orthotrichum pellucidum	rare (1)	-	7000				X					limestone
Orthotrichum pumilum	rare (2)	Park	1700 - 7700	X	X	X		X			X	tree
Oxyrrhynchium hians	rare (4)	-	3400 - 8400			X		X				spring
Philonotis fontana	infreq (5)	-	7600 - 8300		X	X						moist soil; soil
Philonotis marchica	rare (3)	Park	2500 - 2800					X	X			spring; seep
Plagiobryoides vinosula	infreq (7)	Park	1700 - 6400					X	X			seep; spring; riverside
Pleurochaete luteola	infreq (9)	-	1600 - 4100	X	X			X	X			moist soil; limestone; litter
Pohlia camptotrachela	rare (1)	Park/State	8800			X						pond margin; moist soil
Pohlia cruda	rare (2)	-	8400 - 8400			X						moist soil; spring
Pohlia wahlenbergii	rare (2)	Park	5800 - 8400			X		X				moist soil; spring
Polytrichum juniperinum	com (11)	-	7800 - 8800			X		X				soil; soil over rock; spring
Pseudocrossidium crinitum	rare (4)	-	1400 - 6700		X		X	X	X			soil over rock; limestone; riverside

Species	Frequency (Total localities)	New record (Park/State)	Elevation (ft)	GC/Parashant NM	Big Bend NP	N. Rim	S. Rim	Inner Canyon	CO River	Marble Canyon	Lake Mead	Observed habitat
Pseudoleskea patens	rare (1)	Park/State	8100			X						soil; rock
Pseudoleskea radicosa var. compacta	rare (2)	Park	8400 - 8900			X						rock
Pseudoleskeella tectorum	abun (21)	-	1700 - 8800	X		X	X	X			X	limestone; tree; cwd; sandstone
Pterigynandrum filiforme	rare (1)	-	8400			X						soil
Pterygoneurum lamellatum	rare (4)	Park	6800 - 7900			X	X	X				soil over rock; dry soil
Pterygoneurum ovatum	rare (1)	-	5800	X				X				sandstone
Pterygoneurum subsessile var. subsessile	rare (1)	Park	7000	X	X		X					dry soil
Ptychostomum bimum	rare (1)	Park	8300			X						soil
Ptychostomum creberrimum	rare (2)	Park	8000 - 8300		X	X		X				soil; limestone
Ptychostomum pallescens	infreq (6)	-	7900 - 8900			X		X				moist soil; shaded soil; spring; cwd
Ptychostomum pseudotriquetrum	rare (3)	Park	5600 - 8400		X	X		X				spring; moist soil
Ptychostomum turbinatum	rare (3)	-	3800 - 8200		X	X		X				moist soil; spring; streamside
Reboulia hemisphaerica	rare (2)	Park	2000 - 5000					X	X			shaded soil
Rhynchostegium aquaticum	com (10)	-	1700 - 5200					X	X	X		spring; waterfalls; streams; rock
Rhynchostegium serrulatum	rare (1)	Park/State	2400					X				waterfall; wet rock
Riccia glauca	rare (1)	Park	8800			X						pond margin
Rosulobryum flaccidum	infreq (7)	Park/State	5500 - 8500	X		X		X				limestone; soil; soil over rock; tree
Rosulobryum laevifilium	rare (3)	Park/State	8000 - 8400			X						limestone; soil; cwd
Rosulobryum torquescens	rare (1)	Park	4200	O	O			X				soil
Schistidium agassizii	rare (2)	State	8300		X	X						wet rock; moist soil
Schistidium atrichum	infreq (7)	Park/State	4800 - 8400			X	X	X				limestone; sandstone
Schistidium confertum	infreq (8)	Park/State	4800 - 8800			X	X	X				limestone; sandstone; soil over rock

Appendix B. *continued*

Species	Frequency (Total localities)	New record (Park/State)	Elevation (ft)	GC/Parashant NM	Big Bend NP	N. Rim	S. Rim	Inner Canyon	CO River	Marble Canyon	Lake Mead	Observed habitat
Schistidium dupretii	rare (2)	Park/State	6600 - 8400			X		X				limestone
Schistidium frigidum	rare (1)	Park/State	7800			X						rock
Schistidium papillosum	rare (2)	Park/State	8100 - 8300			X						sandstone
Sciuro-hypnum plumosum	rare (1)	Park	7700			X						pond margin
Splachnobryum obtusum	rare (2)	Park	1500 - 1700		X			X	X			travertine; river; riverside
Syntrichia caninervis	com (20)	Park	1700 - 8000	X		X	X	X	X		X	soil over rock; crust; dry soil; limestone
Syntrichia laevipila	rare (2)	Park	4100 - 4200	X	X	X		X				tree
Syntrichia montana	rare (3)	Park	5700 - 7200				X	X				limestone; tree
Syntrichia norvegica	com (12)	Park	6100 - 8400			X	X	X				soil over rock; rock; tree
Syntrichia papillossisima	rare (1)	Park	8400	X		X						cwd
Syntrichia ruralis	abun (51)	-	1500 - 8800	X	X	X	X	X	X		X	soil over rock; soil; tree; cwd
Targionia sp.nov	infreq (5)	Park/State	2200 - 6800	X				X	X			riverside; streamside; shaded & moist soil
Timmia megapolitana subsp. bavarica	com (15)	-	6700 - 8500	X		X	X	X				shaded soil; soil over rock; rock
Tortella alpicola	rare (1)	Park	5900	X			X	X				unknown
Tortula acaulon	infreq (4)	Park	7000 - 7900	X	X		X	X				dry soil; sandstone; crust
Tortula atrovirens	infreq (6)	-	1600 - 7100	X	X		X	X	X			soil over rock; limestone; crust; dry soil
Tortula cernua	rare (1)	Park	7800					X				spring
Tortula hoppeanna	rare (1)	Park	8100			X						rock
Tortula inermis	com (15)	-	1400 - 8000	X		X	X	X	X			soil over rock; shaded soil; sandstone
Tortula lanceola	rare (3)	Park	1700 - 6900				X	X	X			soil over rock; crust; moist soil
Tortula mucronifolia	infreq (8)	-	6600 - 8400	X		X	X	X				soil over rock; rock; moist soil; cwd
Tortula muralis	infreq (5)	Park	7200 - 8200	X		X	X	X				limestone; soil over rock; shaded soil

Species	Frequency (Total localities)	New record (Park/State)	Elevation (ft)	GC/Parashant NM	Big Bend NP	N. Rim	S. Rim	Inner Canyon	CO River	Marble Canyon	Lake Mead	Observed habitat
Tortula obtusifolia	com (10)	-	6800 - 8600			X		X				soil over rock;limestone; shaded soil;sandstone
Trichostomum planifolium	rare (1)	Park/State	2400					X				soil over rock
Trichostomum tenuirostre	rare (1)	Park	1400						X			sandstone
Tritomaria exsectiformis	rare (2)	Park	7800 - 8300			X		X				spring, streamside
Weissia controversa	rare (2)	Park	5700 - 8100		X	X		X				soil over rock; shaded soil
Weissia liguiifolia	com (16)	-	1500 - 6800	X	X	X	X	X	X		X	shaded soil; soil over rock; streamside
Zygodon viridissimus var. rupestris	rare (1)	Park	6800				X					tree

Phylogenetic listing of bryophytes with their traits & distributional data for North America

Phylogenetic listing of bryophytes known to occur in GRCA with mosses (Bryophyta) followed by liverworts (Hepaticophyta). Within each phylum, species are listed in order by family and then genus. Growth form is either pleurocarpous (P) or acrocarpous (A) for mosses and either thalloid (T) or leafy (L) for liverworts. Frequency (Freq) is the number of unique localities at which each species was collected throughout the park. Sexual condition is either monoicous (M) or dioicous (D). Species also known to occur in Mexico and Canada are indicated. Species collected only in mesic habitats (springs, seeps, riparian, ponds, waterfalls) are indicated.

Family	Species	Author	Growth form	Freq	Sex. Condition	Known habitat (Adapted from the Flora of North America)	Only mesic	Mexico	Canada
Phylum Bryophyta (mosses)									
Amblystegiaceae	Amblystegium serpens	(Hedwig) Bruch	P	4	M	Tree trunks, rotten wood, rock, soil, swamps to rather xeric habitats		X	X
Amblystegiaceae	Campyliadelphus chrysophyllus	(Bridel) Kanda	P	1	D	Rocks and soil, frequently temporarily wet, calcareous or otherwise mineral-rich		X	X
Amblystegiaceae	Conardia compacta	(Müller Hal.) H. Robinson	P	11	M	Damp cliffs, especially limestone, swamps on logs, stumps, humus, bark at base of trees		X	X
Amblystegiaceae	Drepanocladus aduncus	(Hedwig) Warnstorf	P	2	D	Wetlands (eutrophic fens, shores, ditches); occasionally submerged in pools and lakes, or in swampy forests		X	X
Amblystegiaceae	HygroAmblystegium varium	(Hedwig) Monkemeyer	P	7	M	Sub-xeric (rocks & trees in hardwood mesic forests) to marsh, fens, ponds, springs, & fast streams	X		X
Amblystegiaceae	Leptodictyum riparium	(Hedwig) Warnstorf	P	6	M	Humus, logs & tree bases in swamps or wet depressions in forests or aquatic on rocks	X	X	X
Battramiaceae	Philonotis fontana	(Hedwig) Bridel	P	5	D	Rock or soil, often in seepy, open habitats	X	X	X
Battramiaceae	Philonotis marchia	(Hedwig) Bridel	P	3	M	Rocks and soil in wet places, roadsides, springs	X	X	X
Brachytheciaceae	Brachythecium collinum	(Schleicher ex. Mull. Hal.) Ignatov & Huttunen	P	30	M	Dry or damp soil, humus, or logs in shadey places			X
Brachytheciaceae	Brachythecium fendleri	(Sullivant) Ochyra & Zarnowiec	P	20	M	Soil, rock, or soil over rock in mts up to 2900m		X	
Brachytheciaceae	Brachythecium frigidum	(Müller) Bescherelle	P	4	D	Rocks and soil in moist or wet areas	X	X	X

Family	Species	Author	Growth form	Freq	Sex. Condition	Known habitat (Adapted from the Flora of North America)	Only mesic	Mexico	Canada
Brachytheciaceae	Brachythecium nelsonii	Grout	P	1	D	Wet to dry soil, humus, logs usually in shaded places at high elevations	X		
Brachytheciaceae	Brachythecium rivulare	Schimper	P	3	D	Submerged in springs and slow-flowing brooks or growing on wet soil, rocks, humus or logs on banks, wet meadows, seepage areas	X		X
Brachytheciaceae	Brachythecium velutinum	(Hedwig) Ignatov & Huttunen	P	1	M	Soil, sometimes rock or tree bases, in dry or moist woods, often on sandy forest trails			X
Brachytheciaceae	Euhrynchiastrum pulchellum var. pulchellum	(Hedwig) Ignatov & Huttunen	P	2	D	Soil in forests, rocks, decaying logs and stumps, tree bases; xeric steppe areas; tundra, granite & limestone		X	X
Brachytheciaceae	Oxyrrhynchium hians	(Hedwig) Loeske	P	2	D	Soil, (open humus) in forest; rocks, rotten logs, tree bases, usually mesic to wet conditions	X		X
Brachytheciaceae	Rhynchostegium aquaticum	A. Jaeger	P	10	M	Rocks, running water of small streams and springs, beds of waterfalls, seepy cliffs, esp. limestone	X	X	X
Brachytheciaceae	Sciuro-hypnum plumosum	(Hedwig) Ignatov & Huttunen	P	1	M	Rocks along creeks (usu. Submerged); wet, shaded rock cliffs/outcrops, occasionally wet soil, rarely tree bases	X	X	X
Bryaceae	Bryum argenteum	Hedwig	A	9	D	Common on soil or soil over rock or in crevices, often in nitrogen enriched sites, usu. disturbed places			X
Bryaceae	Bryum lanatum	(Palisot de Beauvois) Bridel	A	17	D	Common to abundant on soil, soil over rock or rock in drier climates			X
Bryaceae	Gemmabryum badium	(Brid.) J.R. Spence	A	3	D	Rare on dry soil or rock in semi-arid climates at middle elevations			
Bryaceae	Gemmabryum caespiticium	(Hedwig) J.R. Spence	A	25	D	Common on disturbed soil, earth banks, rotten wood, rarely on rocks, abundant in disturbed habitats			X
Bryaceae	Gemmabryum kunzei	(Hornsch.) J.R. Spence	A	21	D	Common on dry sandy soil and rock, often calcareous, in arid to semi-arid regions, temperate regions			
Bryaceae	Gemmabryum subapiculatum	(Hampe) J.R. Spence & H.P. Ramsay	A	1	D	Common on disturbed dry to damp soil and soil over rock, often in agricultural fields	X		X
Bryaceae	Gemmabryum valparaisense	(Thériot) Spence	A	12	D	Damp soil/ soil over rock, usu. at calcareous springs in arid to semi-arid or Mediterranean climates	X	X	
Bryaceae	Imbribryum sp. nov.	J.R. Spence	A	1		Unknown	X		

Appendix C continued

Family	Species	Author	Growth form	Freq	Sex. Cond-ition	Known habitat (Adapted from the Flora of North America)	Only mesic	Mexico	Canada
Bryaceae	Plagiobryoides vinosula	(Cardot) J.R. Spence	A	7		Locally common, damp calcareous rock at springs, including hot springs	X		
Bryaceae	Ptychostomum bimum	(Schreber) J.R. Spence	A	1	syoicous	Locally common on wet soil or soil over rock, occasionally on rock			X
Bryaceae	Ptychostomum crebrimum	(Taylor) J.R. Spence & H.P. Ramsay	A	2	syoicous	Common on damp to dry soil or soil over rock			X
Bryaceae	Ptychostomum pallescens	(Hedwig) J.R. Spence ex D.T. Holyoak & N. Pederson	A	3		Common to abundant on wet soil, soil over rock or rock, often in fens	X		X
Bryaceae	Ptychostomum pseudotriquetrum	(Schleicher ex Schwägrichen) J.R. Spence	A	6	M	Common on damp to wet soil			X
Bryaceae	Ptychostomum turbinatum	(Hedwig) J.R. Spence	A	3	D	Locally common on wet soil in calcareous wetlands	X		X
Bryaceae	Rosulobryum flaccidum	(Bridel) J.R. Spence	A	7	D	Exposed to shaded rock, soil, soil over rock, or rotting wood, rarely on bark		0	X
Bryaceae	Rosulobryum laevifilium	(Syed) Ochyra	A	3	D	Uncommon to locally common and widely scattered, bark, rotten wood, rarely rock or soil			X
Bryaceae	Rosulobryum torquescens	(Bruch ex De Not.) J.R. Spence	A	1	D	Uncommon to locally common, soil or rock over soil, rarely on rotting wood	0	0	X
Cratoneuraceae	Cratoneuron filicinum	(Hedwig) Spruce	P	2	D	Calcareous seepage	X	X	X
Dicranaceae	Dicranoweisia crispula	(Hedwig) Milde	A	14	M	Siliceous rock or gravel, occasionally epiphytic or epixylic		X	X
Ditrichaceae	Ceratodon purpureus	(Hedwig) Bridel	A	21	D	Various: most common on open soil, rock ledges, tree bases, roof tops, old wood, soil post fires		X	X
Ditrichaceae	Distichium capillaceum	(Hedwig) Bruch & Schimper	A	2	M	Soil, rock, crevices, ledges, banks, occasionally bark		X	X
Encalyptaceae	Encalypta rhaptocarpa	Schwägrichen	A	4	M	Soil or soil over rock		X	X
Encalyptaceae	Encalypta vulgaris	Hedwig	A	16	M	Shallow calcareous soil over rock			X

Family	Species	Author	Growth form	Freq	Sex. Cond- ition	Known habitat (Adapted from the Flora of North America)	Only mesic	Mexico	Canada
Fissidentaceae	Fissidens fontanus	(Bachelot de la Pylaie) Steudel	A	1	M	Attached to various substrata in stagnant and flowing water, and in coastal estuaries	X	X	X
Fissidentaceae	Fissidens grandifrons	Bridel	A	5	D	Submerged in rapidly running water in calcareous sites	X	X	X
Fissidentaceae	Fissidens obtusifolius	Wilson	A	3	M	Limestone along streams and waterfalls, sometimes inundated, infrequently on bricks	X		X
Fissidentaceae	Fissidens sublimbatus	Grout	A	5	M	Soil in arid areas, often under overhanging rocks & in the shade of trees and shrubs		X	X
Fontinalaceae	Fontinalis hypnoides	Hartman	A	1	D	Rocks, boulders, base of trees, roots, sticks in streams, swamps, lakes, or ponds; low to high elevations	X		X
Fontinalaceae	Funaria hygrometrica var. calvescens	(Schwägrichen) Montagne	A	1	M	Soil, disturbed habitats such as partially shaded building foundations		X	
Funariaceae	Entosthodon sp.	Schwägrichen	A	3	M	Variable, depending on species			
Funariaceae	Funaria hygrometrica var. hygrometrica	Hedwig	A	9	M	Bare mineral soil in disturbed habitats, greenhouses, campfire sites, and occasionally on wood or gravel			X
Funariaceae	Funaria muhlenbergii	Turner	A	1	M	Bare, apparently alkaline, soils; moderate elevations		X	X
Grimmiaceae	Grimmia alpestris	(Weber & Mohr) Schleicher	A	21	D	Exposed acidic granite and sandstone			X
Grimmiaceae	Grimmia anodon	Bruch & Schimper	A	17	M	Exposed, calcareous sandstone, limestone, and concrete		X	X
Grimmiaceae	Grimmia caespiticia	(Bridel) Juratzkah	A	1	D	Exposed, dry to moist, acidic granite and quartzite, alpine			X
Grimmiaceae	Grimmia longirostris	Hooker	A	4	M	Exposed, dry, acidic granite and quartzite		X	X
Grimmiaceae	Grimmia moxleyi	R.S. Williams in J.M. Holzinger	A	4	M	Dry acidic rock		X	
Grimmiaceae	Grimmia orbicularis	Bruch	A	21	M	Dry basic rocky substrates such as limestone, basalt, and mortar		X	
Grimmiaceae	Grimmia ovalis	(Hedwig) Lindberg	A	6	D	Dry, exposed to partially shaded, acidic, sandstone, granite and basalt			X

Appendix C continued

Family	Species	Author	Growth form	Freq	Sex. Condition	Known habitat (Adapted from the Flora of North America)	Only mesic	Mexico	Canada
Grimmiaceae	Grimmia plagiopodia	Hedwig	A	16	M	Exposed calcareous sandstone, limestone, occasionally concrete, and glacio-lacustrine silt			X
Grimmiaceae	Grimmia pulvinata	(Hedwig) Smith	A	14	M	Various substrates, from acidic to basic rock, old mortar, tree trunks		X	X
Grimmiaceae	Grimmia sessitana	de Notaris	A	1	M	Exposed or sheltered, moist, acidic granite and sandstone			X
Grimmiaceae	Grimmia sp. nov.	Hedwig	A	1	M	Unknown			
Grimmiaceae	Jaffueliobryum wrightii	(Sullivant) Thériot	A	4	M	Dry sandstone or limestone rock, rarely metamorphic rock, open arid to semi-aridlands		X	X
Grimmiaceae	Schistidium agassizii	Sullivant & Lesquereux	A	2	M	Wet or dry rocks in or along water courses and lakes			X
Grimmiaceae	Schistidium atrichum	(Müller Hal. & Kindberg) W.A. Weber	A	7	M	Dry, often shaded mainly limestone rocks; usually high elevations			X
Grimmiaceae	Schistidium confertum	(Funck) Bruch & Schimper	A	8	M	Rocks in somewhat shaded habitats			X
Grimmiaceae	Schistidium dupretii	(Thériot) W.A. Weber	A	2	M	Exposed to semi-shaded rock in dry habitats			X
Grimmiaceae	Schistidium frigidum	H.H. Blom	A	2	M	Rock, rarely on tree bark, in mesic habitats			X
Grimmiaceae	Schistidium papillosum	Culmann	A	1	M	Rock in open to shaded habitats			X
Hypnaceae	Hypnum cupressiforme var. subjulaceum	Molendo	P	2	D	Terrestrial, cliff shelves, horizontal rock surfaces, in exposed or sheltered sites (often calcareous rock)			X
Hypnaceae	Hypnum pallescens	(Hedwig) Palisot de Beauvois	P	1	M	Rocks (boulders); trees (bases) mainly in forested areas	X		
Hypnaceae	Hypnum revolutum	(Mitten) Lindberg	P	15	D	Open sites, earth and rock faces, tree bases, logs in forest, commonly a calcicole			X
Hypnaceae	Hypnum vaucheri	Lesquereux	P	2	D	Generally on rock, esp. calcareous rock, tree bases, mineral soil, decaying logs		X	X
Leskeaceae	Leskeella nervosa	(Bridel) Loeske	P	2	D	Common on bark of trees, occasionally on calcareous rock			X

Appendix C continued

Family	Species	Author	Growth form	Freq	Sex. Condition	Known habitat (Adapted from the Flora of North America)	Only mesic	Mexico	Canada
Leskeaceae	Pseudoleskea patens	(Lindberg) Kindberg	P	1	D	Common on shaded to exposed rocks and outcrops, rarely on mineral soil, often near streams			X
Leskeaceae	Pseudoleskea radicosa var. compacta	(Best) E. Lawton	P	2	D	Locally common on dry siliceous boulders, rare on calcareous rock and mineral soil, subalpine–alpine			X
Leskeaceae	Pseudoleskeella tectorum	(Funck ex Bridel) Kindberg ex Brotherus	P	21	D	Common on shaded calcareous rock or rarely on shaded tree bases or wood			X
Meesiaceae	Leptobryum pyriforme	(Hedwig) Wilson	A	4	M	Wet or damp soil, humus, logs, rocks			X
Mielichhoferiaceae	Pohlia camptotrachela	(Renauld & Cardot) Brotherus	A	1	D	On acid, gravelly or sandy disturbed soil, path banks, stream banks	X		X
Mielichhoferiaceae	Pohlia cruda	(Hedwig) Lindberg	A	2	M	Soil banks, crevices in rocks or under roots, tundra soil and paths	X	X	X
Mielichhoferiaceae	Pohlia wahlenbergii	(F. Weber & D. Mohr) Andrews	A	2	D	On naturally or anthropogenically disturbed clay or rarely sandy soils; path banks, along streams	X	X	X
Mniaceae	Mnium arizonicum	Amann	A	1	D	Damp or dry soil and humus, in crevices of rocks, logs, shady banks	X		
Orthotrichaceae	Orthotrichum alpestre	Hornschuch ex Bruch	A	7	M	Rock crevices and tree bases (common in moist, pine and deciduous forests)			X
Orthotrichaceae	Orthotrichum cupulatum	Bridel	A	4	M	Faces of calcareous cliffs (usu dry) & large boulders in coniferous forests (common in Ponderosa Pine forests & canyons)		X	X
Orthotrichaceae	Orthotrichum hallii	Sullivant & Lesquereux	A	9	M	Calcareous rocks, sometimes granite, quartzite, or basalt, rarely on trunks of deciduous trees, open pine forest, spruce-fir forests or deciduous scrub oak-maple forests, especially common on vertical canyon walls and shaded cliff faces			X
Orthotrichaceae	Orthotrichum obtusifolium	Bridel	A	1	D	Deciduous trees in open areas; in the West, on Juniperus, scrub-oaks, or Populus balsamifera			X
Orthotrichaceae	Orthotrichum pellucidum	Lindberg	A	1	M	Calcareous, rarely siliceous boulders and cliff faces in xeric areas, often found growing in direct sunlight			X
Orthotrichaceae	Orthotrichum pumilum	Swartz	A	2	M	Trunks, lower branches, and bases of deciduous trees, rarely on conifers or in crevices of rocks; common in open, hardwood forests			X

Appendix C continued

Family	Species	Author	Growth form	Freq	Sex. Condition	Known habitat (Adapted from the Flora of North America)	Only mesic	Mexico	Canada
Orthotrichaceae	Zygodon viridissimus var. rupestris	Hartman	A	1	D	Trunks of trees and on rocks; low to middle elevations		X	X
Polytrichaceae	Atrichum selwynii	Austin	A	2	D	Soil, open and shaded habitats, bare roadside banks, overturned tree roots			X
Polytrichaceae	Polytrichum juniperinum	Hedwig	A	11	D	Exposed, well-drained, acid soils in old fields & open woods, post-fire colonizer, on trailside banks, on thin soil over rocks, open ridge tops near timberline, rarely in moist or wet situations		X	X
Pottiaceae	Aloina ambigua	(Bruch & Schimper) E.J. Craig	A	5	D	Low, desert areas, banks and dry washes, soil and limestone		X	
Pottiaceae	Aloina bifrons	(De Notaris) Delgadillo	A	1	D	Sunny sandy soil or soil over limestone in dry areas		X	
Pottiaceae	Barbula bolleana	(Müll. Hal.) Brotherus	A	8	D	Wet limestone, moist areas, wet rocks	X	X	
Pottiaceae	Barbula convoluta var. eustegia	(Cardot & Thériot) Zander	A	5	D	Sandy banks, soil, logs, in pine woods, shores			X
Pottiaceae	Barbula indica var. indica	(Hooker) Sprengel	A	3	D	Soil, clay, limestone, cement, walls	X	X	X
Pottiaceae	Bryoerythrophyllum recurvirostrum	(Hedwig) Chen	A	3	M	Soil, rock (limestone, dolomite, gypsum, siliceous), mortar of wall, bark, in tussock tundra, alpine meadows, bluffs, forested and boggy areas, stream banks, lake shores		X	X
Pottiaceae	Crossidium aberrans	Holzinger & Bartram	A	14	D	Soil and rocks under shrubs, shaded banks or in open sites in dry washes		X	
Pottiaceae	Crossidium crassinervium var. crassinervium	(De Notaris) Juratzka	A	9	D	Soil and rocks, on banks and dry washes, under shrubs in desert areas		X	
Pottiaceae	Crossidium seriatum	Crume & Steere	A	6	M	Sandy soil or rocks, along dry washes, in open or shaded places in deserts		X	X
Pottiaceae	Crossidium squamiferum	(Viviani) Juratzka	A	8	M	Banks, sandy soil or rocks along dry washes; soil, sandy soil or rocks, dry washes		X	X
Pottiaceae	Didymodon australasiae	(Hooker & Greville) Zander	A	5	D	Soil, gypsum, acid rock, ledges, sandstone, silt		X	

Family	Species	Author	Growth form	Freq	Sex. Cond- ition	Known habitat (Adapted from the Flora of North America)	Only mesic	Mexico	Canada
Pottiaceae	*Didymodon brachyphyllus*	(Sullivant) Zander	A	7	D	Soil, limestone, lava, mortar, steppe, road banks, near spring, streamside, arid grassland, soil over lava, sand-stone cliffs		X	X
Pottiaceae	*Didymodon fallax*	(Hedwig) Zander	A	4	D	Soil, silt, conglomerate, dolomite, sandstone, concrete, culverts, gypsum, shale, calcareous rock	X	X	X
Pottiaceae	*Didymodon ne-vadensis*	Zander	A	9	D	Soil, gypsiferous outcrops, limestone boulders, sandy soil			X
Pottiaceae	*Didymodon nich-olsonii*	Culmann	A	2	D	Wet rocks, quartzite, wet silty sand, stream bank, can-yon walls, streamside, chaparral			X
Pottiaceae	*Didymodon rigidulus* var. *icma-dophilus*	(Schimper ex. Müll. Hal.) Zander	A	6	D	Marble, limestone, sandstone, ledges, soil, sand of beaches and dunes, frost boil, old musk ox feces		X	X
Pottiaceae	*Didymodon rigidulus* var. *rigidulus*	Hedwig	A	9	D	Calcareous rock, boulders, cliff faces, soil, outcrops, sinks, ledges, tufa		X	X
Pottiaceae	*Didymodon tec-torum*	(Müll. Hal.) Saito	A	1	D	Limestone shales, riverside, dry shaded rocks, granite cliffs and ledges, north-facing bluff			
Pottiaceae	*Didymodon to-phaceus*	(Bridel) Lisa	A	8	D	Limestone, limy shale, dolomite, cliffs, rock, moist areas, seepage, waterfalls, moist clay		X	X
Pottiaceae	*Didymodon vinealis*	(Bridel) Zander	A	17	D	Soil, calcareous rock, granite outcrop, schist, sandstone		X	X
Pottiaceae	*Eucladium verticil-latum*	(Bridel) Bruch & Schimper	A	15	D	Dripping calcareous or sometimes granitic rock faces or mortar, around springs, dripping bluffs in calcareous regions	X	X	X
Pottiaceae	*Gymnostomum aeruginosum*	Smith	A	3	D	Calcareous rock in wet situations, especially near water-falls, moist gorge walls, rarely soil		X	X
Pottiaceae	*Gymnostomum calcareum*	Nees & Horn-schuch	A	4	D	Damp cliff faces and wet rocks near waterfalls	X	X	
Pottiaceae	*Gyroweisia tenuis*	(Schrader & Hed-wig) Schimper	A	1	D	Thin soil and in rock crevices, sandstone, calcareous rock	X	X	
Pottiaceae	*Hymenostylium recurvirostrum* var. *recurvirostrum*	(Hedwig) Dixon	A	5	D	Calcareous regions, seepy bluffs to moist, seepy ledges and cracks, moist soil along waterfalls, streams and rivers, limestone and calcareous rocks, cedar barrens (sandstone)	X		

Appendix C continued

Family	Species	Author	Growth form	Freq	Sex. Condition	Known habitat (Adapted from the Flora of North America)	Only mesic	Mexico	Canada
Pottiaceae	*Microbryum starkeanum*	(Hedwig) Zander	A	1	M	Bare soil, fields	X	X	
Pottiaceae	*Pleurochaete luteola*	(Bescherelle) Thériot	A	9	D	Exposed clay or sandy soil over calcareous rock, esp in cedar barrens or glades, dry bluffs, ledges		X	X
Pottiaceae	*Pseudocrossidium crinitum*	(Schultz) Zander	A	4	D	Soil, sand, sandstone, limestone, basalt, shale, boulders, ledges, deserts		X	X
Pottiaceae	*Pterygoneurum lamellatum*	(Kindberg) Juratzka	A	4	D	Soil, rock face			X
Pottiaceae	*Pterygoneurum ovatum*	(Hedwig) Dixon	A	1	D	Soil (volcanic, dry saline), frost boil, low desert scrub areas			X
Pottiaceae	*Pterygoneurum subsessile var. subsessile*	(Bridel) Juratzka	A	1	D	Soil (sandy, volcanic), alkali flats			X
Pottiaceae	*Syntrichia canninervis*	Mitten	A	20	M	Soil, deserts and steppe, often forming extensive carpets			X
Pottiaceae	*Syntrichia laevipila*	Bridel	A	2	D	Occasional on bark of trees, rarely on rock		X	X
Pottiaceae	*Syntrichia montana*	Nees	A	3	D	Widespread on soil and rock, occasionally on tree bark		X	X
Pottiaceae	*Syntrichia norvegica*	F. Weber	A	12	D	Soil, rock		X	X
Pottiaceae	*Syntrichia papillosissima*	(Coppey) Loeske	A	1	D	Dry soil, rock		X	X
Pottiaceae	*Syntrichia ruralis*	(Hedwig) Weber & Mohr	A	51	D	Dry to moist soil and rock		X	X
Pottiaceae	*Tortella alpicola*	Dixon	A	1	D	Shaded or exposed, wet or dry rocks, crevices and ledges of granite, quartzite, schist, sandstone and calcareous outcrops on cliffs and in canyons, cracks in a limestone gully, cavern, wet, mesic tundra, wet log, dry limestone cliff face			X
Pottiaceae	*Tortula acaulon*	(Withering) Zander	A	4	M	Soil, lawns, fields, banks		X	X
Pottiaceae	*Tortula atrovirens*	(Smith) Lindberg	A	6	M	Exposed soil, volcanic ash, rock, often calcareous		X	X
Pottiaceae	*Tortula hoppeanna*	(Schultz) Ochyra	A	1	M	Soil, calcareous silt			X

Family	Species	Author	Growth form	Freq	Sex. Condition	Known habitat (Adapted from the Flora of North America)	Only mesic	Mexico	Canada
Pottiaceae	*Tortula inermis*	(Bridel) Montagne	A	15	M	Soil, rock		X	
Pottiaceae	*Tortula lanceola*	Zander	A	3	M	Soil or walls, often in calcareous regions			X
Pottiaceae	*Tortula mucronifolia*	Schwägrichen	A	8	M	Soil, calcareous soil, silt, rock, cliffs, walls			X
Pottiaceae	*Tortula muralis*	Hedwig	A	5	M	Calcareous rock, often on bricks or walls			X
Pottiaceae	*Tortula obtusifolia*	(Schwägrichen) Mathieu	A	10	M	Soil, rock, limestone, calcareous sandstone, stone walls, crevices, ledges			X
Pottiaceae	*Trichostomum planifolium*	(Dixon) Zander	A	1	M	Soil, margins of boulders, rock crevices		X	
Pottiaceae	*Trichostomum tenuirostre*	(Hooker & Taylor) Lindberg	A	1	D	Soil, sandstone, calcareous rock, bluffs, boulders, under overhanging ledges, seepage areas, logs		X	X
Pottiaceae	*Weissia controversa*	Hedwig	A	2	M	Weedy, soil, rock, disturbed areas, roadsides, fields, acid or calcareous substrates		X	X
Pottiaceae	*Weissia ligulifolia*	(Bartram) Grout	A	16	M	Dry soil, rocks, wet crevices, shaded areas			
Pterigynandraceae	*Pterigynandrum filiforme*	Hedwig	P	1	D	Mesic, acidic boulders and rock shelves in the western montane forests and on acidic rocks throughout the eastern Canadian shield country	X		X
Splachnobryaceae	*Splachnobryum obtusum*	(Bridel) Müll. Hal.	A	2	D	Exposed sites on damp or periodically wet limestone, marl, calcareous soil, mortar-work	X	X	
Thuidiaceae	*Abietinella abietina*	(Hedwig) M. Fleischer	P	1	D	Dry, exposed calcareous rocks and soil, sand of partially stabilized dunes, among talus at base of cliffs, and humus in open, coniferous forests			X
Timmiaceae	*Timmia megapolitana subsp. bavarica*	(Hessler) Brassard, Lindbergia	A	15	M	Most often in mesic, calcareous, open or well-vegetated Arctic-montane sites, or in nutrient-rich sites (e.g. cliff bases or around large boulders)		X	X

Phylum Hepaticophyta (liverworts)

Family	Species	Author	Growth form	Freq	Sex. Condition	Known habitat (Adapted from the Flora of North America)	Only mesic	Mexico	Canada
Aneuraceae	*Aneura pinguis*	(L.) Dumort.	thalloid	1	D	Moist soil over rocks; rocks, usually sandstone or limestone	X		X
Aytoniaceae	*Asterella gracilis*	(F. Weber) Underwood	thalloid	1	M	Moist soil over rock usu calcareous in alpine areas	0	0	X
Aytoniaceae	*Mannia fragrans*	(Balb.) Frye & L. Clark	thalloid	1	P	dry soil and sand, typically around boulders	X	X	X

Appendix C continued

Family	Species	Author	Growth form	Freq	Sex. Condition	Known habitat (Adapted from the Flora of North America)	Only mesic	Mexico	Canada
Aytoniaceae	*Reboulia hemisphaerica*	(L.) Raddi	thalloid	2	M	Soil over rock that is commonly but not exclusively calcareous, habitats that are at least periodically moist, temperate areas			X
Cephaloziellaceae	*Cephaloziella divaricata*	(Roth.) Warnst.	leafy	4		humid shaded soil and soil over rock			X
Geocalycaceae	*Chiloscyphus polyanthos var. rivularis*	(L.) Corda	leafy	1		damp to moist soil and sandstone rock	X		X
Jubulaceae	*Frullania inflata*	Gott.	leafy	1		dry shaded soil and bark			X
Jungermanniaceae	*Tritomaria exsectiformis*	(Breidl.) Loeske	leafy	2		damp soil	X		X
Marchantiaceae	*Marchantia polymorpha*	L.	thalloid	2		damp soil and mud along streams, at springs and in shaded sites	X		X
Ricciaceae	*Riccia glauca*	L.	thalloid	1		damp drying exposed mud around margins of lakes, springs	X		X
Targioniaceae	*Targionia sp.nov.*	L.	thalloid	5		damp to drying soil			

Appendix D

Infrequently collected bryophyte species in Grand Canyon National Park

Infrequently collected bryophytes in Grand Canyon NP (GRCA) are listed below along with their observed habitats in the park. All species included have been found at four or fewer unique localities within the park. Species that have been documented to occur in Grand Canyon-Parashant National Monument, Arizona and Big Bend National Park, Texas are indicated. Species that were restricted to mesic habitat (springs, seeps, riparian, ponds, waterfalls) in GRCA are indicated. The growth form for mosses (pleurocarpous, acrocarpous) and liverworts (leafy, thalloid) is included.

Species	Total localities	Growth form	Para-shant NM	Big Bend NP	Collection region	Only mesic	Observed habitat
Abietinella abietina	1	pleurocarp			Inner Canyon		rock
Aloina bifrons	1	acrocarp	X		L.Mead		crust
Anerua pinguis	1	thalloid			N.Rim	X	spring on limestone
Asterella gracilis	1	thalloid			N.Rim		spring; moist soil
Brachythecium nelsonii	1	pleurocarp			N.Rim	X	spring
Brachythecium velutinum	1	pleurocarp			S.Rim		limestone
Campyliadelphus chrysophyllus	1	pleurocarp		X	N.Rim		unknown
Chiloscyphus polyanthos var. rivularis	1	leafy			N.Rim	X	spring on soil over rock
Didymodon tectorum	1	acrocarp			Inner Canyon		rock
Fissidens fontanus	1	acrocarp		X	CO.R	X	travertine riverside
Fontinalis hypnoides	1	acrocarp			CO.R	X	submerged in pool at spring
Frullania inflata	1	leafy	X		N.Rim		limestone
Funaria hygrometrica var. calvescens	1	acrocarp			CO.R		soil
Funaria muhlenbergii	1	acrocarp	X		Inner Canyon		soil
Gemmabryum subapiculatum	1	acrocarp			N.Rim	X	by pond on moist soil
Grimmia caespiticia	1	acrocarp			N.Rim		sandstone
Grimmia sessitana	1	acrocarp			S.Rim		rock
Grimmia sp.nov	1	acrocarp			Inner Canyon		sandstone
Gyroweisia tenuis	1	acrocarp			CO.R	X	seep
Hypnum pallescens	1	pleurocarp			N.Rim	X	streamside

Species	Total localities	Growth form	Para-shant NM	Big Bend NP	Collection region	Only mesic	Observed habitat
Imbribryum sp.nov	1	acrocarp			N.Rim	X	spring
Mannia fragrans	1	thalloid			Marble Can.	X	moist soil
Microbryum starkeanum	1	acrocarp	X	X	Inner Canyon	X	streamside
Mnium arizonicum	1	acrocarp			Inner Canyon	X	seep
Orthotrichum obtusifolium	1	acrocarp			N.Rim		limestone
Orthotrichum pellucidum	1	acrocarp			S.Rim		limestone
Pohlia camptotrachela	1	acrocarp			N.Rim	X	by pond on moist soil
Pseudoleskea patens	1	pleurocarp			N.Rim		soil, rock
Pterigynandrum filiforme	1	pleurocarp			N.Rim	X	soil
Pterygoneurum ovatum	1	acrocarp	X		Inner Canyon		sandstone
Pterygoneurum subsessile var. subsessile	1	acrocarp	X	X	S.Rim		dry soil
Ptychostomum bimum	1	acrocarp			N.Rim		soil
Riccia glauca	1	thalloid			N.Rim	X	lakeside
Rosulobryum torquescens	1	acrocarp	0	0	Inner Canyon		soil
Schistidium frigidum	1	acrocarp			N.Rim		rock
Sciuro-hypnum plumosum	1	pleurocarp			N.Rim	X	pond margin
Syntrichia papillossisima	1	acrocarp	X		N.Rim		cwd
Tortella alpicola	1	acrocarp	X		Inner Canyon		unknown
Tortula hoppeanna	1	acrocarp			N.Rim		rock
Trichostomum planifolium	1	acrocarp			Inner Canyon		soil over rock
Trichostomum tenuirostre	1	acrocarp			CO.R		sandstone
Zygodon viridissimus var. rupestris	1	acrocarp			S.Rim		tree
Atrichum selwynii	2	acrocarp			N.Rim		soil; cwd; spring
Cratoneuron filicinum	2	pleurocarp			N.Rim	X	spring
Didymodon nicholsonii	2	acrocarp	X		Inner Canyon; CO.R		riverside; shaded soil

Species	Total localities	Growth form	Para-shant NM	Big Bend NP	Collection region	Only mesic	Observed habitat
Distichium capillaceum	2	acrocarp			N.Rim		limestone; moist soil springside
Drepanocladus aduncus	2	pleurocarp			N.Rim		limestone; pond margin
Eurhynchiastrum pulchellum var. pulchellum	2	pleurocarp		X	N.Rim		rock; spring
Hypnum cupressiforme var. subjulaceum	2	pleurocarp		X	N.Rim; Inner Canyon		soil; cwd
Hypnum vaucheri	2	pleurocarp	X	X	S.Rim; Inner Canyon		rock; tree
Leskeella nervosa	2	pleurocarp			N.Rim; Inner Canyon		cwd; sandstone
Marchantia polymorpha	2	thalloid			Inner Canyon	X	spring
Orthotrichum pumilum	2	acrocarp	X	X	Inner Canyon; L.Mead		tree
Pohlia cruda	2	acrocarp			N.Rim	X	moist soil at spring
Pohlia wahlenbergii	2	acrocarp			N.Rim; Inner Canyon	X	moist soil at spring
Pseudoleskea radicosa var. compacta	2	pleurocarp			N.Rim		rock
Ptychostomum creberrimum	2	acrocarp		X	N.Rim; Inner Canyon		soil; limestone
Reboulia hemisphaerica	2	thalloid			Inner Canyon; CO.R		shaded soil
Schistidium agassizii	2	acrocarp		X	N.Rim		wet rock; moist soil
Schistidium dupretii	2	acrocarp			N.Rim; Inner Canyon		limestone
Schistidium papillosum	2	acrocarp			N.Rim		sandstone
Splachnobryum obtusum	2	acrocarp		X	Inner Canyon; CO.R	X	travertine riverside
Syntrichia laevipila	2	acrocarp	X	X	Inner Canyon		tree
Tritomaria exsectiformis	2	leafy			N.Rim; Inner Canyon	X	streamside
Weissia controversa	2	acrocarp		X	Inner Canyon		soil over rock; shaded soil
Barbula indica var. indica	3	acrocarp			Inner Canyon; CO.R	X	seep on moist soil; riverside
Brachythecium rivulare	3	pleurocarp			N.Rim; Inner Canyon; CO.R	X	emergent at spring

Species	Total localities	Growth form	Para-shant NM	Big Bend NP	Collection region	Only mesic	Observed habitat
Bryoerythrophyllum recurviro-strum	3	acrocarp	X	X	N.Rim		soil; limestone; spring
Entosthodon sp	3	acrocarp			CO.R		crust; waterfall, soil
Fissidens obtusi-folius	3	acrocarp		X	Inner Can-yon; CO.R; L.Mead	X	travertine river-side; wet rock
Gemmabryum badium	3	acrocarp			N.Rim; Inner Canyon		dry soil; sand-stone
Gymnostomum aeruginosum	3	acrocarp	X	X	N.Rim; Inner Canyon		seep; soil over rock; sandstone
Philonotis marchia	3	pleurocarp			Inner Can-yon; CO.R	X	spring; seep
Ptychostomum pseudotrique-trum	3	acrocarp		X	N.Rim; Inner Canyon	X	moist soil at spring
Ptychostomum turbinatum	3	acrocarp		X	N.Rim; Inner Canyon	X	moist soil at spring; stream-side
Rosulobryum laevifilium	3	acrocarp			N.Rim		limestone; soil; cwd
Syntrichia mon-tana	3	acrocarp			S.Rim; Inner Canyon		limestone; tree
Tortula lanceola	3	acrocarp			S.Rim; Inner Canyon; CO.R		soil over rock; crust; moist soil
Brachythecium frigidum	4	pleurocarp			N.Rim; Inner Canyon	X	spring; emer-gent in spring
Cephaloziella divaricata	4	leafy			N.Rim		cwd; burnt cwd
Didymodon fallax	4	acrocarp		X	Inner Can-yon; CO.R	X	riverside; seep; waterfall
Grimmia longi-rostris	4	acrocarp	X	X	N.Rim; S.Rim; Inner Canyon		limestone; chert
Grimmia moxleyi	4	acrocarp	X		Inner Can-yon; CO.R; L.Mead		soil over rock; soil
Gymnostomum calcareum	4	acrocarp	X		N.Rim; Inner Canyon; CO.R	X	moist soil at spring; stream-side
Jaffeuliobryum wrightii	4	acrocarp	X	X	Inner Can-yon; CO.R		dry rock; dry soil
Orthotrichum cupulatum	4	acrocarp	X		N.Rim; S.Rim; Inner Canyon		limestone; tree
Oxyrrhynchium hians	4	pleurocarp			N.Rim; Inner Canyon	X	spring
Pseudocrossidium crinitum	4	acrocarp		X	S.Rim; Inner Canyon; CO.R		soil over rock; limestone; riverside

Species	Total localities	Growth form	Para-shant NM	Big Bend NP	Collection region	Only mesic	Observed habitat
Pterygoneurum lamellatum	4	acrocarp			N.Rim; S.Rim; Inner Canyon		soil over rock; dry soil
Leptobryum pyriforme	4	acrocarp			N.Rim		moist soil; spring

Appendix E

Bryophyte species vouchers for Grand Canyon National Park

The following 150 bryophyte specimens comprise the modern collection GRCA-05648 (accession number) funded by this project that reside in the Grand Canyon National Park Museum Collection Herbarium. The remaining 6 species reported in the flora are vouchered by historic collections only. Modern collections not included below are available for query on the Southwest Environmental Information Network (SEINet 2011) and are housed at the Deaver Herbarium (ASC) of Northern Arizona University, Flagstaff.

GRCA catalog number	Family	Scientific name	Collector	Collection number	Eleva-tion (ft)	Locality
107135	Amblystegiaceae	*Amblystegium serpens*	T. Clark	113	8079	North Rim, Ken Patrick Trail along stream below Neal Spring
107101	Amblystegiaceae	*Campyliadelphus chrysophyllus*	G. Rink	7658	8280	Milk Spring, along the Point Sublime Road
107174	Amblystegiaceae	*Conardia compacta*	T. Clark	456	8360	North Rim, eastern portion of Robber's Roost
107108	Amblystegiaceae	*Drepanocladus aduncus*	G. Rink	8948	8200	North Rim, about one mile west of Crystal Creek, near the Pt. Sublime Road, south slope
107096	Amblystegiaceae	*Hygroamblystegium varium*	G. Rink	7265	5600	Muav Falls Canyon in Upper Bright Angel Creek, due east of Uncle Jim Point, hanging garden
107204	Amblystegiaceae	*Leptodictyum riparium*	T. Clark	674	1930	along the Colorado River, Artesian spring below Lava Falls, river mile 180.14
107119	Aytoniaceae	*Asterella gracilis*	J. Spence	5903	8350	Basin Spring, North Rim
107110	Aytoniaceae	*Mannia fragrans*	J. Spence	5313	3000	Keystone Spring, downstream from Saddle Canyon
107124	Aytoniaceae	*Reboulia hemisphaerica*	T. Clark	33	5000	Bright Angel Trail
107120	Bartramiaceae	*Philonotis fontana*	L. Stevens	sn	7900	Kanabownits Spring
107111	Bartramiaceae	*Philonotis marchia*	J. Spence	5325	2800	Nankoweap Creek
107140	Brachytheciaceae	*Brachythecium collinum*	T. Clark	125	8800	North Rim, in proximity of the N.Rim lookout tower near N. Rim entrance station
107215	Brachytheciaceae	*Brachythecium fendleri*	T. Clark	831	5695	Grandview Trail, below rim
106702	Brachytheciaceae	*Brachythecium frigidum*	G. Rink	8602	5800	Angel Spring, source of water in Bright Angel Canyon
107121	Brachytheciaceae	*Brachythecium nelsonii*	L.E. Stevens	sn	7600	Big Spring, Big Spring Canyon
107113	Brachytheciaceae	*Brachythecium rivulare*	J. Spence	5337a	2400	Elves' Chasm
107246	Brachytheciaceae	*Brachythecium velutinum*	T. Clark	1212	6972	South Rim, section of Arizona Trail
107107	Brachytheciaceae	*Eurhynchiastrum pulchellum*	G. Rink	8837	7950	Kanabownits Canyon, downstream of Kanabownits Spring

GRCA catalog number	Family	Scientific name	Collector	Collection number	Elevation (ft)	Locality
107098	Brachytheciaceae	*Oxyrrhynchium hians*	G. Rink	7271	5600	Muav Falls Canyon in Upper Bright Angel Creek, due east of Uncle Jim Point, hanging garden/ seep just upstream of where the Old BA Trail crosses this side canyon
107185	Brachytheciaceae	*Rhynchostegium aquaticum*	T. Clark	537	2400	Elves' Chasm; below the falls along the channel connecting the falls to the Colorado River
107106	Brachytheciaceae	*Sciuro-hypnum plumosum*	G. Rink	8799b	7720	Castle Lake, north of Swamp Ridge
107218	Bryaceae	*Bryum argenteum*	T. Clark	871	8003	North Rim, Cape Final Trail
107131	Bryaceae	*Bryum lanatum*	T. Clark	104	8240	North Rim, in forest west of Harvey Meadow off Highway 67, along foot trail in forested gulley recently distubed by fire
107168	Bryaceae	*Gemmabryum badium*	T. Clark	358	8021	North Kaibab Trail
107220	Bryaceae	*Gemmabryum caespiticium*	T. Clark	884	7886	North Rim, Cape Final Trail
107230	Bryaceae	*Gemmabryum kunzei*	T. Clark	1006	1745	Pearce Ferry, < 1 mi east of the park border near the Grand Wash Cliffs
107144	Bryaceae	*Gemmabryum subapiculatum*	T. Clark	143	8800	North Rim, Little Park Lake vicinity (within 3 miles), NE of N. Rim entrance station
107203	Bryaceae	*Gemmabryum valparaisense*	T. Clark	666	1649	along the Colorado River, lower end of Fat City Beach, river mile 180.4
107109	Bryaceae	*Imbribryum*	J. Spence	5906	2500	Basin Spring
107198	Bryaceae	*Plagiobryoides vinosula*	T. Clark	624	1800	Colorado River, Ledges, River Mile 151 vicinity
107102	Bryaceae	*Ptychostomum bimum*	G. Rink	7662	8280	Upper Milk Creek upstream of Milk Spring
107163	Bryaceae	*Ptychostomum creberrimum*	T. Clark	283	8322	North Kaibab Trail
107126	Bryaceae	*Ptychostomum pallescens*	T. Clark	78	8850	North Rim, in forest W of the S section of Upper Little Park, off Highway 67, 1.5 mi south of entrance station
107099	Bryaceae	*Ptychostomum pseudotriquetrum*	G. Rink	7272	5600	Muav Falls Canyon in Upper Bright Angel Creek, due east of Uncle Jim Point, hanging garden
107095	Bryaceae	*Ptychostomum turbinatum*	G. Rink	7048	5800	Perennial stream west of Banta Point in Kwagunt Canyon
107134	Bryaceae	*Rosulabryum flaccidium*	T. Clark	111	8079	North Rim, Ken Patrick Trail along stream below Neal Spring
107172	Bryaceae	*Rosulabryum laevifilium*	T. Clark	429	8384	North Rim, eastern portion of Robber's Roost

GRCA catalog number	Family	Scientific name	Collector	Collection number	Eleva-tion (ft)	Locality
107243	Bryaceae	*Rosulabryum torque-scens*	T. Clark	1133	4150	North Kaibab Trail, < 1/2 mi above Cottonwood Campground
107173	Cephaloziella-ceae	*Cephaloziella divari-cata*	T. Clark	432	8384	North Rim, eastern portion of Robber's Roost
107122	Cratoneuraceae	*Cratoneuron filicinum*	L. Stevens	sn	7600	Big Spring, Big Spring Canyon
107165	Dicranaceae	*Dicranoweisia crispula*	T. Clark	312	8216	North Kaibab Trail
107171	Ditricaceae	*Ceratodon purpureus*	T. Clark	424	8384	North Rim, eastern portion of Robber's Roost
107117	Ditricaceae	*Distichium capilla-ceum*	J. Spence	5470a	8400	North Canyon Spring
107128	Encalyptaceae	*Encalypta rhaptocarpa*	T. Clark	89	8167	North Rim, in forest bordering Harvey Meadow, off Highway 67
107153	Encalyptaceae	*Encalypta vulgaris*	T. Clark	205	6598	Bright Angel Trail
107200	Fissidentaceae	*Fissidens fontanus*	T. Clark	652	1679	Colorado River, Warm Springs, below Lava Falls
107096	Fissidentaceae	*Fissidens grandifrons*	G. Rink	7265	5600	Muav Falls Canyon in Upper Bright Angel Creek, due east of Uncle Jim Point, hanging garden
107180	Fissidentaceae	*Fissidens obtusifolius*	T. Clark	503	2400	Elve's Chasm; below the falls along the channel connecting the falls to the Colorado River
107159	Fissidentaceae	*Fissidens sublimbatus*	T. Clark	259	8286	North Rim, CCC Campground vicinity (near North Kaibab Trailhead)
107205	Fontinalaceae	*Fontinalis hypnoides*	T. Clark	676	1930	along the Colorado River, Artesian spring below Lava Falls, river mile 180.14
107195	Funariaceae	*Entosthodon*	T. Clark	618	1800	Colorado River, Ledges, River Mile 151 vicinity
107112	Funariaceae	*Funaria hygrometrica var. calvescens*	J. Spence	5328	2400	Trinity Camp, CRM 91
107241	Funariaceae	*Funaria hygrometrica var. hygrometrica*	T. Clark	1126	4130	North Kaibab Trail, Cottonwood Campground vicinity
107115	Geocalycaceae	*Chiloscyphus polyan-thos*	J. Spence	2355	7726	North Canyon Spring, North Rim
107161	Grimmiaceae	*Grimmia alpestris*	T. Clark	273	8322	North Kaibab Trail
107149	Grimmiaceae	*Grimmia anodon*	T. Clark	184	6784	Bright Angel Trail, < 1/4 mi from trailhead
107219	Grimmiaceae	*Grimmia caespiticia*	T. Clark	880	7886	North Rim, Cape Final Trail
107245	Grimmiaceae	*Grimmia longirostris*	T. Clark	1209	7092	South Rim, section of Arizona Trail
107148	Grimmiaceae	*Grimmia moxleyi*	T. Clark	176	6946	South Rim, western section of Rim Trail
107190	Grimmiaceae	*Grimmia orbicularis*	T. Clark	569	1998	Colorado River, above Deubendorff, River mile 131.9, river left
107146	Grimmiaceae	*Grimmia ovalis*	T. Clark	171	6874	South Rim, western section of Rim Trail, approximately 1/4 mi from Bright Angel Lodge
107170	Grimmiaceae	*Grimmia plagiopodia*	T. Clark	415	7578	North Kaibab Trail

GRCA catalog number	Family	Scientific name	Collector	Collection number	Elevation (ft)	Locality
107207	Grimmiaceae	*Grimmia pulvinata*	T. Clark	690	1819	Colorado River, mouth of 194-Mile Canyon, river left
107147	Grimmiaceae	*Grimmia sessitana*	T. Clark	174	6946	South Rim, western section of Rim Trail
107244	Grimmiaceae	*Grimmia* sp.nov.	T. Clark	1205	5568	Grand View Trail
107210	Grimmiaceae	*Jaffeuliobryum wrightii*	T. Clark	719	1615	Colorado River, mouth of 205-Mile Creek, River Mile 205, river left
107217	Grimmiaceae	*Schistidium agassizii*	T. Clark	862	8327	North Rim, Ken Patrick Trail
107169	Grimmiaceae	*Schistidium atrichum*	T. Clark	385	7883	North Kaibab Trail
107127	Grimmiaceae	*Schistidium confertum*	T. Clark	87	8173	North Rim, Widforss Point Trail
107154	Grimmiaceae	*Schistidium dupretii*	T. Clark	206	6598	Bright Angel Trail
107138	Grimmiaceae	*Schistidium frigidum*	T. Clark	120b	7837	North Rim, Cliff Springs Trail
107238	Grimmiaceae	*Schistidium papillosum*	T. Clark	1064	8108	North Rim, Widforss Point Trail
107235	Hypnaceae	*Hypnum cupressiforme* var. *subjulaceum*	T. Clark	1023c	8165	North Kaibab Trail
107136	Hypnaceae	*Hypnum pallescens*	T. Clark	114	8079	North Rim, Ken Patrick Trail along stream below Neal Spring
107236	Hypnaceae	*Hypnum revolutum*	T. Clark	1040	8165	North Kaibab Trail, below rim
107123	Hypnaceae	*Hypnum vaucheri*	T. Clark	31	6000	Bright Angel Trail
107226	Jubulaceae	*Frullania inflata*	T. Clark	944	8316	North Rim, Widforss Point Trail
107104	Jungermanniaceae	*Tritomaria exsectiformis*	G. Rink	7700b	8250	Robber's Roost Spring
107141	Leskeaceae	*Leskeella nervosa*	T. Clark	126	8800	North Rim, in proximity of the N. Rim lookout tower near N. Rim entrance station
107137	Leskeaceae	*Pseudoleskea patens*	T. Clark	115	8079	North Rim, Ken Patrick Trail along stream below Neal Spring
107177	Leskeaceae	*Pseudoleskeella radicosa*	T. Clark	480	8384	North Rim, Robber's Roost, W of Route 67
107222	Leskeaceae	*Pseudoleskeella tectorum*	T. Clark	903	7154	South Rim, section of Rim Trail east of Bright Angel Lodge
107100	Marchantiaceae	*Marchantia polymorpha* variety *aquatica*	G. Rink	7288	5200	East side of upper Bright Angel Creek, hanging garden
107142	Mielichhoferiaceae	*Pohlia camptotrachela*	T. Clark	129	8800	North Rim, Little Park Lake vicinity (within 3 miles), NE of N. Rim entrance station
107118	Mielichhoferiaceae	*Pohlia cruda*	J. Spence	5470b	8400	North Canyon Spring
107175	Mielichhoferiaceae	*Pohlia wahlenbergii*	T. Clark	457	8360	North Rim, Robber's Roost
107156	Mniaceae	*Mnium arizonicum*	T. Clark	215	6396	Bright Angel Trail
107176	Orthotricaceae	*Orthotrichum alpestre*	T. Clark	478	8384	North Rim, Robber's Roost, W of Route 67

GRCA catalog number	Family	Scientific name	Collector	Collection number	Elevation (ft)	Locality
107167	Orthotricaceae	*Orthotrichum cupulatum*	T. Clark	344b	8081	North Kaibab Trail
107145	Orthotricaceae	*Orthotrichum hallii*	T. Clark	166	6827	South Rim, western section of Rim Trail
107227	Orthotricaceae	*Orthotrichum obtusifolium*	T. Clark	947	8315	North Rim, Widforss Point Trail
107228	Orthotricaceae	*Orthotrichum pumilum*	T. Clark	992	7720	North Kaibab Trail
107223	Orthotricaceae	*Zygodon viridissimus*	T. Clark	921b	6796	South Rim, section of Arizona Trail near Grand Canyon Village
107103	Polytrichaceae	*Atrichum selwynii*	G. Rink	7666b	8300	Deep limestone sink along the Point Sublime Road southeast of Milk Creek
107125	Polytrichaceae	*Polytrichum juniperinum*	T. Clark	70	8800	North Rim, Upper Little Park off Highway 67, 1.5 mi south of entrance station
107181	Pottiaceae	*Aloina aloides*	T. Clark	505	2400	Elves' Chasm; below the falls along the channel connecting the falls to the Colorado River
107231	Pottiaceae	*Aloina bifrons*	T. Clark	1007	1745	Pearce Ferry, < 1 mi east of the park border near the Grand Wash Cliffs
107202	Pottiaceae	*Barbula bolleana*	T. Clark	660	1679	along the Colorado River, below Lava Falls at Warm Springs
107162	Pottiaceae	*Barbula convoluta* var. *eustegia*	T. Clark	282	8322	North Kaibab Trail
107194	Pottiaceae	*Barbula indica*	T. Clark	606	2431	Colorado River, off Colorado River in Kanab Canyon
107133	Pottiaceae	*Bryoerythrophyllum recurvirostrum*	T. Clark	111	8079	North Rim, Ken Patrick Trail along stream below Neal Spring
107209	Pottiaceae	*Crossidium aberrans*	T. Clark	709	1720	Colorado River, Mouth of Parashant Canyon
107232	Pottiaceae	*Crossidium crassinervium*	T. Clark	1010	1745	Pearce Ferry, < 1 mi east of the park border near the Grand Wash Cliffs
107229	Pottiaceae	*Crossidium seriatum*	T. Clark	1002	1745	Pearce Ferry, < 1 mi east of the park border near the Grand Wash Cliffs
107233	Pottiaceae	*Crossidium squamiferum*	T. Clark	1015	1745	Pearce Ferry, < 1 mi east of the park border near the Grand Wash Cliffs
107206	Pottiaceae	*Didymodon australasiae*	T. Clark	683	1964	along the Colorado River, Hell's Hollow vicinity, river mile 182.3, river right
107239	Pottiaceae	*Didymodon brachyphyllus*	T. Clark	1092	7073	North Kaibab Trail
107196	Pottiaceae	*Didymodon fallax*	T. Clark	619	1800	Colorado River, Ledges, River Mile 151 vicinity
107191	Pottiaceae	*Didymodon nevadensis*	T. Clark	594	2431	Colorado River, off Colorado River in Kanab Canyon

GRCA catalog number	Family	Scientific name	Collector	Collection number	Elevation (ft)	Locality
107199	Pottiaceae	*Didymodon rigidulus* var. *icmadophilus*	T. Clark	646	2266	Honga Rapids, river left
107212	Pottiaceae	*Didymodon rigidulus* variety *rigidulus*	T. Clark	734	1440	Colorado River, Above Three Springs Rapid, River Mile 215.0
107151	Pottiaceae	*Didymodon tectorum*	T. Clark	190	6701	Bright Angel Trail
107186	Pottiaceae	*Didymodon tophaceus*	T. Clark	540	2170	Colorado River, Forster Canyon fan
107129	Pottiaceae	*Didymodon vinealis*	T. Clark	90	8167	North Rim, in forest bordering Harvey Meadow, off Highway 67
107197	Pottiaceae	*Eucladium verticillatum*	T. Clark	620	1800	Colorado River, Ledges, River Mile 151 vicinity
107193	Pottiaceae	*Gymnostomum aeruginosum*	T. Clark	605	2431	Colorado River, off Colorado River in Kanab Canyon
107179	Pottiaceae	*Gymnostomum calcareum*	T. Clark	498	2400	Elves' Chasm; streamside below falls
107189	Pottiaceae	*Gyroweisia tenuis*	T. Clark	560	2233	1 mile above Forster Canyon along the Colorado River
107139	Pottiaceae	*Hymenostylium recurvirostrum* var. *recurvirostrum*	T. Clark	122a	7837	North Rim, Cliff Springs Trail, at the spring
107183	Pottiaceae	*Microbryum starkeanum*	T. Clark	521	2400	Elves' Chasm; below the falls along the channel connecting the falls to the Colorado River
107208	Pottiaceae	*Pleurochaete luteola*	T. Clark	706	1569	Colorado River, River Mile 194.5, 194-Mile Canyon vicinity
107187	Pottiaceae	*Pseudocrossidium crinitum*	T. Clark	540a	2170	Colorado River, Forster Canyon fan
107150	Pottiaceae	*Pterygoneurum lamellatum*	T. Clark	188	6784	Bright Angel Trail
107214	Pottiaceae	*Pterygoneurum subsessile*	T. Clark	790	6996	South Rim, Rim Trail section west of Bright Angel Lodge, at Random Point 79
107221	Pottiaceae	*Syntrichia canninervis*	T. Clark	898	6804	South Kaibab Trail
107242	Pottiaceae	*Syntrichia laevipila*	T. Clark	1127	4130	North Kaibab Trail, Cottonwood Campground vicinity
107157	Pottiaceae	*Syntrichia montana*	T. Clark	232	5747	Bright Angel Trail, above 1.5 mi Rest House
107132	Pottiaceae	*Syntrichia norvegica*	T. Clark	108	8318	North Rim, Ken Patrick Trail along stream below Neal Spring
107160	Pottiaceae	*Syntrichia papillosissima*	T. Clark	260	8422	North Rim, CCC Campground vicinity (near North Kaibab Trailhead)
107130	Pottiaceae	*Syntrichia ruralis*	T. Clark	100	8240	North Rim, in forest west of Harvey Meadow off Highway 67, along foot trail
106685	Pottiaceae	*Tortella alpicola*	G. Rink	7021	5900	Northwest of the saddle between the North Rim and Juno Temple

GRCA catalog number	Family	Scientific name	Collector	Collection number	Elevation (ft)	Locality
107213	Pottiaceae	*Tortula acaulon*	T. Clark	748	6971	South Rim, eastern section of Rim Trail, < 1 mi from Bright Angel Lodge
107158	Pottiaceae	*Tortula atrovirens*	T. Clark	243c	2302	Havasu Canyon, at the intersection of Beaver Creek and Havasu Creek, adjacent to trail near park border
107166	Pottiaceae	*Tortula hoppeanna*	T. Clark	331	8109	North Kaibab Trail, greater than 1/4 mi down from trailhead
107155	Pottiaceae	*Tortula inermis*	T. Clark	209	6396	Bright Angel Trail
107225	Pottiaceae	*Tortula lanceola*	T. Clark	935	6946	South Rim, section of Rim Trail west of Bright Angel Lodge
106768	Pottiaceae	*Tortula mucronifolia*	T. Clark	200	6604	Bright Angel Trail, farther than 1/4 mi down trail
107224	Pottiaceae	*Tortula muralis*	T. Clark	925	7170	South Rim, Shoshone Point Trail
107240	Pottiaceae	*Tortula obtusifolia*	T. Clark	1095	7073	North Kaibab Trail
107192	Pottiaceae	*Trichostomum planifolium*	T. Clark	599c	2431	Colorado River, off Colorado River in Kanab Canyon
107211	Pottiaceae	*Trichostomum tenuirostre*	T. Clark	731	1440	Colorado River, Above Three Springs Rapid, River Mile 215.0
107216	Pottiaceae	*Weissia controversa*	T. Clark	832	5695	Grandview Trail
107234	Pottiaceae	*Weissia ligulifolia*	T. Clark	1017	1676	Pearce Ferry, < 1 mi east of the park border near the Grand Wash Cliffs
107116	Pterigynandraceae	*Pterigynandrum filiforme*	J. Spence	5905	8350	Basin Spring
107143	Ricciaceae	*Riccia glauca*	T. Clark	132	8800	North Rim, Little Park Lake vicinity (within 3 miles), NE of N. Rim entrance station
107201	Splacnobryaceae	*Splacnobryum obtusum*	T. Clark	653	1679	Colorado River, Warm Springs, below Lava Falls
107237	Timmiaceae	*Timmia megapolitana ssp. bavarica*	T. Clark	1045	8000	North Rim, Cape Final Trail

NPS 113/115895, July 2012